THE
LIBRARY

THE
LIBRARY

——— A ———

CATALOGUE

——— OF ———

WONDERS

STUART
KELLS

COUNTERPOINT
BERKELEY, CALIFORNIA

The Library

Copyright © 2017 by Stuart Kells
First published in 2017 by The Text Publishing Company, Melbourne, Australia
First Counterpoint hardcover edition: 2018

Notes on sources are available at www.stuartkells.com.

ISBN: 978-1-640-09020-0

The Library of Congress Cataloging-in-Publication Data is available.

Jacket designed by Donna Cheng

COUNTERPOINT
2560 Ninth Street, Suite 318
Berkeley, CA 94710
www.counterpointpress.com

Printed in the United States of America
Distributed by Publishers Group West

10 9 8 7 6 5 4 3 2 1

CONTENTS

Preface

More than twenty years ago, when I was a young academic working glumly at a social research institute, one of the university colleges held a lunchtime book sale. As soon as I arrived I found a smallish, squarish volume, handsomely printed in old-fashioned type. The binding was distinctively English: dark blue straight-grained morocco (a type of goatskin), the spine boldly gilded and segmented with raised bands in the style of Charles Lewis, the great nineteenth-century bookbinder.

The title page revealed the publication date, 1814, and identified the book as *Pieces of Ancient Poetry from Unpublished Manuscripts and Scarce Books*. I knew "ancient" meant the reigns of Elizabeth I and James I, and "poetry" covered a breadth of ballads and verse.

Otherwise, the book was a little mystery. Just two letters appeared where the author's name should have been: "NY." Nor was the publisher identified.

A footnote revealed ninety-six copies had been printed, plus six "specials" on blue paper. The book in my hands was one of the six. I turned to the back and read the "Disposition of the copies." Though the book kept secret its author and publisher, it named Sheepshanks, Peckover, Pople and the other subscribers who'd agreed in advance to buy a copy—special or otherwise. Several of the listed men were Roxburghers, members of the world's most illustrious and exclusive bibliophile society: Sir Mark Masterman Sykes (a blue copy and a white copy), Archdeacon Francis Wrangham, Sir Francis Freeling, and (enjoying another book purchase before his imminent bankruptcy) George Spencer-Churchill, Marquess of Blandford.

Here, then, in pristine condition and with exceptional pedigree, was a beautifully made and exceptionally scarce collection of rare texts from the time of Shakespeare. In some quarters, leather-bound books are out of fashion. They are "brown books" to go with "brown furniture." But finding *Pieces* was a perfect life moment, the kind of discovery that explains why bibliophiles spend so many hours at flea markets, bookstalls, car boots, and garage sales. Walking home that day, I looked forward to showing the prize to my fiancée, Fiona. We were living in a tower block that used to be a hotel; our apartment still had a minibar-fridge and a wall-mounted hair dryer. Fiona and I grappled with how best to accommodate our VIP guest. Archival box? Shelf to breathe? Would steam from the kitchenette bother the morocco?

Over the following weeks I researched *Pieces*, consulting in the Baillieu Library at the University of Melbourne the *Dictionary of*

Anonymous and Pseudonymous Literature and a nineteenth-century edition of the *Dictionary of National Biography*. "NY," it turned out, was John Fry, a young bookseller from Bristol: N and Y are the terminal letters of his first and last names, a common device of ceremonial anonymity. (Fry's final book was even less anonymous: it identified its editor as "J–N F–Y.")

Fiona and I saved our money and searched for other Frys. Soon, in our tiny flat, we had the world's best John Fry collection (the Folger Shakespeare Library contained his other works but not *Pieces*) and we were beginning to appreciate fully our book-sale find. In strictly monetary terms, *Pieces* was the most valuable thing we owned. But it was more than an asset we could liquidate if we had to. It became for us a talisman. We'd found the nucleus of our future library.

Pieces was also a treasure map, and a portal into multiple strands of a bookish life. John Fry admitted Fiona and me into the circle of gentlemen who, during the reign of King George III, preserved rare books and documents from centuries past. He tutored us on the pillars of good bibliographical method, and exposed us to the most sublime forms of bibliomania. He introduced us to black-letter men, gilt toppers, rough edgers, tall copyists, broadsiders, Aldusians, Elzevirians, Grangerites, pasquinaders, and tawny moroccoites. He initiated us into Elizabethanism and invited us to celebrate the edgy side of Shakespeare's work. And he enlisted us in the search for Shakespeare's missing library.

The discovery sparked an epiphany somewhere between *On the Road* and *Zen and the Art of Motorcycle Maintenance*. I became a student again, determined to learn everything I needed to become a bookman. Nearby universities offered no degrees in holistic bookmanship. Inspired by Fry and his circle, I improvised my own course, plucking units from literature, psychology, philosophy, art, commerce, curatorship, history, law, logic, mathematics—a mixture that made no sense to anyone but Fiona and me. When eventually I graduated, I walked away with a book about bookselling, a master's in book auctions, a doctorate in law, the untidiest transcript in Christendom, and a bespoke qualification in bibliophilia.

On weekends I started "running" books: driving around with a car full mostly of paperbacks, wholesaling them between bookshops. Fiona and I issued catalogues of highlights from our stock. Every book we bought to sell was a puzzle, a judgment to be backed. We relished the chance to work with objects, not just ideas. For us, this was the beginning of a career in books that saw us working side by side in a publishing house, and issuing with delight a series of books about books. We exhibited at bookfairs, and sold books to venerated libraries such as the Mitchell, the Houghton, and the Bodleian, whose users must swear not to remove or deface the objects therein, nor to bring or kindle any fire.

In the course of our work we visited hundreds of libraries. Libraries tidy and chaotic, dry and damp, fragrant and malodorous, welcoming and dangerous, containing nearly every kind of book: loved and neglected, meritorious and meretricious, read and unread. We explored national libraries, workingmen's libraries, subscription libraries, scholarly libraries, corporate libraries, club libraries, plush private libraries, and very modest ones, like the collection of "found" books amassed by a demolition man in the course of his labors, every volume methodically catalogued and lovingly preserved.

We ventured off-catalogue to make exhilarating discoveries on library shelves, like mislaid pamphlets, overlooked signatures, legendary variants, extra-illustrated rarities, and hidden fore-edge paintings. We explored sequestered spaces inside libraries, like the exquisite Shakespeare Room in the State Library of New South Wales, the super-tight spiral staircases deep inside the State Library of Victoria, and the panopticon cavity above the vaulted glass dome of the nearby parliamentary library, modeled on the original Reichstag.

We studied the crimes of book owners, such as the farmers who stored in a woolshed a priceless set (forty-one elephant-folio volumes) of John Gould's marvelous zoological illustrations, and the farmers' town cousins who stored a unique collection of books and manuscripts in a fireplace. We called on the hoarder who cut an indoor pathway to his bathtub, where his most prized possessions were kept. And we swooned over medieval libraries with books shelved spine-inward and attached to chains to prevent escape.

We learned that libraries are much more than mere accumulations of books. Every library has an atmosphere, even a spirit. Every visit to a library is an encounter with the ethereal phenomena of coherence, beauty, and taste. But libraries are not Platonic abstractions or sterile, hyperbaric chambers. They are human places into which humans cry tears, molt hair, slough skin, sneeze snot, and deposit oil from their hands—incidentally the best sustenance for old leather bindings.

How much of themselves did Shakespeare, Donne, Hemingway, and Woolf leave behind in their libraries? And how much of their personalities is discernible from their books? Creating a library is a psychically loaded enterprise. In gathering their bounty, book-lovers have displayed anxiety, avarice, envy, fastidiousness, obsession, lust, pride, pretension, narcissism, and agoraphobia—indeed every biblical sin and most of the pathologies from the American Psychiatric Association manual.

When visitors called on the seventeenth-century Welsh biblio-phile Sir William Boothby, he wished they would hurry up and leave. "My company is gone, so that now I hope to enjoy my selfe and books againe, which are the true pleasures of my life, all else is but vanity and noyse." John Hill Burton described a book collec-tor whose nervous temperament was so sensitive that he could not tolerate an alien book in proximity to his library; "the existence within his dwelling-place of any book not of his own special kind, would impart to him the sort of feeling of uneasy horror which a bee is said to feel when an earwig comes into its cell."

Collectors, having acquired and arranged their books through whichever means, have used every kind of simile to describe their beloved possessions. Garden flowers, verdant leaves, precious fruit, flowing fountains. Ships, houses, bricks, doors, nails, bullets, daggers, scents, elixirs, meteorites, gems, friends, offspring, prison-ers, tenants, soldiers, lovers, wraiths, devils, bones, eyes, teeth. John Baxter imagined the books in his Graham Greene collection rustling and rubbing against each other every night like a colony of insects.

Libraries provide ideal habitats for real insects, which are attracted to quiet, darkish, starchy places. Fiona and I have seen whole shelves of books destroyed by burrowing worms. For me, now, the mounds and trails they left behind are the stuff of genuinely horrifying nightmares. We've also seen whole collections ruined by grazing silverfish, the bibliophile's nemesis. Those monsters relish pulpy paper and the crunchy starch in book glue and book cloth. Seemingly preferring richer inks, they devastate dust jackets with tracks that look fiendishly deliberate.

From our visits to libraries we've learned much about the integ-rity of shelves. Smooth, strong, and open are best. Sagging shelves deform books into painful, non-Euclidean shapes. Abrasive shelves wear away at leather bindings. Books behind glass get sick from breathing their own air. Above all, we've learned that libraries are full of stories. Stories of life and death, lust and loss, keeping faith and breaking faith. Stories of every possible human drama. And via complex, fractal, inter-generational threads, all the stories are connected.

Pieces would be the first in a series of marvelous finds, several of which come instantly to mind. Found piled in a bedroom bookcase on an appraisal visit to a suburban home: two 1625 George Chapman plays, quarto format, in immaculate condition and bound together by one of the world's finest bookbinders, Riviere & Son. At the bottom of a dusty box in a country bookshop: a pre-revolutionary French royal binding, in wonderful condition and with spectacular provenance and rarity. In a secondhand store: Thomas Frognall Dibdin's luxurious catalogue of Lord Spencer's library at Althorp—the catalogue in which Dibdin glamourized the 1623 edition of Shakespeare's plays, the "First Folio."

Though John Fry died nearly two centuries ago, and though it would be years before I properly understood his work in context, he became my book-world mentor, imparting his fascination with the print culture of early-modern England. Under his influence I would write and publish about Shakespeare, and join the search for Elizabethan and Jacobean treasures. I would explore the greatest libraries and the infinite byways of bibliomania. All the while, a young bookseller from Bristol, long dead, would be my counselor and guide. This kind of practical immortality is a large part of why people love books. And why we write them.

Infinity

In 1937, at the age of thirty-eight, Jorge Luis Borges started his first regular full-time job: the "menial and dismal" work of re-cataloguing books at the Miguel Cané municipal library in the Boedo district of Buenos Aires. He worked surrounded by violent, lazy, and loutish colleagues. Often he would disappear to a quiet part of the library and attempt to write. On the way home each day, he walked ten blocks to the tramline, his eyes "filled with tears."

In 1938, on Christmas Eve, Borges ran upstairs and accidentally split his head open on a window casement. Elizabeth Hyde Stevens has described how the wound became poisoned and Borges spent the next week in a sleepless delirium. Suspended between life and death, he was unable to speak—until his mother brought him back to sentience by reading aloud from a book he'd ordered. "On that miraculous day, she looked up from reading C. S. Lewis, notic-ing he had begun to cry. In perfect speech, he told her, 'I'm crying because I understand.'"

One of the first pieces he wrote after his recovery was a short story titled "The Library of Babel"; Borges called it "a nightmare version or magnification" of the hellish Miguel Cané municipal library. The heart of the story is a remarkable vision of a universe consisting of an infinite library composed of interconnected hexagonal rooms, all the same size, all with bookshelves whose dimensions—thirty-five books per shelf, five shelves per side, twenty shelves per floor—mirrored those of the Miguel Cané.

The books themselves are standardized, too. Each one is 410 pages long; each page has forty lines; each line about eighty letters, which are limited to twenty-two phonic characters plus the full-stop and the comma and the space. The books' distribution among the hexagons is apparently random, though many theories exist about the distribution, and many attempts are made to find patterns in the randomness. Most of the books seem to be gibberish, but the library must contain, in every language, every book ever written, every book that might ever be written, and every possible version of every one of those books: detailed histories of the past and the future; faithful and unfaithful catalogues of the library; lost gospels, commentaries, and apocrypha; the lost books of Tacitus; "the treatise the Venerable Bede might have written (and never wrote) on Saxon mythology"; true and false accounts of your death . . .

This metaphor of infinite libraries has been expressed in countless other ways: every possible combination of musical notes; infinite cabinets of things; the set of possible protein sequences; the set of possible mystery-novel plots; tabulations of the secret name of God; the world, nature, and Google as universal libraries; the Bible, the Koran, the First Folio and *Finnegans Wake* as universal texts; monkeys with typewriters; pan-dimensional cryptographs; automatic writing; continuous narratives; nameless cities; formal depictions of mathematical and quantum indeterminacy; the *mare incognitum* and *terra nullius*; the set of all possible tweets. A page of pixels can be used to create not just every page of text, but every image as well. In principle, solids can be sliced into infinitely narrower planes.

In Borges's story, the Library of Babel is an endless subject of wonder for the civiliations that have grown up in its rooms and on its stairs. They construct legends and cults, they debate their theories, they explore the vast expanses of the labyrinth, and, when driven to despair, they jump to fast-slow deaths in the bottomless air shafts that stand between the hexagons.

For nine unhappy years, Borges remained at the Miguel Cané library. Partly on the strength of his literary reputation, he would escape to become director of the National Library of Buenos Aires—a position he remained in for eighteen happier years. Though he lost his sight in his early fifties, he refused to carry a cane and he continued to work. He also continued to visit bookshops. According to Alberto Manguel, who worked at Labach's bookshop in Buenos Aires, Borges would pass a hand over the shelves as though his fingers could see the titles. On one visit to Labach's, Borges was accompanied by his octogenarian mother. The author-librarian searched for medieval English texts. "Oh Georgie," Señora Borges said, "I don't know why you waste your time with Anglo-Saxon instead of studying something useful like Latin or Greek!"

THE
LIBRARY

CHAPTER 1

A Library with No Books

Oral traditions and the songlines

If a library can be something as simple as an organized collection of texts, then libraries massively pre-date books in the history of culture. Every country has a tradition of legends, parables, riddles, myths and chants that existed long before they were written down. Warehoused as memories, these texts passed from generation to generation through dance, gesture and word of mouth. The Kope of New Guinea, the Mandinka griots of Mali, the Ifugao of the Philippines, the Arabs of Palestine, the nomads of Mongolia, the Nambikwara of Brazil, and the Gitksan and Wet'suwet'en of British Columbia—these and other peoples used narrative forms such as *Hudhud* chants, *Hikaye* stories, *Urtiin duu* and *Bogino duu* (long and short songs) to maintain their immaterial libraries.

Cultures that lacked any form of writing could only ever preserve their texts imperfectly. Those cultures, though, adopted elaborate techniques (such as intricate patterns of repetition) and rules (such as social obligations and taboos) to maintain, as best they could, the integrity of their texts. The best examples of mnemonic formulas for preserving oral libraries are from ancient India. Memorizing a single text from the *Vedas* involved up to eleven forms of recitation, including the *jaṭā-pāṭha* ("mesh recitation"), in which every two adjacent words in the text are first recited in their original order, then repeated in reverse order, and finally repeated in the original order.

Perhaps the oldest oral library in the world was formed over a span of tens of thousands of years in the arid lands of central Australia. There, the Arrernte people developed a complex system of tribal knowledge, beliefs, duties, and ethics—what Van Gennep called, in his 1906 *Mythes et légendes d'Australie*, "at one and the same time fragments of a catechism, a liturgical manual, a history of civilization, a geography textbook [and] a manual of cosmography." Indigenous Australians sometimes refer to this expansive system as their "Dreaming" and their "Dreaming stories." The stories reflect the bosom connection between the first Australians, their land, and all its features—tors, plateaux, rivers, billabongs, animals, plants, routes for trade and conquest, and the journeys of totemic beings—giant animals and giant people—from the primordial past.

Travel and geography are so important to the Dreaming that the Dreaming stories are often called "Dreaming tracks," or, especially among the Arrernte, "*tjurunga* lines," a reference to the mysterious *tjurunga* stones that are vital to Arrernte tradition. Rich with sacred meaning, these flat, oblong-shaped stones, about three inches wide, are polished and incised with elaborate patterns and designs—concentric circles and meandering lines, dots, arches, and curves—representing the totems of the groups to which the stones belong. Thought by the Arrernte to have been made by the ancestors themselves, the *tjurungas* are a physical counterpart to the Aborigines' oral libraries. Most *tjurungas* had a central place in "love magic," initiation ceremonies and other ancient rituals. (Versions of the stones tied with women's hair can be swung to make a charmed sound and have been called "bull-roarers" and "wife callers.") When the *tjurungas* were not being used for sacred purposes, male Arrernte elders wrapped them in leaves or bark, hid them in caves, or, when circumstances called for it, carried them overland with great reverence and secrecy.

Every Dreaming track is inherently multifaceted, blending animate and inanimate entities, past and present, fact and belief, ground and sky. It is, as Nicholas Shakespeare writes, "at once a map, a long narrative poem, and the foundation of an Aboriginal's religious and traditional life . . . It is secret and there are penalties for those who transgress." Not surprisingly for a set of concepts that pre-date writing, the tracks resist simple expression in prose.

Nevertheless, the tracks have been the subject of intense scientific and pseudo-scientific study, much of it conducted near Alice Springs at Hermannsburg—a Lutheran mission to the Western Arrernte and Loritja people of remote central Australia. Géza Róheim, the Hungarian-American Freudian, conducted fieldwork there in 1929 with his wife, Ilonka. Freud encouraged and assisted Róheim's work at Hermannsburg as well as in Melanesia, Somaliland, and Arizona. Róheim subsequently wrote about the Arrernte and Pitjantjatjara people and was applauded as the first ethnologist to interpret culture psychoanalytically.

From 1894 to 1922, Carl Strehlow was Hermannsburg's

Lutheran pastor. During his twenty-eight-year calling, he only left central Australia three times. Struck down by dropsy in 1922, he tried to leave a fourth time, to seek medical treatment in Adelaide, but only advanced 240 arduous kilometers before the disease claimed his life; he was buried on the route, at Horseshoe Bend. His son Theodor, known as Ted, grew up among the Arrernte and became an anthropologist of sorts. On a disastrous trip to Europe, he felt shunned by the leaders of the field who frowned at his lack of formal training. He returned to central Australia and continued to study its indigenous people.

In a career spanning four decades, Ted Strehlow undertook fieldwork that was remarkable for its breadth, depth, and fruits. He collected from Arrernte groups some 1,800 objects, most of them sacred, many of them *tjurungas*. He also collected a library of songs, publishing his analysis of them in his 1971 magnum opus, *Songs of Central Australia*. The beauty and complexity of the Dreaming tracks enchanted Strehlow. Attempting to understand them was an epic puzzle, perhaps ultimately impossible, "like opening a door in a secret palace and entering a labyrinth of countless corridors and passages." In *Songs*, Strehlow built an elaborate descriptive and theoretical architecture that linked Arrernte Dreaming with the Western literary canon. Rich with analogies from Greek and Norse mythology, the book received a distinctly mixed reception among the few people who read it. Those people described it variously as "a treasure trove of poetry," "wildly eccentric," and "a dense, often bewilderingly literary work." Five years after Strehlow's death, the British author Bruce Chatwin telephoned Ted's widow, Kath. Chatwin introduced himself and explained that he had read *Songs* and wished to buy another copy of the book. Kath replied, "Let me say hello to the first man in the world who's read it.'

Chatwin had encountered *Songs* soon after its publication. In

1972 he proposed writing a profile of Strehlow for the *Sunday Times*. This was one of several projects left unfinished when Chatwin shot off to South America to write a travel book. He may have become aware of Strehlow's work at an even earlier date: he later claimed to have discussed nomadic art and Strehlow with the Australian archaeologist John Mulvaney in 1970. According to Chatwin's version of that conversation, he met Mulvaney at the Pitt Rivers Museum in Oxford; Chatwin suggested the "walkabout" might be a way to unlock "the nature of human restlessness"; and Mulvaney pointed him in the direction of Strehlow. Mulvaney later confessed to having no memory of this encounter: either he forgot it completely or it never took place at all.

Chatwin's reaction to *Songs* was unambiguous. He saw Strehlow's monolith as "perhaps the only book in the world—the only real attempt since the *Poetics* of Aristotle, to define what song (and with song *all* language) is . . . I feel I'm reading Heidegger or Wittgenstein." Strehlow's *Aranda Traditions*, published in 1947, was for Chatwin another "twentieth century lynchpin: you only have to look at the work of Lévi-Strauss to realise this." On the strength of his reaction to Strehlow's writings, Chatwin traveled to central Australia in January 1983. He would retrace Ted's footsteps and write a serious study of Arrernte culture. Once in Australia, he focused on the *tjurunga* tracks, which held an irresistible appeal as an antipodean analogue to Britain's mystical ley lines. Overbrimming with anthropological mystery, the tracks promised to bridge narrative history and prehistoric migration. Chatwin saw in the Dreaming tracks something vastly grander than anything else mankind had built. "The pyramids are little mud pies in comparison."

Chatwin knew something of the ancient world. At the age of eighteen, straight out of secondary school, he'd joined Sotheby's in London as an assistant porter in the Works of Art department. His job was to dust and move tribal artifacts and European and Oriental pots—tasks he performed poorly. "Bruce would wander around where he wanted. When sales went on view, there would be thirty-five lots missing and things were misnumbered and dirty." Chatwin was nevertheless promoted, working as a junior cataloguer across Furniture, Modern Pictures, and Antiquities. As handsome as he was quick-witted, Chatwin feared Sotheby's directors were using him as "live bait" to ensnare wealthy art owners of both genders.

Now in Australia, Chatwin struck a T. E. Lawrence–like pose: a go-anywhere literary adventurer, highly sexed, unafraid of the desert or of snakes. When he returned to England he appeared on BBC Two alongside Mario Vargas Llosa and—the champion of the literary world's fascination with libraries and mazes—Jorge Luis Borges. Borges was eighty-four, Chatwin forty-three and still riding the success of the experimental travel book, *In Patagonia*, that he'd written while truanting from the *Sunday Times*. He and Borges had more than one thing in common. As Shakespeare noted in his Chatwin biography, "Many of the skills Borges acquired through cataloguing books for the Miguel Cané municipal library, Bruce picked up in Antiquities." Those skills included an understanding of provenance and the ability to juggle masses of detail. The television program was prefaced by a Borgesian parable that resonated with Chatwin's own life and searching. In the parable, a man embarks on a lifelong quest to discover the world. He collects a jumble of images, "of provinces, kingdoms, mountains, bays, ships, islands, fish, rooms, instruments, heavenly bodies, horses and people." Finally, as his death approaches, he realizes that the collection of images has made a composite picture—of his own face.

Chatwin would make a second trip to Australia, in 1984. The results of his work there appeared in 1987 as *Songlines*. The title recalled Strehlow's *Songs of Central Australia* and was Chatwin's word for the labyrinthine Arrernte Dreaming tracks. On one level, the book was simply a travel memoir, and that is how many readers and booksellers received it: another work in a tweedy genre whose authors were, according to the critic Rory Stewart, "celebrated for neither their prose nor their charm." Chatwin, though, had greater ambitions for the book, regarding it as a quintessentially literary work that, like *Madame Bovary*, blurred the line between fiction and nonfiction, which, anyway, Chatwin argued, was an arbitrary boundary invented by publishers. When the Thomas Cook Travel Award short-listed the book, Chatwin asked that it be withdrawn from contention.

Songlines became a *Sunday Times* and *New York Times* bestseller. Hardback sales quickly surpassed 20,000 copies, and Chatwin, in Nicholas Shakespeare's words, "strode into the realm of literary respectability." "I can't say I believe the songlines *literally*," said Colin Thubron. "Maybe any third-year anthropology student could shoot it to bits, but what's wonderful is the passion with which Bruce approaches it." Admirers agreed that Chatwin had created a new type of book. Shirley Hazzard wrote to him: "Things can never again be quite the same as they were ante-B.C." Writing in the *New York Review of Books*, Rory Stewart saw in the book a better, grander, less regular, more exotic English literature, the sharp counterpoint to what Andrew Harvey called in the *New York Times* "Little Englanderism [and] a literary establishment that loves to reward poems to goldfish and novels about the tepid lusts of women librarians."

When the book reached central Australia, though, the reception was quite different. *Songlines* ignited a blast of criticism from historians, ethnographers, and other observers, several of whom could claim direct cultural links to the traditions Chatwin had sought to picture. The basis for the criticism was clear: Chatwin had misunderstood and misstated the place of *tjurunga* tracks in the Arrernte's past and present. In the *Songlines* version of the tracks, Chatwin had dimmed down and generalized the scope and place of the songs and their connection to land and tradition. His lines were too geographical, too explicable, too . . . linear. He'd failed to capture the ineluctable complexity, the genuine wonder, of the Arrernte library.

Critics detected a naive imperial sensibility in *Songlines*. If Chatwin had helped put Aborigines on the international map, it was a map, according to Shakespeare, "superficially exquisite and tasteful like a Mont Blanc pen, and as unrelated to everyday life." After calling the book a tremendous misuse of poetic license, Christopher Pearson quoted Stewart Harris: "If there is one person more damaging to the position of the Aboriginal Australian than the racist, it is the person who idealises them and romanticises them." People who'd met Chatwin in central Australia noted the gulf between the real Bruce and the one in the book. (Among other things, he really was afraid of snakes.) Adopting the persona of a serious academic deploying rigorous methods was just one part of a rankling performance that bordered on deception.

Chatwin was accused of failing to give the Aborigines their due voice. The Arrernte for their part were certain they did not need a white man to mediate their texts and render them intelligible. In many respects the book added insult to the injuries caused by Ted Strehlow, whose irreparable, unforgivable betrayal of the Arrernte had three main limbs: taking the sacred *tjurungas*, and with them a large part of Arrernte culture; passing them on to his second wife, in breach of every Arrernte taboo; and revealing, in the German magazine *Stern*, secrets he'd promised to keep. Taking away the *tjurungas*, and failing to guard their secrets, was as much a library crime as the institutional depredations of notorious book thieves such as Thomas Wise, Count Libri, and James Halliwell.

(In August 1983, Chatwin wrote to the Australian author Murray Bail, asking about "a pulped book on songlines." The book was Charles P. Mountford's 1976 *Nomads of the Australian Desert*. Mountford was a noted Australian anthropologist; his book, which included photographs of indigenous ceremonies, was withdrawn from sale on the grounds that it revealed secrets of the Pitjantjatjara people. This was the first time a book had been withdrawn in Australia for reasons of indigenous cultural sensitivity—a watershed moment in the growth of respect for the first Australians. Though the publisher withdrew the book from normal sales channels, the edition was not pulped. Copies were sold through anthropological societies and remainder dealers. One local author obtained his copy from the Fremantle Prison library.)

The Strehlow–Chatwin account of the oral library of central Australia was a hub of concentric scandals. And yet, despite the blunders in how it was studied and represented, the library does possess the epic grandeur that attracted Strehlow and Chatwin to write about it. That grandeur embraces ancient songs of spectacular richness and diversity. Laws, too, such as the penalties for not killing and cooking a kangaroo correctly. And beautiful word-pictures, like the description of that moment in twilight when the tufts of grass can no longer be distinguished apart, and the moment at dawn, when the eastern sky is aflame with the fingers of the rising sun. The Arrernte narrative tradition is vastly richer than Chatwin had imagined. In the twentieth century, Australia was the perfect place to study oral libraries, but Chatwin and Strehlow failed in their duty as curators.

During his eight-year career at Sotheby's in London and New York, Chatwin had risen to the positions of director, partner, and "expert." But the monkish work of cataloguing took a toll on his eyesight and his state of mind. In February 1965, he left for a long recuperation in the Sudan—the first in a series of dramatic escapes. Though Chatwin returned to Sotheby's and oversaw in Paris the dispersal of Helena Rubinstein's collection of African and Oceanic sculptures, that would be his last major sale for the firm.

At Sotheby's he became notorious for identifying and calling out fakes. He would stride into the salesroom, hurricane-like, and point to Renoirs and Pollocks. "That's a fake. That's a fake. That's a fake." He would also find fakes outside the salesroom, such as the golden eagle necklace, of the Veraguas culture, which researcher Estelle Neumann wore "flapping between her breasts." Often Chatwin was right, but sometimes the "it's a fake" mood would consume him and he would condemn even genuine works. His approach exhausted and alienated his colleagues. Tim Clarke headed the porcelain department. Clarke's wife spoke for "not a few people" within Sotheby's when she said of Chatwin, "We thought *he* was a bit of a fake."

Susannah Clapp, Chatwin's first editor at Jonathan Cape, related the following story. Four years after Chatwin's second and final trip to central Australia, Jonathan Hope (Somerset Maugham's grandson) visited him at the Ritz Hotel in London. Chatwin was bedridden, suffering from the illness that would claim his life. He gave Hope a gift: a small, round, sharp object he'd found in the outback. "An Aboriginal subincision knife," he said—an instrument designed to be used in an initiation rite in which the underside of the urethra is slit open. Holding the object up to the light, Chatwin said it was made from some sort of desert opal. "It's a wonderful colour," he said. "Almost the colour of chartreuse." A few weeks later, James Mollison, Director of the National Gallery of Australia, arrived at Jonathan Hope's house to examine Indonesian textiles. Mollison took the knife from the table, looked at it closely, then announced his verdict. It was amazing, he said, what the Aborigines could make from an old bottle shard.

The pleasure of books

Books, Petrarch wrote, heartily delight us, speak to us, counsel us, and are joined to us by a living and active relationship. Instructing his servants to guard his library as they would a shrine, he kept up an active acquaintance with his books, just as if they were friends capable of talking. The Ottoman poet Abdüllatif Çelebi called each of his books a true and loving friend who drives away all cares. Umberto Eco imagined his books talking among themselves, while Alberto Manguel called the writing of endpaper notes the habit of speaking of a book behind its back.

Elias Canetti's 1935 novel, *Auto-da-Fé*, meditated on the precise nature of books' genial proclivities: "What proof have we that inorganic objects can feel no pain? Who knows if a book may not yearn for other books, its companions of many years, in some way strange to us and therefore never yet perceived?"

Regard for books often goes beyond convivial attachment. Charles Lamb, Samuel Taylor Coleridge, and Thomas Frognall Dibdin are three famous literary men who kissed their books. Henry Crabb Robinson once saw Coleridge kiss the engraved title page of his copy of Spinoza. Thomas à Kempis told his students to take a book "into thine hands as Simeon the Just took the Child Jesus into his arms to carry him and kiss him." During Benedetto Croce's youth, he kissed the pages of Pellico's *Le mie prigioni* in an ecstasy of joy.

Deidre Shauna Lynch wrote an excellent book on the subject of book-love and its physical manifestations. Titled *Loving Literature*, Lynch's monograph chronicles hundreds of instances in which books were kissed, caressed, and even fondled. Seventeenth-century naval administrator, politician, and diarist Samuel Pepys took this game to a whole new level, if we are to believe his account of buying Voragine's 1521 *Golden Legend* on April 10, 1668: "So to piper and Duck Lane, and there kissed bookseller's wife and bought Legend.'

Reading one book while recalling another was, according to the poet Ezequiel Martínez Estrada, one of the most delicate forms of adultery. The Folger librarian Louis Wright wrote of an English wife who parted company with her husband because he insisted upon reciting Shakespeare in the middle of the night. A perhaps less fortunate wife, from Los Angeles, had the same problem except that her husband read Emerson.

Assembling a library is a minefield of etiquette. In the Middle Ages, ecclesiastical and monastic librarians divided sacred from profane books, and were forbidden from placing "unholy" books above holy ones, even in temporary storage. Commenting on a friend's library in the fifth century, Sidonius Apollinaris complained that pagan authors were separated from Christian ones, "the pagans near the gentlemen's seats, the Christians near the ladies." In a similar spirit, an 1863 book of etiquette and deportment instructed book owners to segregate the works of male and female authors, "unless they happen to be married."

Though himself married, Isaac Gosset advocated the bachelor state for collectors. "Never think of marriage," he would say to young book-lovers, "and if the thought should occur, take down a book and begin to read until it vanishes." Bibliophiles frequently refer to themselves as "wedded" to their books; those unable to resist the charms of *human* marriage have been known to keep their purchases secret from their human spouses. To avoid that necessity, the author and librarian A. N. L. "Tim" Munby advised new and prospective husbands that the "education" of wives must be started early: "a visit to at least one bookshop a day throughout the honeymoon is to be recommended." In 1917 Margaret Darwin, granddaughter of Charles Darwin, married the surgeon and bookman Geoffrey Keynes. When the honeymooners visited a bookshop, Margaret complained of feeling faint. Geoffrey "took her outside and made her comfortable, then went back to finish the shop." A long and happy marriage followed.

(Geoffrey's older brother was the famous economist John Maynard Keynes. A member of the liberated Bloomsbury group, Maynard married a ballerina, Lydia Lopokova. Serious and introverted Geoffrey found playful and outgoing Lydia utterly baffling. At Maynard's funeral in 1946, Geoffrey wore a black coat and striped trousers. "Oh, Geoffrey," Lydia said, "you look so sexy." Afterwards, Geoffrey asked several of his friends, "What *can* she have meant?")

An excessive attachment to books can be dangerous. Desiderius Erasmus had clear priorities. "When I have a little money, I buy books; and if I have any left, I buy food and clothes." The French philologist and lawyer Salmasius asked to be locked inside the library at Heidelberg. There he remained for forty-eight hours with neither food nor drink—sustained only by his proximity to treasured books. Leigh Hunt recorded how Elizabeth West, wife of the painter Benjamin West, was so fond of books she became a martyr to them, her physician declaring "she lost the use of her limbs by sitting indoors reading." The Greek philosopher Carneades "was so deeply plunged in an overweening desire for knowledge, so *besotted* with it, that he never had leisure to cut his hair, or pare his nails." The philologist Budaeus showed his commitment in a different way. When a servant rushed into his study to warn him that the house was on fire, Budaeus replied, "Tell my wife that I never interfere with the household," and he went on reading.

CHAPTER 2

The Last Days of Alexandria

Ancient books and their storage

First came oral libraries, then collections of physical books. The roots of the words "library" and "book" derive from different languages—*liber* is from Latin, while *bece, buc,* and *boc* are from the cluster of Germanic languages that includes Old Frisian, Old Saxon, Old Norse, and Old English. Both roots, though, have similar meanings: *liber* is bark, *bece* beech wood. Both etymologies relate to forest materials for book-making. The meaning of these roots is important. As soon as people began writing things down, the properties and availability of book-making materials became intertwined with the history of books and libraries.

Around 1200 B.C., Rameses II assembled a great library of books that included all the principal book materials available in the Nile

Valley. More than ten types of book were represented, among them volumes made from papyrus, palm leaves, bone, bark, ivory, linen, and stone. A single snapshot in 5,000 years of bookish experimentation, Rameses's collection could only ever tell part of the story. In other lands and other times, books would also be made from silk, gems, plastic, silicon, bamboo, hemp, rags, glass, grass, wood, wax, rubber, enamel, iron, copper, silver, gold, turtle shell, antlers, hair, rawhide, and the intestines of elephants.

In the making of books, local availability long dictated what materials would be used, and to what extent; local abundance enabled abundant use. The banks of the Tigris and the Euphrates were heavy with clay, so Mesopotamian scribes naturally used it to make their books. In the Nile Valley, however, clay was scarce— the very first Egyptian tablets were made from bone and ivory. Later Egyptian books, in scroll format, used the plentiful pith of the Nile papyrus. In China, long before Europe, paper was made in large quantities from the abundant bamboo and the by-products of everyday life.

The ancient city of Pergamum, in what is now Turkey, lay at the center of a region of cattle, sheep, and goat grazing. Animal skins for making parchment were therefore plentiful. Experimentally at first, parchment was used to supply Pergamum's large library. At that time, there was already a long history of people using animal parts to keep written records; animals had given much in the history of the book, and they would give much more still. Parchment is made by washing and stretching a split skin and rubbing it smooth. A single flawless sheep yields one folio sheet. As Lewis Buzbee noted in *The Yellow-Lighted Bookshop*, twenty skins might be needed to make a small book, "but you could eat the leftovers. And yes, that's why a diploma is called a sheepskin." In the year 1000 C.E., an average-sized book consumed the skins of dozens, even hundreds of animals. A 1,000-page Bible, for example, needed 250 sheep. In *Curiosities of Literature*, Isaac D'Israeli marveled that the volumes written by Zoroaster, entitled *The Similitude*, were said to have taken up the space of 1,260 cattle hides. The largest surviving medieval manuscript, the *Codex Gigas* or Devil's Bible, is thought to have been made from the skins of 160 donkeys.

Quality issues always loom large when using animal hides, especially those of wild animals. Kangaroo skins, for example, have been used for bookbinding, but their quality is notoriously variable. Male kangaroos have long, scraping claws. Raw roo leather often arrives scratched and scored with what are known in the leather trade as "mating marks." In the Middle Ages, scribes sometimes had to work with parchment that was similarly holed by wounds or insects. Some blemishes were repaired with silk thread, others incorporated into the illuminator's design. At Durham there is a delightful gospel book, dating from the seventh or eighth century, in which the improvising scribe has carefully decorated the edges of several insect bites.

Vellum, the most deluxe and tragic form of parchment—made from the skin of bovine fetuses—is smooth, white, and highly workable. Thomas Frognall Dibdin, the illustrious nineteenth-century bibliographer and book kisser, regarded vellum-bound books as the pinnacle of bookish treasure. He called them "membranaceous bijoux." Vellum is also highly durable. When Tim Munby was librarian at Cambridge University's King's College, he co-owned a 1925 type 40 Bugatti, "which was regularly taken to pieces by the roadside." On one trip, when one of the car's gaskets kept blowing, Munby had a few of his own rare manuscripts to hand. After a process of experimentation, the gasket turned out to respond to vellum. An old antiphonal that had been ruined by water was cut up and put to use,

> and this, when enthusiasts asked the Bugatti's age, enabled one to indulge in a little piece of lifemanship and reply nonchalantly, "Parts of it date back to the fifteenth century."

Scholars have noticed a relationship between the availability of writing materials, the vibrancy of literary activity, and the growth of libraries. According to Herodotus, by 500 B.C. papyrus was the preferred writing material on the Grecian peninsula. When Athens imported large quantities of Egyptian papyrus, a flood of Athenian literary work followed and the city's libraries prospered. Those libraries, such as the great research collection formed by Aristotle for the Lyceum (c. 335 B.C.), were the location for two important beginnings: the inception of Western scholarship, and the creation of architectural features—spaces for reading, writing, and conversing—that distinguish all subsequent academic, monastic, and public libraries through the classical era to the Middle Ages, the Renaissance, and beyond.

Five centuries after the Athenian library boom, the same sequence was repeated in Rome: plentiful papyrus led to a flourishing of Roman book-making and library formation. (Conversely, a second-century Ptolemaic embargo on Egyptian papyrus exports caused difficulties for writers and readers throughout the classical world.) The pattern would continue. In early Christian times, increased supplies of parchment—favored as a more reliable alternative to papyrus—made possible the monastic output of codices. Along with printing, the greater use of paper in the sixteenth century underwrote the spectacular literary output of Elizabethan England.

The library of Rameses II contained books made from papyrus but not from true paper; book-makers would not use that material until much later. But the library did contain clay tablets, which had been imported from the Fertile Crescent to the northeast. Dating from before 3100 B.C., the very first libraries of physical books are thought to have appeared in that region. The libraries were modest storerooms, containing tens of thousands of square and rectangular clay tablets, each one about half the length of a *tjurunga* stone, each one covered with markings. The tablets were carefully organized on shelves and in trays. Tablet rooms at Ebla, Mari, and Uruk are examples of these simple libraries. Throughout Mesopotamia, scribes used a complex script, known as "cuneiform," to write Akkadian, Elamite, Hattic, Hittite, Urartian—a total of fifteen languages from the nursery of civilization, the area of modern-day Syria, Iraq, and western Iran.

To write cuneiform, Mesopotamian scribes used chevron-shaped styli to impress precise signs (representing sounds) into wet clay. Thomas Hyde, Regius Professor of Hebrew and Laudian Professor of Arabic at Oxford University, gave cuneiform its name; the signs brought to mind for him *cuneus*, the Latin word for "wedge." The script was so complex that some of the first modern archaeologists denied it was a script at all. In Hyde's 1700 book on Persia, for example, the double professor confessed he regretted the survival of the cuneiform inscriptions at Persepolis because they were a triviality, "likely to waste a lot of people's time." The inscriptions, he said, proved cuneiform could not be writing: the characters in the inscriptions were never repeated; they must just have been a playful experiment, an attempt to see how many different combinations the artist could create from a single element—a set of signs, in other words, as unhelpful as the mysterious Voynich manuscript or the nonsense books in Borges's infinite library.

The doubters, however, were wrong. Today, not only can we understand the writing, we can even pronounce the words, more or less as they were spoken thousands of years ago. Apart from official records, the cuneiform tablets captured epic poems and stories—such as the tale of Utnapishtim and Gilgamesh—that had first been composed long before the arrival of writing. In the twentieth century, the earliest Albatross and Penguin paperbacks were color-coded by genre. In contrast, the first clay tablets were shape-coded: square for financial accounts, round for farming records, and so on. Some featured both text and images, making them the first illustrated books.

Tablets of special importance received special protection. Each one of a group of Assyrian tablets, now in the British Museum, was encased in a clay shell. Readers could only access the tablets by breaking the shells—the very first book covers—like walnuts. Just as the Mesopotamians did, the first Egyptian scribes made tablets, but they used different materials and a different script, namely hieroglyphics. That iconic, pictorial script was first used at around the same time as cuneiform, and seems to have been influenced by it, though the relationship between the two scripts is not at all clear. Cuneiform's precedence over hieroglyphics was for many years a settled question in academia. Recent discoveries, though, have thrown the order of invention into contention. The debate is lively, and paleographers have begun taking sides.

Both camps can point to early stories about the invention of writing. A Sumerian legend gives that invention to Enmerkar, lord of Kulaba. He is said to have sent an emissary to another lord to ask for materials with which to rebuild the residence of the goddess Inanna. The emissary ferried back and forth between the two lords, passing on their messages, until he lost track—Enmerkar's instructions became too difficult to memorize. According to this story, the lord of Kulaba invented writing so he could be sure his messages were getting through. The myth on the Egyptian side contains some familiar characters. According to Plato, Socrates told Phaedrus that the Egyptian god Theuth invented writing, and demonstrated it to the god Thamous (Amon) as a means to "increase the intelligence of the people of Egypt and improve their memories." Neither story is very helpful to the debate: Enmerkar existed too late—more than four centuries after the first Mesopotamian tablet books—and Theuth probably never existed at all.

Papyrus is well suited to scrolls. The libraries of the ancient world—patrician, official, scholarly, domestic—stored their scrolls in chests, niches, and hatbox-like containers known as *capsae*. One of these is shown in a beautiful fresco at Herculaneum, near Pompeii. Herculaneum's Villa of the Papyri is an example of the scroll libraries that were common in ancient Rome. Eighteen hundred scrolls were unearthed there in the eighteenth century—the most well-preserved library from antiquity.

Much is known about how scrolls were produced, and about who did what in the production process. The *librarii* copied the author's manuscript; the *librarioli* ornamented the copies and supplied titles and other ancillary matter; and the *bibliopegi* bound the copies by evening up the margins, squaring the ends, polishing the blank sides with pumice, and attaching wooden rods (taller than the scroll was wide) to each end—these aided rolling and reading, and helped protect the scroll from damage. The rods could also be slotted into a desk to keep the scroll open.

The greatest scroll library in all history was assembled downstream from the main source of papyrus. A port city in northern Egypt, Alexandria was a key capital in the Hellenic empire established by Alexander the Great and his generals. Around 300 B.C., the Greek-speaking Ptolemaic dynasty founded the Great Library of Alexandria inside the fortified walls of the royal palace, on a spit of land between an intertidal lake and the man-made port at Pharos. The library's *bibliothekai* or bookshelves were probably set in recesses along a wide covered passageway. The precise layout of the collections is uncertain, but the Italian classicist and historian Luciano Canfora surmised, "Every niche or recess must have been dedicated to a certain class of authors, each marked with an appropriate heading." Above the *bibliothekai* was an inscription: "The place of the cure of the soul.'

The library adopted an admirably inclusive and international ambition: to assemble books from all the known countries and in all the languages. During the third century B.C., Ptolemy III sent messages to kings, lords, and rajas asking for books to copy. While in reality most of the texts obtained by the library were Greek, it did succeed in gathering substantial numbers of books from India, the Near and Middle East, and elsewhere in the Alexandrine world— books that represented a multitude of philosophies and creeds.

The library was also the venue for important translations, such as rendering the Torah from Biblical Hebrew into Greek— the famous Septuagint. Ptolemy II Philadelphus was behind this project. He asked seventy-two Jewish scholars to undertake the translation. According to the Tractate Megillah of the Babylonian Talmud, a miracle of congruency followed.

King Ptolemy once gathered seventy-two Elders. He placed them in seventy-two chambers, each of them in a separate one, without revealing to them why they were summoned. He entered each one's room and said: "Write for me the Torah of Moshe, your teacher." God put it in the heart of each one to translate identically as all the others did.

Philo of Alexandria suggested that the number of scholars was determined by selecting six scholars from each of the twelve tribes of Israel.

The internationalism of Alexandria's acquisitions policy had a Sumerian antecedent. Discovered in 1849 by the amateur archaeologist and adventurer Henry Layard, the royal library at Nineveh was an attempt by King Ashurbanipal to collect all available knowledge in one place. The Ptolemies picked up where Ashurbanipal left off. At its peak, Alexandria's library held hundreds of thousands of scrolls. Some accounts have put the number at half a million, others 1 million, plus another 40,000 in a building attached to the Temple of Serapis, in the old Egyptian quarter of Rhakotis.

Despite the labels on the outside of Alexandria's scrolls, readers struggled to find specific volumes—there were just too many books. A solution, though, was at hand. The famous poet and teacher Callimachus of Cyrene would help keep the books in order, and help scholars navigate through the collections. In other words, he would be a librarian.

From ancient writers such as Strabo, Athenaeus, Epiphanius, and the Byzantine authorities Suidas and Tzetzes, we know much about the operations of Alexandria's library. The so-called

Oxyrhynchus fragment no. 1241 is especially informative. That damaged fragment is from a group of papyri discovered in the late nineteenth and early twentieth centuries at a site near the modern Egyptian town of el-Bahnasa. The site was an ancient rubbish dump. Like other landfill found there, the manuscripts span the first six centuries A.D. They include thousands of Greek and Latin books and documents. Dating from the second century and written in a careful uncial script, the anonymously authored fragment 1241 is "a characteristic product of the Alexandrian erudition which exercised itself in antiquarian research and tabulation." Along with military and mythological information, and short catalogues of famous sculptors and painters and grammarians, the document contains a priceless chronological list of the head librarians at Alexandria.

Thanks to this and other sources, we know not only the names of the first half-dozen librarians—such as Zenodotus of Ephesus and Aristophanes of Byzantium—but also their duties and achievements—Callimachus was responsible for the library's catalogue, for example. We also know that, under the Ptolemies, the office of Alexandrian librarian was a high one, suitable for royal tutors and superannuated military men.

To expand the great library's famous collections, the authorities at Alexandria adopted a famous policy. Whenever a ship arrived at the city's port with scrolls on board, the scrolls were taken to the library for copying. When the copying was finished, the new facsimiles were returned to the ship, and the originals stayed in the library. Books obtained in this way were identified in the catalogue as "from the ships." Alexandria's assertive collections policy seems to have been applied in other ways, too. When the library borrowed the works of Sophocles, Euripides, and Aeschylus from Athens in order to make copies, the copies rather than the originals were sent back to Greece. Once Alexandria became notorious as a book moocher, other cities and libraries refused to lend their books unless the Ptolemies staked large security deposits. According to Galen, the great library could only keep the Athenian books by forfeiting an enormous bond of fifteen talents (450 kilograms) of gold or silver.

Alexandria's acquisitions policy was a precursor to a law passed by the King of France more than a thousand years later. Established in 1537 by the *Ordonnance de Montpellier*, "legal deposit" prevented printers and publishers from selling a book unless a copy was given to the royal library at the Château de Blois. The law covered all new books, regardless of their size, cost, genre, or language. (After reestablishing this right of legal deposit, the post-revolutionary Bibliothèque Nationale would also assume the power to preemptively purchase books at auction sales.) In this and other respects, Alexandria is an important waypoint in a continuum that links the collections, policies, and practices of the world's ancient and modern libraries.

Through a private agreement with the Stationers' Company, Sir Thomas Bodley established England's first legal deposit scheme in 1610. The company agreed to send to the Bodleian Library "a copy of every book entered in their Register on condition that the books thus given might be borrowed if needed for reprinting, and that the books given to the Library by others might be examined, collated and copied by the Company." Unlike the Egyptians and the French, Bodley seems to have intended the scheme to be selective rather than comprehensive. Tellingly, he reprimanded the University Librarian, Thomas James, for cataloguing many "idle bookes and riffe raffes" unworthy of the Bodleian. In 1662 the scheme was extended to the Royal Library and the Cambridge University Library, and these collections too obtained much "riffe raffe."

With such a concentration of books and scholarship, Alexandria was naturally home to spectacular achievements in medicine, astronomy, and geometry. Eratosthenes worked out ninety-nine percent of the circumference of the Earth. Archimedes worked out 99.9 percent of pi. In the history of Western thought, the library came to rival Athens as an intellectual powerhouse. Alexandria's collection was specifically a scholars' library; the Ptolemies regarded men like Archimedes, Eratosthenes, and Euclid as the ideal users. A whole other class of user, though, also had a stake in the library.

Not far from Alexandria's perilous red-light district, the city's merchant quarter hosted a boisterous array of booksellers. "Disreputable" and "unscrupulous" were the words most often used to describe them. They survived on several rackets, one of which was to bribe the librarians to remove scrolls from the collections; the scrolls were then copied, and the booksellers sold the piratical versions locally and abroad.

The Ptolemies' appetite for the classics was voracious. Apart from mandating the copying of texts, the king sent his agents far and wide to borrow and buy more and more books. This appetite created another opening for book-world entrepreneurs. A class of para-literary workers on the fringes of the library produced forgeries, then collaborated with the booksellers to distribute them, and, often, to sell them to the library. Apocryphal Aristotelian treatises were a favorite, and were produced to a convincingly high standard. Only after centuries of subsequent research were they proven to be bogus.

Even legitimate-seeming scholars produced fraudulent works for sale to the library. Posing as an Athenian contemporary and confidant of Thucydides, the scholar Cratippus wrote *Everything Thucydides Left Unsaid*, "in which he made happy use of bombast and anachronism." The book found its way into the collection, where it was treated as a legitimate text. Dionysius of Halicarnassus and Plutarch both took the manuscript seriously. This style of work, parasitically piggy-backing on the reputation of a valued author, would become a staple of fraudulent publishing in the early-modern era and well into the Enlightenment. Names as famous as Shakespeare, Johnson, and Swift would appear on books cobbled together by opportunistic and anonymous authors.

Elias Canetti's *Auto-da-Fé* is a lurid retelling of the shadowy history of Alexandria's library. Herr Doktor Peter Kien, the novel's main protagonist, is a middle-aged Sinologist and voracious book-buyer. In Kien's childhood he had stowed away in a bookshop overnight— just so he could be, like Salmasius, with the books. Now in adulthood, he assembles in his apartment a personal collection of 25,000 volumes, the most important private library in Vienna. He surrounds himself with so many books that he must wall up his windows to accommodate more shelves. Kien's world is full of dangers, especially those of social interaction and bacteriological infection. One dread, though, stands out above all others. Kien's insatiable appetite for books is matched by a fear that they will be lost in fire.

Conned by everyone around him, Kien marries his housekeeper Therese—"a sturdy peasant type," who has "her eye on the main chance"—with the idea that she will dust his books and help keep them safe. Within days of the marriage she begins to take charge.

Kien must give up three-quarters of his library as a living space for his new wife. Then he is forced out of his apartment altogether. Homeless, he enters a nightmarish underworld of seedy bars, bungling police, apparitions, molesters, cutthroats, and con-artists.

Descending into madness, Kien employs Fischerle, an unscrupulous, chess-playing, hump-backed dwarf, to catalogue the library that exists in the bibliophile's head. At the local pawnshop, Kien appoints himself principal book-rescuer. Whenever customers arrive with books to pawn, Kien pays for them and sends the would-be hocker away with a lecture on the proper care of books. This gives Fischerle an idea. He and his gang assemble fake parcels of worthless volumes, then take them to the pawnshop. Again Kien pays for them, and the gang members share the proceeds.

While Kien is thus engaged, Therese searches the flat for her husband's bank book, and for a dead body or some other clue to his cumulative mania. Things come to a head when she appears at the pawnbrokers to sell a pile of his books. At the novel's climax, Kien returns to his book-filled apartment, sets it alight, climbs to the sixth rung of a ladder, and waits, laughing. The book ends in fire and madness, with Kien's library destroyed. The Great Library of Alexandria flourished for three centuries, or perhaps as many as nine—from around 300 B.C. to 642 A.D.—no one knows for sure. But it, too, ended in mass destruction.

Many different stories have been told about how the library came to an end. Perhaps an accidental blaze destroyed it in 47 B.C. Perhaps it was a casualty of a first-century pagan revolt against Alexandria's Christianization. Or perhaps Roman Emperor Aurelian's troops destroyed it in 273 A.D. when they set fire to Alexandria's royal quarter. According to the most colorful story, the seventh-century Caliph Omar ordered the library's books to be distributed among the city's bathhouses, where they were burned to heat the waters. It took six months, so the story goes, to burn them all. An altogether different school of thought is that, long before Omar, the manuscripts had simply worn out. Papyrus is a terrible material for preserving texts. Without a large and unwavering commitment to conservation and copying, a library of papyrus scrolls will readily and unceremoniously disintegrate—especially in the damp conditions of a river delta. Alexandria's library might have just faded away.

Whatever the cause, virtually every scroll in the library was destroyed. In Greek drama alone, the losses were devastating: 83 of Aeschylus's 90 plays were lost, along with 62 of Euripides's 80, and 113 of Sophocles's 120. Some books, though, including those backstreet bootleg copies, found their way into collections in Greece, the Levant, and especially Constantinople. Today, the editions pirated by booksellers account for a high proportion of the surviving texts from Alexandria.

For however many centuries, Alexandria had preserved and promoted the Greek literary heritage. In turn, that tradition passed to the great libraries of Constantinople—the Imperial, Patriarcha, and University libraries—which maintained it for another thousand years. Though scholars at those libraries produced little that was new or creative, they edited, annotated, and elucidated the standard classical texts, thereby guarding them for the future.

In 1453 Constantinople fell to the Ottoman Turks. Many of the Greek scholars who'd established schools on the shores of the Bosphorus left for Italy. Italians at the same time rushed to those shores to acquire books. The Sicilian humanist, Hellenist, and manuscript collector Giovanni Aurispa went to great lengths to obtain manuscripts there: "I remember having given up my clothes to the Greeks in Constantinople in order to get codices—something for which I feel neither shame nor regret.'

By sea and by land, along trade routes and pilgrim routes, the books and texts from Constantinople fed Eastern and Western monasteries and other public and private collections such as the papal library, the Ambrosian, and the Laurentian. The collapse of the Byzantine Empire elevated Rome, Milan, and Florence as centers of classical learning. It also helped make Venice a center for trade in Greek manuscripts. Impacts were felt further afield, too, at emerging and later libraries such as the Bodleian, Königsberg, and Wolfenbüttel. Ultimately, books and texts from Constantinople nourished the world. The histories of humankind's libraries are intricately interwoven. Occurring over millennial time frames, the interlibrary movement of books and ideas marked out nonlinear trails of study, editing, translation, exchange, innovation, and appropriation—tracks that are just as arcane and marvelous as the sacred songlines of ancient Australia.

Books in bed

Books will sleep with you. The seventeenth-century Belgian politician and bibliophile Charles van Hulthem assembled a personal collection of 32,000 volumes, "all excellent copies," many of them great rarities. In *Great Libraries*, Anthony Hobson wrote of how the books "filled to overflowing one house in Brussels and another in Ghent. Books were heaped on every table, so that there was never room to spread a tablecloth, and stood in piles in the alcove where he slept." Van Hulthem allowed no fire in the house—that would be just too dangerous. On cold nights he kept warm in bed by spreading folios on his feet. The best book for this purpose was Barlaeus's voluminous account of Maurice of Nassau's expedition to Brazil. Van Hulthem would sometimes be found "contemplating with infantile pleasure an engraving of a fine female torso"—his sole contact with the opposite sex.

The Medici librarian Antonio di Marco Magliabecchi was renowned as a literary glutton who possessed a memory "like wax to receive and marble to retain." According to Holbrook Jackson, author of *Anatomy of Bibliomania*, Magliabecchi "lived in a cavern of books, slept on them, wallowed in them";

> they were his bed and board, his only furniture, his chief-
> est need. For sleep he spread an old rug over a heap of

them and so composed himself; or he would cast himself, fully clothed, among the books which covered his couch.

Jackson describes another bibliomaniac, active at the start of the nineteenth century. His collection was "choice, costly, and copious," and no man loved more to "embed himself" among the books and documents:

> his pillow-case, Columbus's *Letter* of 1493, stitched to the original *Challenge* of Crichton; his counterpane, the large paper *Hearnes*, formerly in Dr Mead's library, "still glittering in their primitive morocco attire"; his mattress, large paper *Dugdales*; his bed-curtains, "slips of the original Bayeux Tapestry."

Jeanette Winterson is another bibliophile who slept on a bed of books. Her parents were strict Pentecostal evangelists. In her childhood the outside toilet was the best venue for clandestine reading. There, Winterson first read Freud and D. H. Lawrence, "and perhaps that was the best place, after all," she remarked. A rubber torch was the only source of reading light. "I had to divide my money from a Saturday job, between buying books and buying batteries." Winterson's mother knew exactly how many Evereadys were needed "to illuminate the gap that separated the toilet paper from its function."

> Once I had tucked the book back down my knickers to get it indoors again, I had to find somewhere to hide it, and anyone with a single bed, standard size, and paperbacks,

standard size, will discover that seventy-seven can be accommodated per layer under the mattress.

As her collection grew and her bed began visibly to rise, Winterson worried that her mother might notice. When in fact she did, the books fed the fire.

The designers of the British Museum's famous reading room have achieved the wonderful illusion that the enormous dome is suspended, like Jeanette Winterson's mattress, on layers of books.

CHAPTER 3

———— ❦ ————

In Pursuit of Perfection

The rise of the codex

Throughout the classical world, the papyrus scroll was the dominant form of book. The days of scroll libraries, though, were always numbered. As a surface for writing, parchment is demonstrably superior to papyrus. More tolerant of folding and of damp, it is also easier to obtain and therefore harder to monopolize. Unlike papyrus scrolls, sheets of parchment will happily take ink on both sides. Cut and folded into rectangular gatherings, parchment can be used to make hinged books—called codices—that store more information with less space. The reader can jump to a chapter or passage without manually scrolling through nine meters of papyrus. Codices also suit reference guides such as contents pages, indexes, and page numbers—guides that are practically useless in scrolls. Gradually, the parchment codex replaced the papyrus scroll.

If we search back through history to find the very first codex, we can point to several contenders for that honor. Starting in 1978, Australian and North American archaeologists excavated the Dakhleh Oasis in the Sahara. They found an accounts book that dated from the fourth century. The book has been called the earliest complete example of a codex. Each of its thin wooden leaves, thirteen by thirty-three centimeters, was bored with four holes on the left side, to be bound with cord into eight-leaf gatherings. The effect was not unlike the even earlier "tablet books" that ancient Greeks carried on their belts as a signifier of learning. Made by hinging clay, wood, or metal tablets together into a diptych or polyptych, these stiff books, and the Dakhleh wooden version, are not true codices—but they helped prove the concept.

Another proto-codex in the classical era was made with sheets of papyrus, stabbed and laced at one end. Cicero, in his *Epistles to Atticus* (56 B.C.), suggested that papyrus sheets may also have been *glued* into codex form. The poet Martial, in his first-century *Apophoreta*, praised the compactness of the codex format and commended it to his readers in words that later sellers of pocket classics and paperbacks would also use. "Assign your book-boxes to the great, this copy of me one hand can grasp." Whether stabbed or glued, such brittle papyrus codices could only ever be a temporary solution.

The first recognizably modern codices, with strong and flexible parchment pages, did not arrive until around 100 A.D., or perhaps a little later. That model was perfected over subsequent centuries until, probably in an early monastic workshop, an inventive binder fastened gatherings of parchment leaves to cords and (crucially, for strength) to each other. The binder then bonded the sewn gatherings by applying glue to their back. This method resulted in a book block that would hold its shape, open flat on a table, and protect the text when the book was not in use. C. S. Lewis remarked that the codex was one of the two most important innovations of the so-called Dark Ages. The other was the stirrup.

The genesis of parchment codices may owe a debt to another development in the late classical period. In Roman times, shortly before the Christian era, the growing use of desks led writers to prefer square sheets of parchment, which in turn were well suited to the codex format. The intimate relationship between furniture design, book formats, and library layouts would persist over the next 2,000 years or so.

In the Middle Ages, most of Europe's libraries were attached to cathedrals and monasteries, and most ecclesiastical and monastic books were codices. The era of the monastic library began with Cassiodorus and St. Benedict, whose monasteries of Vivarium and Monte Cassino were founded in the sixth century. Reading and copying came together as the basis for the great tradition of monastic scriptoria, in which books were painstakingly copied and decorated.

Many scribes in the classical world were slaves. Now, in the monastic scriptoria, the scribes were freemen, more or less, who took pride in their work. The tradition of elaborate, exuberant pictorial frontispieces and initials arose in this spirit of individual creativity. Even the most senior priests participated in manuscript production. The very act of carefully copying out texts by forming each stroke and each letter by hand was itself an act of observance and devotion. As Lewis Buzbee observed, "the books that held the true word incarnate had to be works of art." The scribes toiled at lecterns arranged like church pews. Manuscript production was holy work.

"Illuminated" manuscripts were the height of the medieval scribe's art. Illumination refers to the use of elaborate decoration—initial letters, frontispieces, marginal decoration—and rich colors such as red, purple, lapis lazuli, and especially silver and gold. (In pre-modern times, lapis lazuli came from as far away as Afghanistan, while purple ink was derived from the glands of Mediterranean snails. About one and a half grams of the dye cost 12,000 snails their lives.) The talented and inventive monks created enchanting images, sometimes with microscopic precision. Rabbits, cats, and mice frolicking and murdering each other in the margins. Intricate lacework patterns that explicitly recall the masterpieces of Celtic enamelwork. Cartoonish caricatures and drolleries with startling vitality. Despite many tragic losses, thousands of painted manuscripts have survived to the present day. Indeed, the manuscripts that accounted for a large proportion of monastic effort now account for a large proportion of the extant artistic output of the Middle Ages—and of our knowledge of what delighted, appalled, and terrified the people of the time.

The seventh-century volume known as the Lindisfarne Gospels is one of the most marvelous illuminated manuscripts to survive from the Middle Ages. The initial page of the Gospel of St. Luke features 10,600 dots of red lead: these alone would've taken the illuminator at least six intently focused hours to apply. The scribe Eadfrith, the Lindisfarne monastery's future bishop, was a master of manuscript illumination. He was responsible for many of the gospels' finest illustrations, most notably the interwoven Celtic "carpet" designs of exceptional complexity and beauty. But Eadfrith introduced deliberate errors into his designs: an interlocking pattern of the wrong color, a bird lacking its wing, and so on. These have been interpreted as a way to stop just short of perfection—because perfection was the preserve of the Creator.

For almost 1,000 years, Europe's libraries held almost nothing but Bibles, church-sanctioned religious tracts, and selected classical works of science and philosophy that were accessible only to a privileged class. A typical Christian monastery possessed fewer than one hundred books. Not until the end of the Middle Ages were monastic libraries likely to have more than two or three hundred. The Italian monastery of Bobbio was an exception. Founded by Irish monks, it housed 666 manuscripts in the tenth century—still a very modest number compared to the libraries of classical times, and compared to the myth, popularized in fiction and film, of the extensive medieval library. In 1200, the "large" medieval library at Durham—equally exceptional—numbered only 570 volumes. After the fall of Rome, 1,000 years would pass before western libraries had as many codices as Herculaneum had scrolls.

Some large libraries did flourish in the middle of the Middle Ages. Those libraries were in the Arab world and the Far East. In the year 1011, Korean monks founded the Tripitaka Koreana—a library of over 80,000 immaculate woodblocks for printing a complete set of the Buddhist scriptures. The greatest libraries of medieval Islam rose in Córdoba, Baghdad, Cairo, and Fez. They held thousands of scrolls and codices but, by the end of the twelfth century, these had largely been scattered.

In medieval Christian libraries, the first codices were kept in chests and on lecterns rather than in bookcases. The practice of storing books on shelves came later. Titles were seldom displayed on the outside of books. With so few about, there was no need— the abundance of Alexandria and its labeled scrolls was a distant memory, if remembered at all. Whenever a medieval scholar wished to consult a book, he or she could know which book was which by its size, shape, color, and placement. (Book spines in the infinite Library of Babel are labeled, but with random letters unconnected to the books' contents except by chance.)

Typically, monastic codices were much larger than run-of-the-mill modern books. The heaviest book at the Benedictine monastery of St. Gall weighed 22.5 kilograms. The Devil's Bible weighed 74.8 kilograms. Size added legibility and grandeur, but was also a way of preventing theft. In an 858 A.D. letter to Archbishop Hincmar, Lupus of Ferrières explained why he'd been reluctant to send a copy of Bede's *Collectanea*: the book was too large to conceal on one's person or to hide in a bag and, even if it could be, "one would have to fear an attack of robbers who would certainly be attracted by the beauty of the book." Later, as the average size of books shrank, the rate of theft would rise, and librarians would have to resort to a portfolio of techniques to keep their books safe.

In the late Middle Ages, as the number of books grew, they began to be shelved standing up, alongside each other, on bookshelves. To accommodate this new arrangement, books had to be made to conform to verticality. We take it for granted today that books can slide in and out of shelves smoothly. In the transition to uprightness, though, changes had to be made. Bindings had to be strong enough to stop the text block from drooping in the binding, or dropping out of it altogether. Some changes were overt, even drastic. At the Spanish royal library of El Escorial, silver mounts and clasps were removed from the outer covers of books so that adjacent bindings would not be scratched; the recovered metal was sold to scrappers and goldsmiths.

Evolving incrementally from lecterns, bookshelves brought a host of thermodynamic and monosyllabic problems: sag, lean, fall, cram, hook, squash. Displaying a peculiar mathematical beauty, the rate of shelf-sag occurs proportionally to the shelf's length, to the power of four. In light of such bookshelf calculus, the modern library reformer Melvil Dewey thought the optimal shelf length was one meter. Any longer and sagging was inevitable without costly reinforcement.

Samuel Pepys—a recognizably modern collector with his taste for English literature, science, and maritime voyages—could not tolerate even the slightest deviation from straightness. Fastidious to the point of mania, he buttressed his shelves with elegant brass rods. Pepys had even less patience for the ragged line that occurs when books of different heights are shelved together. He commissioned tailor-made blocks—little wooden plinths disguised with leather—and placed them under his books so that the tops would be exactly even. Each block was rounded and gilded to match its burden.

Some collectors have been known to carry tape measures to bookshops, to be sure to buy volumes that are precisely the right size for the gap they are meant to fill. "Inchrule" Brewer, for example, earned his nickname by carrying in his pocket a folding ruler, "with which he measured rare books and bought them by length and breadth." The diplomat Pablo Manguel assembled a private library in Buenos Aires by instructing his secretary to purchase books "by the yard" and to put them in green leather covers that matched precisely the uniform height of his bookshelves. To fit the books to this tight specification, the binders armed themselves with scissors and guillotines and invaded the top and bottom margins, even going so far as to obliterate the top lines of text.

(Manguel's books were thoughtlessly chosen and thoughtlessly abridged, but the eclectic library was perfect for his son Alberto. With the cut-down books, young Alberto completed his sexual education by reading *Lolita*, *Peyton Place*, *Main Street*, and, in the Espasa–Calper Spanish encyclopedia, the harrowing entry on gonorrhea.)

Tim Munby noticed the propensity of books to fill room after room with the inevitability of the rising tide. It is a curious fact of bookcase history that shelves, in their evolution from the lectern

43

desk, first extended upwards towards the ceiling. Only later did they reach for the floor. The medieval shelves that are still in place in the library of Queen's College, Cambridge, demonstrate neatly the gradual transformation of lecterns into shelves. Founded in 1448, the college's original library of chained books featured bi-level, standing lecterns, with desks sliding out from underneath a single shelf. The ends of the lecterns were carved in an ornate, late Elizabethan or early Jacobean style. Around the year 1600, carpenters cut off the sloping tops of fourteen of the lecterns and replaced them with single shelves, retaining the decorative ends, which became the sides of the lower part of what were now bookshelves. At a later date, extra shelves were inserted in the mid-level. At a still later date, sometime before 1650, the final stage in the ascension was completed: the open bottoms of the old lecterns were filled with more shelves. As a result of this history, the surviving bookcases feature striking remnants of the original lectern desks.

At Queen's and other English libraries of the same period, the rising shelves created something new in the history of book storage: little private spaces—libraries within libraries. Placing bookcases perpendicular to exterior walls, just as the original lecterns had been placed, is known as the "stall" system. First used, it is believed, at Merton College in 1590, this system came to characterize early institutional libraries in England.

The opening of Leiden University's library in 1594 was one of several catalysts for Thomas Bodley's decision to revive at Oxford the library that had been dispersed and dismantled in the Reformation. On February 23, 1598, Bodley wrote to the vice-chancellor:

> I will take the charge and cost vpon me, to reduce it again
> to his former vse: and to make it fitte, and handsome

with seates, and shelfes, and Deskes, and all that may be needfull, to stirre vp other mens benevolence, to helpe to furnish it with bookes.

For the revived library, Bodley adopted the new stall system. The Bodleian formally opened on November 8, 1602. The shelves were well stocked with 299 manuscripts and over 1,700 printed volumes. Just as Bodley had hoped, the library proved to be a book magnet; a mere three years later, when the first printed catalogue was published, there were about 6,000 volumes. In European libraries, in contrast, bookcases were usually arranged parallel to and against the walls. This "wall" system was first adopted on a large scale at the Escorial. The Wren Library, at Cambridge's Trinity College, used a combination of the wall and stall systems.

Whether oriented in parallel or perpendicularly, the full-height bookcase is just one example of a bibliographical technology that was once novel but is now ubiquitous. Punctuation is another example. Separating words with blank space, and using punctuation marks and colored inks and upper- and lowercase letters to make easier sense of the words on the page—all these date from the time of Charlemagne (c. 747–814). Not until then was writing organized into sentences and paragraphs, with a capital at the beginning of each sentence and a full stop at the end. Books without spaces and punctuation look utterly forbidding. An example is the *Vergilius Sangallensis*, the Virgil manuscript in the abbey library of St. Gall. Produced in Rome late in the fourth or early in the fifth century, the manuscript was written from start to finish in capital letters without breaks or punctuation: one very long capitalized word that is exhausting for our modern eyes to read.

Today, the numbering of pages—called "pagination"—is

ubiquitous. But this, too, was not always so. "Foliation"—numbering leaves rather than pages—predominated in the sixteenth century. Pagination only gained its ascendancy after 1600. Like the books that preceded printing, the first generation of printed books (those printed before 1475) hardly used any numbering at all.

Throughout history, different cultures have written and read in different directions on the page. Cuneiform was written and read left to right; Arabic right to left; Chinese top to bottom; and Ancient Greek, for a time, back and forth ("*boustrophedon*" or "ox-turning"), like plowing a field. Some Etruscan texts were also written in the *boustrophedon* style. (Lemuel Gulliver documented the manner of writing among the Cascagians—bottom to top—and in the land of Lilliput—"aslant, from one corner of the paper to the other, like ladies in England.")

In the fifteenth and sixteenth centuries, different tastes and traditions also governed how books would stand on bookshelves. Decisions about whether to shelve books spine-inward or -outward dictated whether titles would appear on spines or fore-edges (the outer extremities of the leaves). Famous early libraries that shelved their books spine-inward include Dublin's Trinity College Library and Spain's Escorial and Colombina libraries. At the Bodleian, chained folios were placed with their fore-edges facing outwards. Book spines and edges can be read to reveal much about how books were used and stored.

With strikingly photogenic effect, Odorico Pillone shelved his books spine-inward and commissioned the artist Cesare Vecillio to paint 172 of their fore-edges with colorful images relevant to the books' contents. (A photograph of twelve of his painted fore-edges standing on a shelf is one of the most shared bibliophile images on the internet.) Vecillio was an excellent artist but a fallible bookman. Images on two of the volumes were painted upside down.

In the seventeenth century, an opulent fashion introduced a new twist to fore-edge decoration. Fore-edge paintings were concealed under layers of gold, so that each image would only become visible when the leaves were splayed like a fan. Samuel Mearne pioneered this secret art. He was royal bookbinder to Charles II from the Restoration to 1683. The fore-edge painting on Charles's 1622 *Book of Common Prayer* is a beautiful example. The painting consists of five vertical pictures showing the agony, betrayal, crucifixion, resurrection, and ascension of Christ. It was effected in watercolor, probably by a hired artist working on the fanned pages "with as dry a brush as possible." When the paint dried, the finisher squared the pages, then coated them (using camel hair or a sponge) with a mixture of red chalk, black lead, water, and muriatic acid, finally cutting the gold leaf to size and placing it on the surface. The technique is so effective that many book owners fail to notice the magical, disappearing paintings in their collections. Finding them is a supreme delight. Every book with a gilt fore-edge should be searched for buried treasure.

Libraries grow according to their own version of Moore's Law. Don Tolzman estimated that America's major libraries were doubling in size every twenty years from the 1870s to the 1940s, and every fifteen years after that. Globally, the British Library was the first collection to surpass 100 million items. The Library of Congress was not far behind. As early as the seventeenth century, people worried about the rate at which books were proliferating. Leibniz remarked, "if the world goes on this way for a thousand years and as many books are written as today, I'm afraid whole cities will be made up of libraries." Noticing the explosion of printed titles, Thomas Coryat observed, "methinks we want rather readers for bookes than bookes for readers."

(In his 1622 *Problema Arithmeticum de Rerum Combinationibus*, Pierre Guldin formally calculated the number of libraries that would be needed to accommodate all the books that could be written using terms from an alphabet of twenty-three letters. His research generated an answer of Borgesian precision: seventy thousand billion billion words, recorded in 1,000-page volumes with one hundred lines per page and sixty characters per line, would require exactly 8,052,122,350 libraries, each one measuring 132 meters per side.)

Apart from filling public libraries, books infiltrated households and formed themselves into private libraries. From the beginning of the first century B.C., prosperous Roman households maintained libraries, along with staff who worked as readers and scribes. Books could be obtained as war booty, and through dealers in the Greek-founded southern Italian cities such as Syracuse and Naples. The great villa libraries, described by Pliny and Seneca, are examples of a fashionable way to display wealth and learning, almost certainly in that order.

The Renaissance saw a revival of private libraries. From the mid-fifteenth century, Italian citizens of means began to have small studies built into their homes. According to John Hale's *The Civilization of Europe in the Renaissance*, these were places in which to store family papers, but they were also sanctuaries, "where the head of a busy household could retreat to read his favourite books, often at night when others were asleep." The origins of the English private library date from no later than the sixteenth century. In the 1530s John Leland, venturing through the restive north of England, "rejoiced to find in the tower of a castle belonging to Henry Percy, Earl of Northumberland, a study-room with desks and book-rests." The earl called his book room "Paradise."

Fools in love

Bibliophiles must endure all manner of insults. Critics have accused book-accumulators of being irrational, peculiar, life's voyeurs, obsessed with inanimate lovers, the classic cold fish. The Irish-born diplomat Shane Leslie wrote, not very diplomatically, that the book-collector is the hermaphrodite of literature: neither a reader nor a writer. As soon as books were common enough to collect, bibliophiles were the subject of ridicule. Sebastian Brandt's 1494 *Ship of Fools* is a roll call of dunces, and the foremost dunce is the man who collects "useless books" he cannot read.

A dialogue in Petrarch's *De remediis utriusque fortunae* rails against the accumulation of unread books. The Latin poet and rhetorician Decimus Magnus Ausonius wrote similarly in one of his opuscules:

> You've bought books and filled shelves, O Lover of the
> Muses.
> Does that mean you're a scholar now?
> If you buy string instruments, plectrum and lyre today:
> Do you think that by tomorrow the realm of music will
> be yours?

In 1607 Cardinal Federico Borromeo founded Milan's Ambrosian Library. (It was inaugurated in 1609.) Borromeo's own writings reveal an immense and wide-ranging intellectual curiosity. Why do birds sing? How do angels and demons speak? Do angels have proper names? Why do some animals live longer than others? What do Icelanders eat? What do the people of Guinea believe? When and where was writing invented? Borromeo had little patience for the veneration of books as physical objects. When a bibliophile showed him a well-printed, well-preserved, and handsomely bound Cicero, the cardinal replied, "I should like it more if it were a little less clean and a little more used.'

Edward Gibbon, commenting on the worldly achievements of the third-century Roman emperor Gordian the Younger, noted approvingly:

> Twenty-two acknowledged concubines, and a library of sixty-two thousand volumes attested the variety of his inclinations; and from the productions which he left behind him, it appears that both the one and the other were designed for use rather than for ostentation.

The eighteenth-century English barrister Thomas Rawlinson was lampooned as a learned idiot who accumulated a large collection of books, then read little more than their title pages. He was said to have gathered books "much as a squirrel gathers nuts." After Rawlinson lost money in the South Sea Bubble, his books were dispersed—in sixteen auctions between 1722 and 1734—and other collectors gathered up his nuts with relish.

Unsympathetic portraits of book-lovers picture them as oddballs and outcasts, fussing over gaps, misalignments and asymmetries in their private libraries. Tim Munby sided with the bibliomaniacs. "To be thought a lunatic by one's fellow men . . . is an insignificant price to pay for a lifetime's enjoyment." So did Walter Bagehot:

> In early days there is an opinion that the obvious thing to do with a horse is to ride it; with a cake, to eat it; with a sixpence, to spend it. A few boyish persons carry this further, and think that the natural thing to do with a book is to read it. The mere reading of a rare book is a puerility, an idiosyncrasy of adolescence.

CHAPTER 4

⸺ ⚬ ⸺

"A damned sewerful
of men"

Renaissance rediscoveries

In the depths of the Dark Ages, Western Europe was scarred by war and imperial collapse. There was, however, an unlikely patch of cultural light. In Ireland and on Scotland's remote northwest coast, Celtic Christians pioneered a monastic culture that helped keep European art and civilization alive. In the sixth and seventh centuries a vanguard of Irish and Scottish missionaries (the Hiberno–Scottish Mission) set out from Iona and other refuges, crossing to the Continent, where they founded some of Europe's most important monasteries—and libraries. Wherever they appeared, the missionaries brought manuscripts and an extraordinary zeal. In France, Belgium, Germany, Switzerland, and Italy, at Disibodenberg, Besançon, Lure, Cusance, Langres, Toul, Liège, Péronne, Ebersmünster, Cologne, Regensburg, Vienna, Erfurt, Würzburg,

Annegray, and Fontaine-lès-Luxeuil, communities adopted the way of life modeled by Columba of Clonard and Columbanus of Bangor. In a richly symbolic development, the monastery at Annegray was established in an abandoned Roman fortress.

Fast-forward to the fourteenth century and the Catholic church was again in trouble. Between 1378 and 1417, first two and then three concurrent popes claimed authority over western Christendom. Each contender maintained his own Sacred College of Cardinals, and his own administrators and offices. The causes of the split were political rather than theological. The followers of the rival popes were divided, in large part, along geographical lines. Naturally, the spectacle of the Great Schism seriously eroded the prestige of the church and the papacy.

In 1414 a general council of the church convened in Constance with a view to mending the schism. The council was a logistical exercise with few precedents. Apart from 30,000 horses and 700 prostitutes plus scores of jugglers, more than 20,000 cardinals, abbots, monks, friars, and priests converged on the Swiss town. The council lasted four and a half years, and ultimately succeeded in obtaining the resignation of the Roman pope, Gregory XII; dismissing the Avignon pope, Benedict XIII; neutralizing the Pisan pope, John XXIII; and, in November 1417, electing Martin V as the sole pope.

In the summer of 1416, three Tuscan secretaries—Cencio Rustici, Bartolomeo da Montepulciano, and Gian Francesco Poggio Bracciolini—took a break from their work at the general council. Hearing rumors that a nearby monastery guarded an ancient library, they set out on the thirty-kilometer journey to St. Gall (now St. Gallen).

The monastery's roots traced back to the same vanguard of Irish missionaries who'd founded Bobbio in Lombardy. Early in the seventh century, Colombanus of Bangor (also known as Columban the Younger) had led his missionaries across Europe. When the party reached mountainous country near Brigantia on Lake Constance, a monk named Gallus tripped. Taking this as a sign, it was said, he set up a hermit cell. By chance or design, he'd stumbled at a beautiful spot: near the waterfall in the wooded valley of the River Steinach, in the Forest of Arbon. Residing in an austerely appointed hermitage, Gallus kept a small library of liturgical works for use in daily worship. The cell and its hermit became well known in the local area. People went to Gallus for instruction and protection. A prayer house was built, more monks came, and soon the hermitage had grown into a monastery.

A century after Gallus broke march by the waterfall, a priest named Otmar built an abbey on the site and became the first abbot of the monastery of St. Gall. Under their second abbot, in 747, the monks joined the Benedictine order. A series of astute and diligent successor abbots—Waldo (782–84), Gozbert (816–36), Grimald (841–72), Hartmut (872–83), and Salomo III (890–920)—built St. Gall into an important religious center.

Books were pivotal to Benedictine monastic practice. St. Benedict's precepts mandated daily readings. Also, at Lent, every monk had to read the Holy Scriptures solo, from cover to cover. All this reading required Bibles. St. Gall's scriptorium dates from no later than 760, early in the monastery's history. Apart from Bibles, the first scribes at St. Gall produced commentaries, hagiographies, and grammars. After overseeing growth in the monastery's library, Abbot Waldo moved to Reichenau Abbey in southern Germany where he founded a great library. (He was abbot at Reichenau from 786 to 806.) Under Waldo, St. Gall's scribes had made do with parchment that was, according to Anthony Hobson, "dirty yellow in colour and full of tears and holes." Under Gozbert, however, high-quality white vellum became available. Thus equipped, as many as a hundred scribes set to work enlarging the monastery's inventory of books. In the decade from 820, a separate, two-story library building was constructed—scriptorium below, book collection above—the first of its kind in Europe. (Preserved in the abbey library is the oldest extant plan of a monastery. Dating from the early decades of the ninth century, it shows a large, two-story library—a perfect cube—and seems to be a plan for the "ideal monastery," of which only the library–scriptorium building was actually built.)

In the new scriptorium, the art of illuminated initials flourished. St. Gall's distinctive style blended Irish, English, German, Latinate, and Byzantine elements—to beautiful effect. Apart from producing their own manuscripts, St. Gall's monks also swapped them with books produced elsewhere, and received books through bequests and commerce. Most of the books, though, were made on-site by talented monks such as Notker the German and Notker the Stammerer.

A catalogue written sometime after 850 and before 890 recorded, in the main library, 294 volumes containing 426 texts; some texts were bound together. The monastery also boasted a scholar's library, a church library, and the abbot's private library. St. Gall was a place of books. The first history of the abbey appeared in 890. Written by the monk Ratpert, it was called "The Vicissitudes of the Abbey of St Gall." Many vicissitudes would follow.

Late in the ninth century, the monks moved their books to a fortified building, adjoining the church, called Hartmut Tower— named after the recently deceased abbot. In the tenth century, ahead of an imminent Hungarian invasion, a devout, prescient recluse named Wiborada advised the monks to move the library to an even safer place: the island of Reichenau on Lake Constance. When the invaders came, the monks sought refuge in a nearby fortress, but Wiborada remained in her recluse's cell at the church of St. Magnus. Killed by the intruders at the beginning of May 926, she became in 1047 the first woman in the history of the church to be canonized. Today, she is honored as the patron saint of libraries and bibliophiles.

After surviving the 937 fire that destroyed much of the abbey, St. Gall's library entered a long period of stasis. From the eleventh century until the Renaissance, additions to the library "amounted to little beyond a handful of legal books and a few works by Bernard, Anselm and later authors." In the year 1200 or thereabouts, the scriptorium was shut altogether. Two centuries later, the abbey and town of St. Gall became an independent principality, the abbot a prince of the Holy Roman Empire.

The library, though, remained a prize. In 1416, as soon as the three Tuscan secretaries arrived, they found wonderful treasures. A complete copy of Quintilian's *Institutiones oratoriae*, a treatise on the theory and practice of rhetoric—a book the Tuscans had hitherto known only in a very imperfect form. They also found Silius Italicus's *Punica*, a seventeen-book, 12,000-line saga on the Second Punic War (which was fought from 218 to 201 B.C.)—the longest poem in Latin literature. Plus two historical and legal commentaries by Asconius Pedianus on Cicero's speeches. And, dedicated to Vespasian and written by Valerius Flaccus "in shimmering and powerful verse falling not far short of poetic majesty," the epic poem *Argonautica*—a "free re-handling" of the story, already told by Apollonius of Rhodes, of the quest for the golden fleece.

An amazed Cencio Rustici wrote to Francesco da Fiano, gushing about these and other marvels at St. Gall: by Vitruvius, *On

Architecture, the most important ancient work on that subject; by the grammarian Priscianus (who flourished around the year 500), a schoolbook commentary on Virgil's poetry. And by Lactantius, a book "small in size but prodigious in the quality of its eloquence and wisdom," in which the author, writing on the creation of mankind, "plainly refutes the reasoning of those who have declared the human condition to be lower and more wretched than that of the beasts." The volume was probably Lactantius's *De officio hominis*.

Several of the works and their authors were largely or entirely unknown in Italy. Poggio Bracciolini remarked of Quintilian, for example, "among us in Italy, he had been so mutilated, so mangled, ravaged, no doubt, in the toils of time, that it was impossible to recognize in him his form or his nature." Only one half of Quintilian's *Institutiones oratoriae* was known in Italy, and that half was "in a very mutilated state." The rediscovery at St. Gall of Quintilian and other Roman authors would reverberate far and wide. And the discoveries kept coming. When Cencio Rustici found a papyrus manuscript by Isidore of Seville, he took it in his arms and hugged it, "on account of its holy and incorrupt antiquity." The magical experience of encountering impossibly old and rare books filled the men with joy.

But the men's joy soon turned to sadness and anger at the abbot, Heinrich von Gundelfingen. In Hartmut Tower, as reported by Poggio and Rustici, the Tuscans found "innumerable books" in wretched condition. Rustici recorded how the men "broke out in tears" when they saw "the unsurpassed glory and honour of the Latin language"

> debased and defiled by dust, worms, dirt and all other things pertaining to the destruction of books . . . Surely

if this library were able to speak for itself, it would shout: "Lovers of the Latin language, do not allow me to be annihilated by this awful neglect: rescue me from this prison, whose darkness even the light of learning cannot illumine." The abbot and monks who dwelled in that monastery were completely illiterate. What barbarous foes of the Latin language, what a damned sewerful of men!

In a letter to Guarino Guarini of Verona, Poggio described how the books were filthy with mold and dust.

For these books were not in the library, as befitted their worth, but in a sort of foul and gloomy dungeon at the bottom of one of the towers, where not even men convicted of a capital offence would have been stuck away.

Vividly, Poggio imagined how the cultivated, elegant, conscientious, humorous Quintilian volume must have suffered in "the foulness of that prison, the filth of that hole, the savagery of the guards."

Dejected, dressed in tatters as though in mourning, with unkempt beard, hair matted with dirt, he seemed by his face and bearing to declare that he had been sentenced to an unjust execution. He seemed to reach out, to implore the citizens of Rome to protect him from unfair judgement, to rage and complain that he who had once by his support and eloquence defended many, now could find neither patron to take pity on his misfortune nor anyone at all to look out for his welfare or save him from being subjected to an unjust punishment.

Subsequent authors have expressed doubts about the Tuscans' melodramatic accounts of the book room in Hartmut Tower. One of the men in particular has attracted skepticism. Poggio would later be styled "the greatest book hunter of the Renaissance," the prototype "bird dog" collector. Perhaps the man who relished finding and taking away old books had overstated the monastic disarray as a cover and a justification for making off with some of the abbey's choicest volumes. In the course of his work, Poggio certainly did not remain squeaky clean. He demonstrated a knack for talking himself into monasteries; at least once he exaggerated his credentials and achievements as a book finder. Ever ready to accuse others of lying, cowardice, theft, hypocrisy, heresy, and perversion, he himself was labeled a cheat, and was not above using underhanded means to obtain books from monasteries. He bribed a monk, for example, in an attempt to remove a Livy and an Ammianus from the library of Hersfeld Abbey.

While working as a papal official, Poggio fathered fourteen children with his mistress, Lucia Pannelli. At the age of fifty-six he married seventeen-year-old Selvaggia de'Buondelmonti, with whom he produced a further six children. (In 1436 he penned a famous dialogue, *On Marriage in Old Age*.) Over the span of a varied and colorful career, Poggio, like Shakespeare, used his wits to amass a substantial fortune. After selling a Livy manuscript in 1434, he used the proceeds to build a villa in the Valdarno, which he filled with coins, inscriptions, and antique busts. Also like Shakespeare, Poggio improved his apparent standing by purchasing a bogus coat of arms. (A silver-gilt reliquary bust, in the form of a mitered bishop and bearing the arms of Poggio and Selvaggia, is now in the Metropolitan Museum of Art.)

And then there is the small matter of the *Facetiae*, the fifteenth century's most scandalous book of rude jokes. Poggio wrote the *Facetiae* between 1438 and 1452. Some of the jokes are about church politics and current affairs. Most are about sex. Jokes about lusty parishioners, lecherous merchants, magical orifices, gullible patients, lewd factotums, randy hermits (St. Gallus must have turned in his grave), simple-minded grooms, libidinous peasants, seductive friars—and the woman who tells her husband she has two vaginas (*duos cunnos*), one in front that she would share with him; the other behind—for the Church. Building on this theme, Poggio's joke number CLXXXI is an "Amusing remark by a young woman in labour."

> In Florence, a young woman, somewhat of a simpleton, is on the point of giving birth. She has long endured acute pain, and the midwife, candle in hand, inspects *secretiora ejus*, in order to ascertain if the baby is coming: "Look also on the other side," the poor creature says. "My husband has sometimes taken that road."

Joke number CLXI presents a new theory about personal destiny.

> A quack doctor claims he can produce children of different types—merchants, soldiers, generals—depending on how far his member penetrates. A foolish rustic, hoping for a soldier, hands his wife over to the scoundrel, but then, thinking himself sly, springs from his hiding place

and hits the quack's backside to push his member further in. "Per Sancta Dei Evangelia," the rustic shouts triumphantly, "hic erit Papa!" "This one will be Pope!"

CLIV is about "A mountaineer who thought of marrying a girl."

A mountaineer from the village of Pergola is inclined to marry the quite youthful daughter of one of his neighbours. But, after close inspection, he finds her too young and delicate, and refuses. "She is riper than you think," the ignorant father says. "She has already had three children by the Vicar's clerk.'

Though frowned upon by the church for obvious reasons, manuscripts and printed editions of the book were so popular, "they flooded all Italy and overflowed into France, Spain, Germany, England and every other country where Latin was understood." Leonardo da Vinci owned a copy, as did J. P. Morgan four centuries later.

Apart from complicating his reputation by authoring the *Facetiae*, Poggio also attracted a certain amount of guilt by association. He was at the general council in his capacity as secretary to Baldassare Cossa, better known as Pope John XXIII, or the Anti-Pope. One of the three papal contenders, John had in fact initiated the general council; he did so under pressure from Sigismund, the Holy Roman Emperor. But, once the council was underway, things went badly for him. So badly that he was forced to flee Constance under the cover of darkness, dressed as a postman and flanked by a loyal crossbowman. During his absence he was formally charged with incest, rape, sodomy, simony, piracy, immorality, torture, murder, ambition, schism, tyranny, "bad conduct," and heresy—the latter through denying the reality of the resurrection. Tried in absentia, he was found guilty on all counts. According to Edward Gibbon, though, "The most scandalous charges were suppressed; the vicar of Christ was only accused of piracy, rape, sodomy, murder and incest." He spent a few months as Sigismund's prisoner before buying his way out by paying a large ransom. He made amends with the new pope, who absolved him and named him cardinal bishop. A few months later, he died.

For these and other reasons, the name Poggio carries baggage. Some modern authors have come straight out and called him a thief. Library historian Alfred Hessel wrote of Poggio, "When he could do nothing else, he copied texts, but he preferred to 'save' them by thrusting them under his robe." This picture of Poggio resembles the nineteenth-century book thief James Halliwell, another biblio-phile who famously "rescued" books by stealing them. E. V. Lucas recalled of Halliwell, "If he ever chanced to see anything in anyone else's house or in a museum that he thought he was more worthy to possess, he had no scruples about taking it."

There are other reasons to doubt Poggio's account. The story of the Tuscans' discoveries has a familiar ring to it. There are many other early descriptions of encounters with books in strange and frightful circumstances. Together, these stories constitute a hoary genre in which the thoughtful, archetypal book-lover "rescues" manuscripts from misuse and neglect. The genre depends on a differ-ence in values for its dramatic force. On one side of the difference are those who recognize and appreciate rare manuscripts. On the other side are those who regard them without respect or sentiment. Often, the difference between these viewpoints is excruciating.

Take, for example, the "greatest coup" of Milan's Ambrosian

Library, which, in the seventeenth century, swapped a selection of "more useful" modern books for part of Bobbio's ancient library. Bobbio at that time owned a magical and priceless collection— including most of those 666 books it had held in the tenth century, one of the very few substantial surviving groups of Italian pre-Caroline manuscripts—and it swapped them for the latest outputs of the printing press. Another seventeenth-century Ambrosian coup is also informative about the difference in values. Antonio Salmazia spent a year in Corfu hunting Greek manuscripts for the library. He succeeded in buying a total of 113 manuscripts there. In today's interior-design magazines, suppliers advertise old leather-bound books at a price per meter. The manuscripts from Corfu suffered an even ruder slight: being sold by weight. Each Corfiote pound-weight of manuscript cost Salmazia five Milanese lire.

A classic of the "manuscript rescue" genre is the description of Boccaccio's visit to the monastery library at Monte Cassino. Boccaccio was escorted to a store of "noble manuscripts" in a doorless loft that was reached by a ladder. Inside, he found books white with dust; books with whole sheets ripped out; books with their margins cut away. A weeping Boccaccio demanded to know how such precious volumes could be so ill-used. A monk told him that whenever his brethren needed money, they would cut out enough parchment leaves from a Bible to make a little psalter, then sell it. They also sold the cut-away margins.

Boccaccio's visit brings to mind the emptying of the library of the University of Oxford—the predecessor to the Bodleian. In 1550, at the height of the Reformation, all the books in that library, including more than six hundred manuscripts, were sold to bookbinders and other tradesmen for the value of the vellum and parchment. The Dean of Christ Church led the purge; he was intent on eradicating all traces of Catholicism, and all "superstitious books and images." Six years later, Christ Church College bought the emptied bookcases. For the next forty-two years, individual colleges had libraries, but the university itself had none. Thanks to this and other disposals, bibliophiles made wonderful finds in unlikely locations. Sir Robert Cotton was at his tailor's shop when he saw by chance an ancient document that the tailor was about to cut up and use as a tape measure. On examination, the sheepskin parchment turned out to be an original Magna Carta—one of as few as four that King John had signed in 1215—still with "all its appendages of seals and signatures" attached.

Rafael Tabares left behind another account of manuscript neglect: the story of the Biblioteca Colombina. At the age of fourteen, Fernando Columbus—the son of Christopher Columbus and Beatriz Enríquez—had accompanied his father on his fourth voyage across the Atlantic. When "tall, most amiable and very fat" Fernando obtained his maturity, he acquired a fortune in property and slaves that made him one of the richest men in Spain. In 1526 he built a house in Seville on the banks of the Guadalquivir. He planted the garden with American trees, and filled a large room with more than 15,000 books.

After Fernando's death, the Biblioteca Colombina was moved to Seville Cathedral. In 1552 the books were installed in a cathedral annex that was built into the wall of a former mosque. Two decades later, King Philip II of Spain ordered the earliest manuscripts to be transferred to the library of the royal monastery at El Escorial. Fourteen years after that, the Colombina collection came under the scrutiny of the Inquisition. The Basel 1528 edition of St. Cyril's *Works*, edited by the German Protestant Oecolampadius, had most of its second volume and the whole of the third removed. Other books were condemned to total destruction.

For the books that remained in the Colombina library at Seville, the seventeenth century was a period of prolonged contempt, with occasional moments of care, such as in 1683 when many of the books were rebound in vellum. The eighteenth century was a time of appalling neglect. Tabares, Colombina's under-librarian, described how "in his youth he and other children were allowed to play in the room and run their fingers over the illuminated manuscripts and books of prints." The building fell into disrepair; the gutters leaked and water ran into the library, drenching several volumes. Light, damp, and misuse transformed other neglected volumes into "powdery nuisances." Tabares helped set things right, but, in the nineteenth century, the losses mounted due to further damage and through theft and secret sales of books. As at 1970, only about 5,500 titles of Fernando Columbus's bequest survived in the Colombina. Almost 10,000 volumes had been lost.

Yet another example from this baleful genre has a picturesque setting. In 1801 Edward Daniel Clarke, a Fellow of Jesus College, Cambridge, anchored his small caïque in the port of Scalea, on the Greek island of Patmos, and walked the four winding kilometers from the quay, past a concentration of "generally handsome" local women, to the highest part of the island. There sat an Orthodox monastery, founded in 1088: the Monastery of Saint John the Theologian. Clarke was accompanied by his pupil and friend from Jesus, John Marten Cripps, and an interpreter called Riley. (On this tour, Clarke and Cripps had first set out from England in May 1799, initially with Malthus—the writer on population—and William Otter—a future bishop of Chichester. Malthus and Otter "soon dropped off.")

On Patmos, Clarke and Cripps carried impeccable credentials: letters of introduction from the Capudan Pasha, Grand Admiral in the Turkish Sultan's government, commander-in-chief both of the fleet and of the army. At the monastery they were received by the abbot and his subordinate the bursar. Clarke presented a letter from the Capudan Pasha. It was written in Turkish, so Riley interpreted. Among other courtesies, the letter enabled the foreigners to order bread from the island for their voyage.

Escorted by the abbot and his colleague, the Englishmen were taken on a tour of the monastery. They were shown a small rectangular chamber lined with shelves and nearly filled with books. The shelves were packed with printed volumes, "for these, being more modern, were regarded as the more valuable." The old parchment manuscripts, in contrast, "were considered only as so much rubbish" and were heaped and thrown about on the floor, some with covers and some without, prey to damp and worms. A quantity of manuscripts had been cut up to serve "any purpose for which the parchment might be required." At the end of the chamber was a pile of Greek codices, some of them evidently of great antiquity. The party asked the abbot what they were. Turning up his nose with an expression of indifference and contempt, he replied, "χειρόγραφα! Manuscripts!"

Clarke and Cripps calculated the number of volumes in the bookroom to be about 1,000, of which more than 200 were manuscripts. After the Englishmen made plans for a rescue, Riley opened negotiations with the abbot, and Clarke and Cripps "fell on the contemned heap" where, almost immediately, they discovered Arethas's *Plato*. Neither the abbot nor the bursar could read. They agreed to sell five of the manuscripts, so long as the sale was kept secret from the Patmosians, some of whom, the abbot feared, were spies for the Turkish government. Excited but apprehensive, the travelers returned to their boat and waited. In due course a monk appeared carrying the manuscripts in a large basket on his head.

As he came alongside, he said aloud, so the nearby islanders could hear, that he'd brought the loaves of bread that the Englishmen had ordered via the Capudan Pasha.

Some of these stories of book discovery are surely apocryphal. There is considerable doubt, for example, as to whether Cotton really did find an original Magna Carta at his tailor's shop. The abbot at Patmos might not have been as much of a philistine as Clarke related. Which brings us back to the question: were Poggio and Rustici telling the truth about St. Gall?

Alfred Hessel certainly did not think so. "In the customary manner," Hessel wrote, Poggio "uttered bitter complaints about the state of the libraries in these places and declared it his duty to free the treasures of antiquity from their bonds." And yet, in the centuries after Poggio's arrival, other visitors to St. Gall painted a similar picture of neglect. Johann Stumpf, for example, inspected Hartmut Tower in 1548 and found its manuscripts lying "in a disorderly heap." Most damning for the monks of St. Gall, though, is the appalling evidence that they committed book crimes far worse than neglect. The case of the *Vetus Latina Gallensis* is a tragic example.

An exceptionally early version of the Latin Bible, the *Vetus Latina* pre-dated St. Jerome's Vulgate Bible. When later and "better" Bible texts came available, the monks of St. Gall cut their *Vetus Latina* into strips of parchment and used them as reinforcement in the spines and covers of newer manuscripts. An early Vulgate manuscript at St. Gall was also sliced up; a total of 110 fragments of that exist today. They date from the fifth century and together are the oldest "surviving" (barely) translation of St. Jerome's gospels. Other equally significant St. Gall manuscripts were similarly cut up, including an important Lombard law book.

Naturally for a place founded by an Irish monk, St. Gall held early Irish manuscripts. Numbering fifteen volumes in all, they dated from the seventh to the ninth century, the foundation years of the monastery. Priceless artifacts from the era in which Irish and Scottish missionaries helped preserve and renew European Christianity, all fifteen were of worldwide importance for the history of religion, culture, language, and paleography. One of them, for example—the *Grammatica Prisciana*, c. 845—is today the main source for the philology of Old Irish. How, then, did the monks of St. Gall treat the Irish manuscripts? Out of the fifteen, a total of eleven were cut into fragments. Apart from breaking and cutting up books, the monks at St. Gall also washed and scraped manuscript leaves to remove the original ink so the parchment could be reused.

The library historian and bookman Anthony Hobson accepted Poggio's and Rustici's accounts as truthful, and it seems that the Tuscans were indeed telling the truth about St. Gall. They were book heroes in a world over-endowed with book villains. St. Gall's Abbot Von Gundelfingen allowed the Tuscans to take away to Italy five gems of classical Roman literature: Flaccus's *Argonautica*, Italicus's *Punica*, Pedianus's two commentaries, and Quintilian's *Institutiones oratoriae*. With characteristic drama, Poggio wrote of the Quintilian manuscript: "By Heaven, if we had not brought help, he would surely have perished the very next day." Poggio and his fellows had rescued this unique star of the Roman firmament "not merely from exile, but virtually from annihilation."

St. Gall was not the only abbey that Poggio visited during the Council of Constance. He called on other Swiss abbeys, as well as Swabian and French ones such as those at Reichenau, Weingarten, and Cluny. Nearly everywhere he went he made spectacular discoveries. At Cluny, he found two orations of Cicero's, previously only known in incomplete versions. At Monte Cassino, a manuscript of Frontinus's late first-century *De aquaeductu*—a treatise on Rome's waterways. At Langres and Cologne, Cicero's *Oration for Caecina* and another sixteen Ciceronian orations, many of them hitherto unknown.

He also found works by Nonius Marcellus, Flavius Caper, Probus, and Eutyches; Cicero's *Pro Sexto Roscio*; Festus's *De significatu verborum*; Manilius's *Astronomica*; Ammianus Marcellinus's *Res gestae*; the *Silvae* of Statius; and Apicius's work on cooking. And he found Eden.

In 1416 Poggio traveled, "for the benefit of the waters," to the opulent German bath town of Baden, "to which I am come to try whether they can remove an eruption which has taken place between my fingers." From the town he wrote an excited letter to his friend Niccolò Niccoli.

Much is said by the ancients of the pleasant baths of Puteoli, which were frequented by almost all the people of Rome. But in my opinion, these boasted baths must, in the article of pleasure, yield the palm to the baths of Baden. For the pleasantness of the baths of Puteoli was founded more on the beauty of the circumjacent country, and the magnificence of the neighboring villas, than on the festive manners of the company by which they were frequented. The scenery of Baden, on the contrary, has but few attractions; but every other circumstance relating to its medicinal springs, is so pregnant with delight, that I frequently imagine that Venus, and all her attendant joys, have migrated hither from Cyprus. The frequenters of these waters so faithfully observe her institutes, so accurately copy her manners, that though they have not read the discourse of Heliogabalus, they seem to be amply instructed by simple nature.

The public baths, "exposed to view on every side," were frequented by people of all ages and of each sex. The male and female bathers, "entertaining no hostile dispositions towards each other," were separated "only by a simple railing"; at other baths, the barrier was a flimsy partition with low windows,

> through which they can see and converse with, and touch each other, and also drink together; all which circumstances are matters of common occurrence. Above the baths are a kind of galleries, on which the people stand who wish to see and converse with the bathers; for every one has free access to all the baths, to see the company, to talk and joke with them. As the ladies go in and out of the water, they expose to view a considerable portion of their persons; yet there are no door-keepers, or even doors, nor do they entertain the least idea of any thing approaching to indelicacy.

Men and women were separated in the water but they came and went via a common passage, the setting for frequent "very curious encounters." Poggio was especially struck by the young women—"good looking and well-born and in manner and form like a goddess"—and their mode of dress—"linen vests, which are however slashed in the sides, so that they neither cover the neck, the breast, nor the arms of the wearer." Thus attired, some of the young women played harps in the shallows.

In January 1417, in the monastery at Fulda in Germany, Poggio encountered *Agrimensores*—an illustrated ninth-century Roman manuscript on agriculture and land surveying. There he also made his most famous find: the only known manuscript of Lucretius's *De rerum natura* ("On the Nature of Things"). Written in Latin, the manuscript is a poem of 7,400 lines, divided into six books and giving a full description of the world as viewed by the ancient Greek philosopher Epicurus. John Addington Symonds's 1877 book, *Renaissance in Italy: The Revival of Learning*, and Stephen Greenblatt's 2011 book, *The Swerve: How the World Became Modern*, chronicled Poggio's discovery of the Lucretius manuscript—and how it turbocharged the Renaissance, the Reformation, and modern science.

Poggio assembled a priceless personal collection of manuscripts that was surpassed in Florence only by the superb collection of eight hundred manuscripts assembled by Niccolò Niccoli. Poggio's books ultimately found a home in Florence's marvelous Laurentian Library—the place where Michelangelo proved he was a genius of architecture as well as sculpture and painting.

Starting in 1523, Michelangelo planned and guided the library's construction under the patronage of the Medici pope Clement VII. The artist's bold and lively architectural innovations, which create the impression of organic movement, mark out the library as an exemplar of Mannerism. Michelangelo attended to every aspect of the design, and made three-dimensional models so that the builders would realize his vision precisely. In January 1559, he sent a model and a letter to his collaborator architect Bartolomeo Ammannati:

I wrote to tell you I had made a little clay model of the Library staircase; I'm now sending it to you in a box, and

71

as it is a small affair, I have not been able to do more than give you an idea, remembering that what I formerly proposed was freestanding and only abutted on to the door of the Library. I've contrived to maintain the same method; I do not want the side stairs to have balusters at the ends, like the main flight, but a seat between every two steps, as indicated by the embellishments. There is no need for me to tell you anything about bases, fillets for these plinths and other ornaments, because you are resourceful, and being on the spot will see what is needed much better than I can. As to the height and length, take up as little space as you can by narrowing the extremity as you think fit. It is my opinion that if the said staircase were made in wood—that is to say in a fine walnut—it would be better than in stone, and more in keeping with the desks, the ceiling and the door.

Michelangelo had to discard the idea of making the stairwell in walnut: the squeaking timber stairs would have distracted the monks. He and Ammannati made do with monumental marble. John Shearman wrote of the library in his 1967 book on Mannerist art:

> The principal development here is an application of licence to all architectural members, major and minor. It is the first building that seems to have been turned outside in, for the massive treatment of the interior walls belongs by tradition to exteriors.

The walls feature purely decorative volutes that are oversized and "seem to hang there like tongues." James Ackerman noticed how, in the corners, the giant volutes "seem to mate rather than meet."

Despite its exceptionally picturesque foundation story, St. Gall continued to be a place of tragedy. Soon after the Tuscans' visit, the monastery was again devastated by fire (the manuscripts in Hartmut Tower once more escaped extinction). The Toggenburg War of 1712, the last sectarian war of the old Swiss Confederation, saw victorious troops from Zurich and Berne occupy and loot the abbey, setting back its rococo revival. Designating the manuscripts and printed works as war booty, the victors took half of them to Zurich and the rest to Berne.

Upon the signing of a peace treaty in 1718, most of the books were returned to St. Gall, but Zurich retained approximately one hundred items, including a few dozen important medieval and early-modern manuscripts, as well as a quantity of printed books, paintings, astronomical devices, and Prince-Abbot Bernhard Müller's cosmographical globe. The globe, whose diameter is more than 120 centimeters, was made before 1575, probably in northern Germany. A masterpiece of mapmaking and globemaking, it shows both terrestrial and celestial terrains—the constellations were drawn in the oceans.

Later in the eighteenth century, St. Gall entered a new golden era, not of book production but of book curatorship and display. The abbot engaged master builders and master craftsmen to construct a perfect home for all the books that had survived the perils of scissor-happy monks; squalid, moldy, wormy confinement in the basement of Hartmut Tower; the rescuing hands of papal secretaries from Tuscany; invasion and war in 926 and 1712; and the fires of 937 and 1418. Construction of the new library commenced in 1758 and lasted a decade. The elderly master builder Peter

Thumb was responsible for the new structure. Working in cherry, walnut, olive, and pine, the cabinetmaker Gabriel Loser crafted the elaborate timber fittings and the floor. Johann and Matthais Giggel completed the stuccowork. The deliberate imperfections encountered in early manuscripts had no place in the realization of the library. Featuring an undulating gallery, ornate Corinthian columns and pilasters, and a pinewood floor inlaid with walnut, the new hall at St. Gall came very close to aesthetic perfection; it is one of the best surviving examples of baroque and rococo architecture.

Roman numerals from I to XIV divide the hall into sections, each with a particular subject matter. Plaster cherubs represent the different subjects: poet, physician, botanist, singer, painter, gardener, composer, merchant, geographer. Josef Wannenmacher painted the elaborate ceiling in 1762 and 1763. It shows the Virgin Mary (representing Divine Wisdom) and, in the lunettes over the four large window embrasures, the Greek and Latin Church Fathers—Gregory the Great, Gregory of Nazianzus, Anselm of Canterbury, Cyril of Jerusalem, Ambrose, Augustine, Athanasius, Basil, Jerome, John Chrysostom—as the guiding lights for the monastery. Executed in an illusionistic, trompe l'oeil style called *quadratura* (popularized in the seventeenth century by Jesuit monk Andrea Pozzo), the ceiling creates an illusion of bookcases extending upwards into the heavens. Surrounded by clouds and cherubs, St. Augustine sits atop a celestial, three-dimensional throne of books. All fantasy and show business, the library is a masterpiece.

Pozzo's treatise *Perspectiva pictorum et architectorum*, published in two volumes in 1693 and 1700, codified a "scenographic" approach to architecture—one that would flourish in Italy and be highly influential throughout Europe for over a century. In the German baroque library of Wiblingen Abbey, the trompe l'oeil is so effective that visitors struggle to tell which architectural features are real and which are illusory. Widely translated, Pozzo's treatise was addressed to "the Lovers of Perspective." Arguing that "Perspective never appears more graceful than in Architecture," Pozzo provided a hundred almost obsessive examples of how to achieve perfect perspective.

At St. Gall, the library ceiling's rococo plasterwork created separate fields in which Wannenmacher depicted the first four ecumenical councils: Chalcedon, Constantinople, Ephesus, and Nicaea. The three-dimensional illusion achieves its greatest visual impact when the images are viewed from the ends of the library's main hall. Above the windows, the artist painted more *quadratura* scenes of the great Church Fathers. And finally, a series of smaller monochrome images between the hall's windows show the order's monks at work. Over the entrance to the library there is a Greek inscription that echoes the one from Alexandria and that reads, loosely translated, "Sanatorium for the soul."

The history of St. Gall is rich with tragedies, and the next one to befall St. Gall was especially bitter. No sooner had the monks built the perfect library than it was taken from them.

In 1803 the Napoleonic *Act of Mediation* elevated St. Gall as a sovereign canton. Two years later, the canton abolished what had been, according to St. Gall historian Werner Vogler, "one of the most illustrious, flourishing and scholarly monasteries of the Western world." The monastery was dissolved, the monks "thrown out." Other nearby monasteries and convents were also secularized, such as the island abbey at Lindau on Lake Constance. At St. Gall, parts of the abbey complex became the canton's offices. The abbey itself became the cathedral for a new bishop. A decree of 1813 transferred responsibility for the abbey's archives and library to the Catholic administration of the state of St. Gall. Once again, the library survived.

Mean-spirited collectors

Not all collectors approach the hunt in good spirit. Born in 1836, David Scott Mitchell became Australia's greatest collector of Australiana. As the rate of his buying accelerated, his home at 17 Darlinghurst Road, Sydney, began to bulge with books. A. H. Spencer, who early in his bookman career visited the home regularly as a messenger boy for the booksellers Angus & Robertson, described Mitchell's living space thus: "Books, pamphlets, maps, pictures, newspapers, manuscripts, filling a vast amount of shelving and stacked upon the floor, tables and chairs in every room, and up the staircase." The books even infiltrated the maid's attic.

Mitchell developed a toxic rivalry with another collector, Alfred Lee. When a local doctor passed away, a local bookseller (William Dymock) purchased the doctor's library. Lee got to it first and put aside a choice pile of books. When Mitchell arrived at the shop he saw Lee's pile.

"What are those there?" he asked the bookseller.

"Oh, they were picked out by Mr Lee."

"How much do they come to?"

"Three hundred pounds, Mr Mitchell."

"Put them into my cab at once," Mitchell said, "or I'll never come into this shop again." The bookseller did as he was told while Mitchell went on making his own selection. When Lee discovered what had happened, his reaction "could only be printed on asbestos."

Lee owned an especially desirable prize: Sir Joseph Banks's manuscript journal. Having tried several times to induce Lee to sell it, Mitchell gave it one last go. Lee refused, declaring he would sell his library before he parted with that treasure.

"Well," Mitchell said, "put a price on the lot."

"Seven thousand pounds."

"Done. When will you call for your cheque?"

At the appointed time, Lee knocked at 17 Darlinghurst Road. The door opened a crack and Old Sarah the housekeeper poked out the envelope. "Good morning," she said, then closed the door.

Holbrook Jackson wrote of an almost demonic figure: a wealthy Irish book collector who was known "by many hard names" such as "Vampire" and "Dragon." The collector's hoard of books filled garrets, cellars, and warehouses, "not for his own delight, but to prevent others enjoying them." Possessing an instinct for knowing what other people wanted, the collector snatched at auctions those volumes most desired by his rival bidders. The rivals, though, settled on a solution. By feigning interest in cheap books, and by running them up to high prices, the rivals beat "the devouring monster," who "disappeared as mysteriously as he had come."

CHAPTER 5

Free for All

The abundance of books in the printing era

Printing reached England in 1476 when William Caxton set up his press at Westminster. He had already operated a press, in Bruges, and had first encountered printing in Cologne. By 1500, there were five printers working in London. By 1523, there were thirty-three. The growth of printing in England was intimately linked to the availability of a viable alternative to parchment.

John Tate set up England's first paper mill in 1490 near Stevenage, in Hertfordshire. Bartholomaeus Anglicus mentions Tate's mill in the 1495–96 book *De Proprietatibus Rerum*, which was translated by John Trevisa and printed by Wynken de Worde, on Tate paper. A poem printed in the colophon stated:

And also of your charyte call to remembraunce
The soule of William Caxton, first prynter of this boke
In laten tonge at Coleyn hymself to avaunce
That every well disposyd man may thereon loke
And John Tate the yonger, Joye mote he broke
Whiche late hathe in Englonde doo make this paper
   thynne
That now in our englyssh this boke is prynted inne.

Tate's mill failed, possibly due to competition from discounted Dutch paper, but in 1588 Sir John Spilman established a commercially successful mill at Dartford in Kent. The queen granted Spilman special privileges for the collection of rags. Late in the sixteenth century and early in the seventeenth, other mills were established in Buckinghamshire, Staffordshire (at Cannock Chase), Oxfordshire, Surrey, and near Edinburgh. Paper was also imported from the Continent, as was, until about 1567, most printing type.

For seven centuries the Chinese guarded the secret of paper manufacture. They also tried to eliminate other Asian centers of paper production, to ensure the kind of monopoly the Ptolemies had enjoyed over papyrus. The paper monopoly, though, was inherently fragile. At the Battle of Talas, in 751, the Ottoman Turks defeated the T'ang army. Prisoners were taken to Samarkand, where the local people learned the secrets of papermaking. Soon the people of Samarkand were producing paper in large quantities for export. Thereafter, the technology as well as the product spread inexorably. Paper production was important in Baghdad late in the eighth century. Arab traders brought paper to Europe as early as 1085. Damascus was a major supplier of paper to Europe until the fifteenth century. Two of papermaking's first footholds on the European continent were in Muslim Spain, at Toledo and Xàtiva.

France had a paper mill by 1190, and by the early fourteenth century Italy had mills at Fabriano, Treviso, and elsewhere.

The craft of papermaking is surprisingly simple. First, rags are boiled with lime and washed and beaten to a pulp that is transferred to a vat and agitated. A frame stretched with a fine wire screen is then dipped into the pulp and shaken to spread the fibers. When the excess liquid has drained off, the frame is dismantled and the raw paper is pressed on a sheet of felt. A stack of felts interlaced with paper sheets is then placed in a press and squeezed to remove moisture. The sheets are then hung to dry. Signs of this procedure are revealed when the paper is held up to the light. "Chain lines" are left by the metal frame and show up as widely spaced lines running at right angles to the closely set parallel wire or "laid" lines. Gradually, just as parchment had replaced papyrus, paper superseded parchment as the principal material for making books.

Like papermaking, the technology of printing with movable type arrived in Europe having already proven itself in the Far East. An early and simple form of printing—the "block book"—was developed in China and Korea in the eighth century as a way to print images. Building on these foundations, the Chinese made movable type from wood and clay in the eleventh century. In Korea, as early as the fourteenth century, individual characters were cast in metal. When the technology reached Europe, a young engraver and gem-cutter refined it even further. In so doing, he kicked off a revolution in the shape and size of libraries, and the shape and size of world culture.

Johannes Gensfleisch zur Laden zum Gutenberg was born in Mainz around the year 1400. By the late 1430s, he was still in Mainz and was borrowing money for an entrepreneurial venture that required quantities of lead and a wooden hand-press, like the ones used by vintners and bookbinders. In 1450 he borrowed a further 800 guilders from Johannes Fust, a wealthy goldsmith, lawyer, and moneylender. Like most entrepreneurs, Gutenberg would soon run out of funds; two years after the first Fust loan, he borrowed a further 800 guilders from the goldsmith.

The central insight of Gutenberg's invention was that much could be gained in speed and efficiency if the letters of the alphabet were cut in the form of reusable type. Each page of text could be printed from individual letters locked in a frame; the letters could then be unlocked and reused to print further pages. The development of his method of printing took him several years of trial, error, and experimentation. For it to work, the method required dozens of subsidiary and complementary innovations, such as suitable paper, fine metalworking, and oil-based inks. One of the most difficult stages to perfect was the casting of individual letters from a suitable alloy. (The screw-press was not the only element of Gutenberg's technology to have been influenced by bookbinding. The metal punches with which binders decorated leather were a precursor to Gutenberg's punches and type.)

In the beginning, Gutenberg's bread-and-butter printing included papal indulgences; the earliest of these to come from his printery carries a date of 1454. Even before that date, Gutenberg was working on a much grander and more ambitious project: a large, two-volume Bible containing over 1,200 pages of Latin text, printed in two columns of forty-two lines each. The titles, chapter headings, and initials would be added by hand, just as they had been in illuminated manuscripts. (The forty-two-line Bible is sometimes referred to as the "Mazarin Bible" because its first rigorous bibliographical description was made for the great Parisian library of Cardinal Mazarin.)

Sometime near the year 1452, Peter Schoeffer joined Gutenberg as an apprentice. Schoeffer knew Gutenberg's backer: Fust had sent Schoeffer to Paris to train at the university as a calligrapher, engraver, and manuscript copyist. Assisted by Schoeffer, Gutenberg produced about 180 copies of the forty-two-line Bible, some on vellum but most on paper.

There are European printed books that pre-date Gutenberg's. Block books were produced in Europe by the mid-fifteenth century, as were single devotional woodcut prints. Laurens Janszoon Coster of Haarlem printed around the time of Gutenberg's first experiments, and may in fact have been the first European to print with movable type. But his productions were of a low standard; Coster was a less exacting craftsman than the gem-cutter from Mainz. Gutenberg was the first craftsman in Europe to make letterpress printing viable and beautiful. He took sample pages of his Bible to the Frankfurt Trade Fair (*Frankfurter Messe*). Enea Silvio Piccolomini saw them, and in 1455 he wrote to the cardinal of Carvajal in Wiener, Neustadt. The Bible featured "very clear and very proper lettering, and without any faults, which Your Eminence would have been able to read effortlessly with no glasses." Even before the books were finished, customers came forward to buy them.

Things were going well for Gutenberg, until disaster struck. Fust expected a prompt return on his 1,600 guilders, but Gutenberg was taking too long. In 1455, even though the Bible was all but finished, Fust foreclosed on the original loan and took Gutenberg to court. The moneylender prevailed and took over the valuable security: the printer's equipment and edition. Gutenberg was ruined.

After the trial, Schoeffer continued the business in partnership with Fust. The former apprentice knew where his future lay; he cemented the partnership by marrying Fust's only daughter, Christina. (In court, Schoeffer had been the principal witness against Gutenberg. Schoeffer's Fustian links led to talk of a pact to bring down the printer from the inside and take control of his marvelous innovation.) Fust and Schoeffer would soon produce the landmark 1462 Mainz Bible. In the history of the book, Gutenberg was shunted aside. His former financier and his former apprentice made no mention of him in their productions. He died in 1468; decades would pass before he received any credit for his future-shaping achievements. In 1499 Ulrich Zell, the first printer of Cologne, stated emphatically and definitively that Johann Gutenberg was the true inventor of printing.

In the first fifty years after Gutenberg, printing presses sprang up in virtually every significant urban center in Europe. Though the technology took hold only gradually, and though the first printers preferred to use parchment and took pains to replicate the look and feel of manuscripts, the world had undergone a sea change in book media. The advent of printing enabled books to be produced in far greater numbers. It is estimated that, before the printing press, there were 50,000 books in the whole of Europe. Fifty years after Gutenberg's first Bible, the number of books exceeded 8 million, the number of editions 28,000. An efficient printer could produce in one day what a competent scribe could accomplish in six months. In the first hundred years of printing, more books were produced than in the previous thousand years of scribework. This revolution drove a thousand innovations in how ideas and knowledge were spread, and an equal number of innovations in libraries.

(Medieval scribes may have introduced deliberate imperfections into their manuscripts, but the arrival of printing opened the way for a new kind of error. The first Bibles to be printed in English are noted, and indeed classified—as He bibles, She bibles, Breeches bibles, Wicked bibles and so on—for their typographical and editorial idiosyncrasies, some of which are highly regrettable. The

Wicked Bible of 1631, for example, left out a critical word, rendering the seventh commandment as, "Thou shalt commit adultery." The whole edition was recalled; Barker the printer would never print again; and scarcely a copy of that now sought-after version exists today.)

Book-makers targeted their wares not only at the clergy and the aristocracy, but also at scholars, who could now debate books over long distances by citing page numbers and diagrams from identical printed copies. A yet more important target was the newly extensive middle class. Publishers and printers fed the appetite for editions of a manageable size. The great Venetian printer Aldus Manutius produced, in an octavo format, a series of well-edited and limpidly printed "pocket" editions of the classics, suitable for carrying around and even more so for displaying in bookcases at home. Aldus introduced new typefaces that were both beautiful and economical. The "italic" font, for example, allowed more words to fit on the page, without sacrificing legibility or elegance. The Bolognese punch-cutter Francesco Griffo created that font, building on the scriptorial innovations of Poggio's friend Niccolò Niccoli.

Aldus had set up his press in 1490, shortly after arriving in Venice. An ardent admirer of the ancient literature of Athens and Alexandria and Constantinople, he employed humanist scholars and Greek compositors to issue scholarly editions, in Greek, of classics by Aristophanes, Euripides, Herodotus, and Sophocles, then Latin classics by Virgil, Pliny, and other authors. Apart from the first italic typeface, Francesco Griffo also produced for Aldus a Greek font and fine Roman ones.

In 1499 Aldus printed the *Hypnerotomachia Poliphili*. Attributed to Francesco Colonna, a Dominican monk, the book is an epic allegory of the search for lost love. Cleverly concealed in the book, the author's name is revealed by taking the first letter from each chapter.

The letters spell out *Poliam frater Franciscus Columna peramavit*: "Brother Francesco Colonna loved Polia tremendously." Regarded as one of the finest books ever made, the *Hypnerotomachia Poliphili* is renowned for the beauty of its design, and how seamlessly it integrated Griffo's Roman type with 174 woodcuts. The book was highly influential: among other reverberations, it caused French printers to switch from Gothic to Roman typefaces.

Aldus's books came to be prized by libraries and collectors around the world. In the nineteenth century, upon the death of the Marquis of Hastings—better known as a horse man than a bookman—the Marquis's possessions were to be auctioned. Andrew Lang tells the story of how Didot, the biographer of Aldus, had a sixth bibliographical sense that led him to guess the Marquis "might have owned something in his line." Didot sent his agent to the English town where the auction was to be held. Among the books "dragged out of some mouldy store-room"—what Lang called (with words that Poggio and Rustici might have used) "a rubbish heap in an English cellar"—was the large-paper copy of Homer that Aldus had printed then presented to King Francis I of France, the monarch who also owned Leonardo da Vinci's *Mona Lisa*. When Didot's agent found the book, "part of the original binding [was] still clinging to the leaves." Once it was in Didot's hands he sent it to "the hospital for books"—the fine binder who only worked for "dukes, millionaires and Rothschilds," and who restored the king's arms and devices on the book's cover.

To reach the world's new readers, and their public and private libraries, printer-publishers exploited the newly dug channels of international commerce. The Frankfurt Book Fair, or *Frankfurter Buchmesse*, began in 1478 or thereabouts. It convened each year towards the end of Lent—just as the Benedictine monks were finishing their annual read-through of the scriptures—and in late summer. Though many books continued to be written and printed in Latin, more and more books in the vernacular languages appeared. The Renaissance was an era of translation. By 1528, for example, Livy, Suetonius, Thucydides, and Xenophon were all available in French. This made the texts accessible to an audience that was neither academic nor clerical.

William Caxton translated with vigor. Of the hundred or so surviving Caxton editions, about seventy were published in English. Many of these—including the first book printed in that language, *Recuyell of the Historyes of Troye*—were translated by Caxton himself. To Lady Margaret Beaufort, the Queen Mother, he dedicated his translation of a romance, with these words:

> Bysechynge my sayd ladyes bountyuous grace to receyve this lityll boke in gree of me, her humble servaunt, and to pardoune me of the rude and comyn Englyshe, where as shall be found faulte; for I confesse me not lerned ne knowynge the arte of rethoryk ne of suche gaye termes as now be sayd in these dayes and used. Bat I hope that it shall be understonden of the redars and herers—and that shall suffyse.

Greater access to books and learning in turn promised greater social mobility. In 1507, the biographer of a German aristocrat warned that his caste had neglected learning, "whereas the children of peasants have taken to study and thereby come to large bishop-rics and high legal offices . . . so that, as the common proverb says, the chairs have jumped upon the table."

In October 2014, nineteen-year-old Kendra Sunderland simultane-ously filmed and pleasured herself on the sixth floor of the Valley

Library at Oregon State University. The film became one of the most watched on the internet. Copycat productions appeared, breathing life into memes, GIFs, spin-offs, and the "sexy librarian" topos. Sunderland was charged with public indecency. In court she pleaded guilty—the evidence was incontrovertible—and the judge fined her $1,000. A career in digital porn followed.

Though the incident caused a scandal at the library, Sunderland can claim affinity with a tradition that dates back at least as far as ancient Rome. A remarkable number of explicit sculptures and implements and murals have been found in excavations at Pompeii and Herculaneum. A famous example from the library at Herculaneum's Epicurean Villa of the Papyri is the marble statue of Pan making unmistakable love to a she-goat. The word "pornography" entered English after these discoveries. Webster's 1864 dictionary defined the word with reference to "licentious painting employed to decorate the walls of rooms sacred to bacchanalian orgies, examples of which exist in Pompeii."

Eighteenth-century Italy and France were enormously productive of printed pornography and other forbidden books. Subjects spanned the arts of seduction, prostitution, and flagellation. Ladies and gentlemen from across Europe gathered choice examples for their private libraries. But printed smut was not solely the preserve of the upper classes. On the eve of the French revolution, the restive masses gobbled up pamphlets and broadsides—*chroniques scandaleuses*—on lurid topics such as the king's impotence and Marie Antoinette's bisexuality.

Despite the popularity of erotica, its collection has always carried a stigma. In his 1877 series of satirical dialogues that went under the title *The New Republic*, W. H. Mallock pictured Walter Pater in the guise of "Mr Rose."

> Mr Rose . . . is more than a little odd. He is made to show undue interest in certain books of a curious character, including the *Cultes Secrets des Dames Romaines*, which occupy a locked compartment of his host's bookcase. There is a faint suggestion that his languid enthusiasms are not only sickly but even a bit dubious in morality.

Erotic collections have been assembled in unlikely places. Garages, vicarages, workingmen's cottages. One of the largest collections of pornographic literature in Latin America was formed by beloved children's book author Constancio C. Vigil. Major institutional libraries also collected pornography and erotica. For most of the past century, an air of secrecy and coyness surrounded such holdings as the British Museum's "Secretum," the Bibliothèque Nationale's Enfer collection, and the library at San Francisco's Institute for the Advanced Study of Human Sexuality. In 1950, after viewing Henry Fuseli drawings in the British Museum, the Folger librarian Louis Wright observed that some of the drawings were regarded as so pornographic they were fit only for specialists who were allowed just a few scientific peeks. (One superintendent at the museum was asked for permission to consult a pornographic book in the collection. "Are you a doctor or a psychologist?" he asked. The reader answered "No," and access was refused.) Erotic books in the New York Public Library—identified in the catalogue with a discreet triple-star code—spent many decades locked in cages.

During the Cold War, the Russian State Library stockpiled publications banned by the Soviet government for being "ideologically harmful." Known as the *spetskhran* ("Special Storage Section") the hoard included thousands of erotic and pornographic works from around the world, ranging from Japanese Ukiyo-e engravings to Nixon-era romance novels. (In her introduction to *The House of Mirth*, Edith Wharton recalled a conversation with Henry James in which she mentioned the type of novel "that used euphemistically to be called 'unpleasant.'" "You know," Wharton told James, "I was rather disappointed; that book wasn't nearly as bad as I expected." James replied with a twinkle, "Ah, my dear, the abysses are all so shallow.")

For people who grew up in the West in the present century, censorship is almost an alien and antique concept. Few books are banned; the *Anarchist's Cookbook* comes to mind, along with one or two other dangerous manuals. But for people who grew up in the twentieth century, censorship was commonplace. And censorship was mostly about sex. Think *Lady Chatterley's Lover, Tropic of Cancer, Portnoy's Complaint, Ulysses, Lolita*. (In 1972 Oakland County's circuit judge found many reasons to ban *Slaughterhouse-Five* from local public schools, accusing it of being depraved, immoral, psychotic, vulgar, and anti-Christian. The following year, a school board in North Dakota destroyed thirty-two copies of the novel in the school's coal burner.)

In the first years of censorship, things were very different. Sex was the least of the censors' worries. In England, for example, the primary concern of the Tudors was the eradication of heretical and treasonous works. Except in the most extreme cases, lewd and bawdy literature was tolerated.

The initial period of printing was somewhat of a free-for-all. With all the reading and translating and jumping on tables, something just had to be done. Censorship began in Germany in 1475. Soon after, Pope Sixtus IV empowered the University of Cologne to license the publication of books. Producers, sellers, and readers of unauthorized books faced a plethora of punishments.

Offenders could be fined or excommunicated. Their books could be burned, or they themselves could be. (In 1512 in The Hague, for example, the Inquisition burned a "relapsed heretic," Herman of Rijswijk, along with his books.)

The first censors' justifications would be reused many times: books had become much more accessible, especially to the "less instructed and more excitable" middle and lower classes; new ideas were springing up, including worryingly unorthodox social and religious ones; unfettered distribution of books threatened political, moral, and doctrinal values. Control of print was necessary to ensure the safety and stability of church and state. A decade after the Cologne license, a similar regime came into force in the archdiocese of Mainz, Johannes Gutenberg's hometown.

In 1501 Pope Alexander VI extended censorship to the whole of Germany. Bishops or their deputies punished the printers of unauthorized religious works by excommunication and fines. The introduction of religious censorship in Italy followed a similar pattern. Venice, 1480; Treviso, 1491; and by 1515, coverage of the whole peninsula. When the religious and secular authorities of other countries followed suit and initiated censorship, many of them used German and Italian models.

Book-burners set fires on both sides of the Protestant Reformation. In 1520 there were public burnings of Luther's works at Cologne and Louvain. Luther burned papal edicts and decretals in Wittenberg. He also sought bans on works by Protestants with whom he disagreed.

The 1521 Edict of Worms was the instrument through which the Holy Roman Emperor Charles V prohibited the printing, possessing, and reading of any works by Luther. The Bavarian State Library in Munich imposed special conditions on unorthodox works. "Protestant theology, on the papal legate's advice, was separately shelved and in theory available only in exceptional circumstances." Thomas Platter left behind a diary that is important for sixteenth-century evidence about the literary culture of the time. In 1599 he visited London where he saw, at the Globe Theatre, an early production of *Julius Caesar*. Platter also recorded a 1595 visit to the Jesuit College at Tournon. Young Platter and his companion, Dr. Collado, saw there a copy of the Calvinist Geneva Bible. "Collado wanted to open it, but one of the fathers angrily forbade it, saying that it was a work of the damned."

The year after censorship began in Cologne, William Caxton set up his printing press at Westminster. In medieval England, political troublemakers had been prosecuted under old laws of treason and heresy. Now, the Tudor monarchs made new regulations to control printing and the spread of books. Henry VIII's first act of censorship was to stem the importation and distribution of Lutheran tracts. In 1520 and 1529 lists were compiled of Lutheran writers whose works would be prohibited in England. Ecclesiastical courts were empowered to prosecute printers and owners of the forbidden books. When, in 1534, Henry broke with the Catholic Church, this apparatus was retained but its targets changed. The king also went further by establishing a preventative form of censorship. The Proclamation of 1538 was created to "expel and avoid the occasion of errors and opinions opined." Before a book could be printed, it had to be authorized by the king, the Privy Council, or a bishop. To prevent foreign books from slipping past the censor, books printed abroad were banned altogether.

Henry's daughter Mary Tudor expanded censorship even further by creating the Stationers' Company, a London guild of printers and booksellers and binders. In 1557 she granted the company a royal charter to regulate the printing trade and ensure no treasonous or seditious works were issued. Members of the company could seize and destroy unlicensed books. Only members of the company could own a printing press.

For the Catholic faithful, the Vatican banned bawdy books and purged the most racy and anticlerical passages from literary classics such as the *Decameron*. References to God replaced references to the role of Fortune in human affairs. The works of heretics, occultists, and Machiavelli were placed on the banned list, as was Lorenzo Valla's book about the forged Donation of Constantine, and Poggio's book of jokes. In 1559 the church included the *Facetiae* in the *Index* of banned heretical, anticlerical, and suspect books. In all, the *Index* contained the entire works of approximately 550 authors, plus some individual titles. The *Tridentine Index* of 1564 extended the list of forbidden books. It included a ninth-century theological work, the *Libri Carolini*; fourteenth-century writings by John Wycliffe (including *De Sacramento altaris*, in which he denied the transubstantiation of Christ); Reuchlin's speculative *Der Augenspiegel* (1511); and a variety of theological, medical, botanical, zoological, and legal books by Protestant scholars. Later editions of the *Index* included Diderot's *Encyclopaedia*, whose first volume appeared in 1751. The twentieth and final edition of the Vatican's *Index* appeared in 1948. Pope Paul VI formally discontinued the *Index* on June 14, 1966.

Curiosities

In Tolkien's Middle-earth, a "mathom" is any portable object for which a Hobbit has no immediate use, but is unwilling to throw away. The "mathom house" is a museum where the Shire's antiquities, some of them of questionable value, are displayed. Individual Hobbit families keep their mathoms in studies, libraries, and cupboards—most Hobbits live underground and do not have attics.

According to Peter Gilliver, Jeremy Marshall, and Edmund Weiner, Tolkien revived "mathom" from Old English, where it meant "something valuable, an item of treasure." The word has Gothic and Germanic roots that relate to the gifts warriors exchanged to cement friendships and alliances. *Beowulf* described an ancient king's funeral at which a treasure of mathoms was laid upon his bosom. The *Old English Chronicle* from the year 1110 described an English princess taking mathoms to Germany as part of her dowry. *Ormulum* (c. 1200) discussed the three kings visiting the infant Jesus, each of them presenting "hiss hord off hise madmess" (mathoms).

Gilliver, Marshall, and Weiner note how Tolkien repurposed the term.

> Tolkien brought it down in the world, for among the hobbits it denotes a piece of bric-a-brac, something that is only subjectively a treasure because you don't want to part

with it, although at the same time it is clear that the giving of presents, many of which were probably mathoms, was a highly important part of hobbit life.

Tolkien's use of the word befits the Shire, whose Hobbit citizens are neither aristocratic nor militaristic.

The concept of a mathom house had its analogy in the eighteenth and nineteenth centuries. Popularized as an Enlightenment-age expression of wonder at the physical world, the "cabinet of curiosities" was a feature of many libraries, public and private. Also known as a *Kunstkabinett* and a *Wunderkammer,* the cabinet might be a piece of furniture or an entire room dedicated to displaying intriguing objects (not all of them authentic) from nature, art, archaeology, and ethnography, very broadly defined. Grand or humble, each cabinet tried to capture the richness of the universe on a miniature scale.

Bruce Chatwin's grandparents maintained a cabinet of curiosities that was said to contain "a piece of brontosaurus"—actually part of a giant sloth, an inspiration for his wanderings in Patagonia. The striking and grotesque curiosities kept at the Bodleian included a mummy, an Irish skull, a Jamaican crocodile, Chinese books, the Tsar of Russia's lambskin coat, and a whale that had been caught in the River Severn.

St. Gall's cabinet of curiosities contains the jaws of a shark, citrus fruits, coins, artifacts from East India (shoes, textiles, and a basket), and the mummified remains of Schepenese, a young Egyptian princess from Thebes—believed to date from about 610 B.C. A visitor to the library in 1962 noted that the ebony-skinned mummy had "such delicate features, as well as beautiful teeth."

CHAPTER 6

———— ✦ ————

"What the Barbarians did not do"

The Vatican Library

English Grand Tourists visiting the Vatican were always shown Greek and Roman antiquities, a papyrus leaf, a breviary said to have belonged to St. Gregory, more Chinese books, and, pivotal to England's break with the Roman church, prized documentary treasures such as the manuscript of Henry VIII's *Assertio septem sacramentorum*, as well as adulterous love letters he sent to Anne Boleyn. Other treasures in the Vatican include a reliquary for the head of St. Sebastian; the granite torso of Pharaoh Nectanebo I; the smiling Polynesian god Tu, sturdily built from wood; a reddish stone sculpture of Quetzalcoatl, the Plumed Serpent; the *Gabinetto Numismatico o Medagliere*, which contains the world's largest collection of papal and Roman coins; and figures in ivory, bronze, enamel, glass, terra-cotta, and cloth, many of them taken from the Roman catacombs.

Today, the Vatican's book collections, especially the fabled Secret Archive and prohibited books, present a hypnotically alluring prospect for book-lovers. More than one bibliophile has fantasized about infiltrating the secluded holdings, which are pictured as an inaccessible wonder, stretching back to ancient Rome and the birth of the Church, and containing all the best books, and all the worst ones. In several important respects, that picture is a false one.

The Vatican Library is believed to have begun around 385 A.D. as the personal library of Pope Damasus I. He and other early popes collected scrolls and codices: "there was always need of liturgical books to conserve and transmit evidence of the Church's spiritual life." Apart from liturgical works, those popes also collected histories, commentaries, and biographies; works of the Greek apologists; and Greek and Roman classics.

Early in the thirteenth century, Pope Innocent III created the *Regestes*—the first thorough listing of papal documents. Less than a century later, under Boniface VIII, the papal collection of illuminated manuscripts had grown to become one of the most important in Europe. The next century, though, brought a series of calamities. In 1303 soldiers loyal to King Philip IV of France attacked Boniface VIII's palace at Anagni, southeast of Rome, and plundered the papal library. The next pope (Clement V) moved 643 valuable codices to the sacristy of the monastery in Assisi. That town, too, was attacked and further losses ensued.

In 1308, under Clement V (his run of ill luck continued), fire destroyed the principal temple of the Catholic world: the Cathedral of St. John Laterano in Rome. The following year, the "Babylonian captivity" began: the exiled pope resided at Avignon under French authority. Exile forced reorganization of the papal library, but it also led to many additions. At Avignon, the growing collection was stored in the Angel's Tower of the Papal Palace.

After the Council of Constance and the mending of the Great Schism, the papal library was unambiguously Rome's. Pope Nicholas V is credited as the true founder of the Vatican Library. He used as a model the Medici library at the Dominican convent of San Marco in Florence. He employed copyists and illuminators from Bologna and Florence to create and embellish codices. He sent representatives to search East and West for valuable manuscripts. When Constantinople fell to the Turks, he tried in vain to save the famous imperial library. Unswayed by concerns that Renaissance humanism threatened the church and its teachings, he encouraged the study of classical authors—thereby continuing a long-standing papal tradition. He appointed Lorenzo Valla as the library's Latin expert, and he commissioned the translation of Greek works into Latin. (Valla's translation of Thucydides is one of the Vatican's treasures.)

Applying his linguistic expertise, Valla achieved major scholarly breakthroughs, especially in the field of sniffing out fakes, such as those bogus texts from Alexandria. He had already demonstrated, in 1440, that a document called the Donation of Constantine, allegedly composed by the emperor who converted the Roman Empire to Christianity, was in fact a clever forgery. In the donation, Constantine supposedly transferred power over the western provinces of the empire, including Italy, to the Church. The document's exposure as a forgery was a calamitous blow to the Vatican's prestige.

In the jubilee year of 1450, however, pilgrims still flocked to Rome. Revenues from alms enabled rapid expansion of the library. Nicholas V funded the purchase, the copying, and the illustration of manuscripts on a scale never before seen. He sent agents all over Europe to search for valuable books. His librarian, Tortelli, organized the rapidly expanding library. It contained about 1,200 entries, of which more than eight hundred were Latin manuscripts and approximately four hundred were Greek. Nicholas V's successor, the Spanish canonist Calixtus III, was appalled. When shown the library, he exclaimed, "Just see what the property of God's church has been wasted on!"

Fortunately, Pope Sixtus IV had a different attitude to books. On June 15, 1475, he issued the bull *Ad decorem militantis Ecclesiae*, which formally established the library and endowed it with the space and funds it needed—including space for a chained library, accessible to the public, in a prized location: on the ground floor beside the Sistine Chapel (which Sixtus IV also brought into being). The stated priority of the library was "the convenience and honour of the learned and studious." The humanist Bartolomeo Sacchi, known as Platina, was appointed librarian. The collection had already grown to 2,527 codices. Platina oversaw even more rapid expansion. His 1481 catalogue includes 3,500 items, representing almost forty percent growth in six years. The library had become nothing less than the largest collection of books in the Western world.

During the years 1471 to 1484, under Sixtus IV, the library was generously endowed. To be given permission to study and work there was a great honor; and an even higher goal for scholars was to be named Vatican Librarian. A fresco dating from around 1478 shows Sixtus IV and Platina standing in front of rows of lecterns paved with about fifty codices, all of them looking most fine in their leather covers adorned with clasps, studs, hinges, bosses, and blind tooling. During his six years of office, Platina was entitled to a monthly salary of ten ducats, plus wood, candles, oil, brooms, and food for himself, three assistants, and a horse. The assistants worked as copyists and general laborers. In all, the library occupied four large new rooms that were elaborately painted by Melozzo da Forlì, Antoniazzo Romano, Domenico and Davide Ghirlandaio. A fifth room accommodated Platina, his assistants, and a bookbinder. The library's marquetry cupboards, the work of the Florentine architect Giovannino de'Dolci, were later fixed to the anteroom walls of the Sistine Chapel. The cupboard inlays depict doors that are partly ajar and reveal books lying down inside.

Over the next century, growth in the collection led Pope Julius II to assign more rooms. The library continued to prosper under Leo X. And then, in May 1527, disaster struck. Under Emperor Charles V of the Habsburg dynasty, the mutinous imperial army sacked Rome. For the most part, Charles's army consisted of bandits, deserters, and unpaid Lutheran infantrymen. A contemporary letter describes a scene of devastation in the Vatican Library, with manuscripts' covers and clasps wrenched off, and books "mutilated, torn, cut in pieces and thrown among the rubbish." Pope Clement VII took refuge in the Castel Sant'Angelo.

In 1587 or thereabouts, Sixtus V commissioned Domenico Fontana to design a new building for the library, between the Cortile del Belvedere and the Cortile della Pigna. A capacious top-floor room, measuring sixty by fifteen meters, housed the library's books and manuscripts. Showcasing precious codices, the room is lavishly decorated with painted ceilings, frescoes and other ornamentation. Sixtus V also moved the papal printing works to the new building.

In the 1590s the collections of Cardinal Antonio Carafa and Fulvio Orsini were incorporated in the library. In 1618, under Paul V, twenty-eight early manuscripts were transferred from Bobbio. In 1623 the marvelous Heidelberg Library, a "prize of war" offered by Maximilian I, Elector of Bavaria and leader of the Catholic League, to Pope Gregory XV, arrived in Rome. Known as the mother of all German libraries, the Heidelberg collection was added to the Vatican Library, although it retained a separate identity therein as the *Biblioteca Palatina*. From that time on, whenever the Vatican acquired an important collection, the acquisition was designated as a "*fondo*" (bequest) and maintained its individuality as such. (The collection in existence at the library until 1622 is referred to as the *Fondo Vaticano*.)

From the Renaissance until today, the story of the Vatican's collections is a story of irrepressible growth: a marvelous cascade from donors intent on saving their books, and their souls. The stream of acquisitions created enchantment and envy everywhere. Acquired gradually from 1654 to 1759, for instance: the *Fondo Reginense*, the library of Queen Christina of Sweden, which contained 2,120 Latin manuscripts and 190 Greek ones, not counting the queen's fifty-five manuscripts from the library of Pius II—the "fun-loving" pope who wrote the erotic novel *The Tale of Two Lovers* (*Historia de duobus amantibus*). (Published by Ulrich Zell in Cologne between 1467 and 1470, that book became a fifteenth-century bestseller.)

And acquired in 1658: the *Fondo Urbinate*, rich in Renaissance manuscripts, from Federico da Montefeltro, Duke of Urbino. In 1746: the *Fondo Capponiano*, 288 codices collected by a Roman bibliophile. In 1748: the *Fondo Ottoboniano*, the manuscript collection of Cardinal Marcello Cervini of Montepulciano, purchased by Benedictus XIV from the heirs of Cardinal Pietro Ottoboni the Younger and comprising 3,394 Latin and 473 Greek manuscripts, some from the University of Avignon, some from the Greek monasteries on Mount Athos. Acquired in 1902: the *Fondo Borgiano*, an exceptionally international collection of 768 Latin, 276 Arabic, 178 Syrian, 136 Coptic, eighty-eight Armenian, eighty-one Turkish, forty-one Tonkinese, thirty-seven Ethiopic, thirty-seven Indian, twenty-seven Greek, twenty-four Persian, twenty-two Illyrian, nineteen Hebrew, fifteen Georgian, two Siamese, and two Irish manuscripts, as well as one each in Icelandic and Precolumbian Mexican, and 543 Chinese texts, most of them printed. In 1885: the vast collection of Count Leopoldo Cicognara of Ferrara, a great traveler and connoisseur (who had already given the Vatican 4,300 volumes). Also in 1885: a further 1,445 valuable volumes collected by Cardinal Angelo Mai, a Jesuit scholar, formerly scriptor of the Ambrosian and prefect of the Vatican Library, and a specialist in the study and decipherment of palimpsests. Acquired under Leo XIII: the *Fondo dei Neofiti*, the *Fondo della Cappella Sistina*, and the *Fondo Borghese*, which includes manuscripts from the library of the Avignon popes. And the greatest coup under Leo XIII: the *Fondo Barberiniano*, a wonderful collection of books assembled in the Palazzo Barberini by the spendthrift prince Cardinal Francesco Barberini.

Bernini and Borromini built Prince Francesco's palace, in part using stones from the Colosseum and tiles from the Pantheon, an expedient that prompted the mocking epigram, "*Quod non fecerunt Barbari, fecere Barberini*" ("What the Barbarians did not do, the Barberini do"). The prince acquired 36,049 printed volumes, 10,041 Latin manuscripts, 595 Greek manuscripts, and 160 Oriental manuscripts. Totti's 1638 Roman guidebook observed that the Barberini library could be visited and that, "because it can be of use to the public, there are custodians." The prince's approach to acquiring books attracted the same criticism as his pillaging of ancient stones. "The Cardinal also did not hesitate to acquire some of his manuscripts in like manner. He confiscated what he wanted at the Abbey Grottaferrata which, for centuries, had been a centre of Greek–Byzantine studies."

Into the first decades of the twentieth century, the creation of new *fondi* continued with gusto. Acquired in 1921: the *Fondo Rossiano*, the library of Roman nobleman Giovan Francesco de

Rossi, comprising 196 manuscripts, 6,000 rare prints, and 2,500 "incunabula" (printed books from the fifteenth century). Acquired in 1923: the *Fondo Chigiano*, the last great collection of a noble Roman family, comprising 3,916 manuscripts in total, including fifty-four early Greek manuscripts, an eleventh-century Horace, the *Summa Dictaminum* of Pier delle Vigne, the *Chronicle* of Giovanni Villani (with 225 fourteenth-century miniatures), and the famous *Codice delle sei Messe*. As well as important works by Cicero, Virgil, Sallust, Juvenal, Pliny, Dante, Petrarch, and Boccaccio, the *Fondo Chigiano* includes original drawings by Bernini, seventeenth-century music, and books on war, hunting, and dance. Acquired in 1926: the *Fondo Ferrajoli* comprises 885 manuscripts and 100,000 autographs. Under John XXIII and Paul VI the *Fondo Cerulli Persiani* and *Fondo Cerulli Etiopici* were acquired, swelling the library's holdings of Persian drama and Ethiopic manuscripts.

All these *fondos* added up to 80,000 late-antique, Byzantine, medieval, and Renaissance manuscripts in dozens of languages, from Aramaic to Old Church Slavonic. Many of the world's greatest documentary treasures. Codex B, a fourth-century manuscript of the Bible in Greek. One of the earliest versions of Virgil's *Aeneid*. The oldest Hebrew book in existence. One of the oldest copies of the Pythagorean theorem. An autograph of Thomas Aquinas. Eight thousand incunabula. A hundred thousand maps, prints, engravings, and drawings. Nearly 2 million printed books. Seventy-five thousand reference volumes. All housed in the building commissioned by Sixtus V, next to the Cortile del Belvedere—a small city of halls, offices, laboratories, reading rooms, and strongrooms.

Established by Paul V in 1612, and now part of the Vatican Library, the *Archivio Segreto Vaticano*—the "Secret Archive"—runs to 35,000 volumes and comprises the Vatican's collection of the Papacy's own papers, including those from Avignon. One of the papers is a threatening note from Genghis Khan's grandson demanding that Pope Innocent IV "pay service and homage" to the Mongols. There are also accounts of the trial of the Knights Templar held at Chinon in August 1308; the 1493 papal bull that split the New World between Spain and Portugal; Leo X's 1521 decree excommunicating Martin Luther; and letters from Elizabeth I, Voltaire, Abraham Lincoln, and, written on fragile birch bark, a group of Christian Ojibwe Indians. (Addressed to Pope Leo, or "the Great Master of Prayer, he who holds the place of Jesus," that letter is postmarked, "where there is much grass, in the month of the flowers.") Mostly bound in cream vellum, the Secret Archive volumes, some more than a foot thick, are housed in the Tower of Winds, whose rooms are lined with more than eighty kilometers of dark wooden shelves.

In 1714 Humfrey Wanley recommended that a new library should have "sines that may keep off loiterers, peepers, and talkative persons." At the Bodleian, which was well endowed with such signs, any "gentleman stranger" from abroad could apply for permission to study in the library. The first "Extraneus," admitted on February 15, 1603, was a Frenchman. Students from Protestant Europe came in substantial numbers. Other readers before 1620 included Spaniards, Italians, and one Ethiopian.

The Ambrosian Library was referred to as the "Catholic counterpart of Bodley's creation." When Richard Lassels visited the Ambrosian in the seventeenth century, he concluded it was one of the best libraries in Italy, "because it is not so coy as the others, which scarce let themselves be seen; whereas this opens its dores publikly to all comers and goers, and suffers Them to read what book they please." He was able to handle amazing treasures, including the album of drawings by Leonardo da Vinci that was formed by the sculptor Pompeo Leoni and was known as the *Codice Atlantico* for its large size. And a copy of *Il Saggiatore*, which Galileo presented, along with a covering letter, to Cardinal Borromeo, "not because I think it worthy to be read by you, but for my own esteem and to procure life and reputation for the work, in itself low and frail, in your most Illustrious and Reverend Lordship's heroic and immortal library." The Ambrosian also included manuscript treasures from the monastery of Bobbio.

In 1726 Charles VI declared Vienna's Hofbibliothek open to all except "idiots, servants, idlers, chatterboxes and casual strollers." At Trinity College, Dublin, arrangements were in place should students abuse their access privileges. If, for example, a volume was missed, "a stringent search should be made" of the dorms and studies—such as when, in 1793, an undergraduate was caught selling library books on the quays. At the Bibliothèque de l'Arsenal in Paris, the borrowing of books was forbidden; "the single recorded exception was disastrous: a volume of costume plates lent to the Duc de Luxembourg and "miserably torn" by his children."

Prior to 1692 the French national library was closed to the public; "even a scholar of the eminence of Isaac Vossius could only gain admittance through influence at court." This all changed when a curious appointment was made. For a significant part of the reign of Louis XIV, François Michel Le Tellier, Marquis de Louvois, was Secretary of State for War. In the last decades of his life he was the most powerful of the king's ministers. In 1684 Louvois purchased the office of Royal Librarian for his fourth son, as a ninth-birthday present. The incumbent librarians and their agents were unceremoniously fired. The new librarian, Abbé de Louvois, turned out to be a precocious savant and an erudite and able librarian. In 1692, he began opening the library to the public for two days a week, and he invited scholars to dine and converse with him on those days.

At the Vatican Library, the idea of allowing scholars to consult the collections was first broached in the middle of the fifteenth century, during the brief but energetic pontificate of polymath and bibliophile Nicholas V. He intended the library's treasures to be used "for the common convenience of the learned." Nicholas died before this vision could be implemented, but, in June 1475, the new pope crystallized the idea with a bull that opened the library to people outside the Vatican. "Serious students" were allowed to access books and even to borrow from the library, just as they could from the Medici collections in Florence.

After this apogee of liberality, though, access became more and more difficult. In the seventeenth century, John Evelyn complained that the Vatican's books were "all shut up in Presses . . . and not expos'd on shelves to the naked ayre." Clement XIII was the notoriously prudish pope who put fig leaves over the rude bits of the Vatican's nudes. In 1765 he issued a bull limiting access to the manuscripts, locking many of them away "under double keys." At the end of the eighteenth century, things were so bad that a Spanish priest, Juan Andres, denounced the library as not so much a *biblioteca* as a *bibliotaphio*, a tomb for books. The regulation of access to the Secret Archive was especially strict. Absolutely no browsing allowed. In the nineteenth century, during the long librarianship of Cardinal Mai, the main collections were still largely off-limits. Readers could consult neither indexes nor catalogues, and were given only a small, ill-lit room in which to work. There were other restrictions, too. As late as the 1970s, the shoulders of visiting female scholars had to be completely covered.

Today, however, the picture of the Vatican Library as forbidding and inaccessible is largely a myth. In the nineteenth and early twentieth centuries, a succession of brilliant directors—Father Franz Ehrle (1895–1913; he became a cardinal), Monsignor Achille Ratti (1913–22, formerly librarian of the Ambrosian, and later Pope Pius XI), Monsignor Giovanni Mercati (1922–36, another future cardinal), and Monsignor Anselmo Albareda (1936–62, ditto)—transformed the library into one of the world's most progressive and efficient libraries, notwithstanding those covered shoulders.

The antiquity of the library is another myth. For more than 1,000 years after the fall of Rome, the papal collections grew, but the growth was halting and haphazard. Losses due to fire were many, as were those due to theft, plunder, and conservation ignorance. None of the ancient manuscripts for which the Vatican Library is now famous were obtained before the fifteenth century—a time when the church was much less centralized and papalized, and when other Catholic collections overshadowed the pope's library. (The capitular library of St. Peter's, for example, possessed more early codices, thanks to a generous bequest from Cardinal Giordano Orsini.) Very few of the Vatican's current holdings were acquired prior to 1600, and many key acquisitions date from much later than that. Though a symbol of religion and the early papacy, the Vatican Library is in fact a product of the Renaissance and the Enlightenment.

Delicacies

The olfactory sense has a proud place in bibliographical research. Much can be discovered by smell, though some odors continue to confound scholars. A uniquely sweet and smoky scent, for example, adheres to some of T. E. Lawrence's books. The precise source of the aroma is the subject of debate. Is it from fruity pipe tobacco? Motorcycle exhaust fumes? Tea and biscuits? Decaying leather? Ink, glue, mold, ashes, licorice? Or camel?

John Seely Brown and Paul Duguid studied a twentieth-century medical historian who could determine, by sniffing eighteenth-century papers in old archives, how far a cholera outbreak had traveled. The telltale smell of vinegar, a disinfectant, still adhered to the papers after the passage of two centuries. Books can also be dated by their smell. Volatile organic compounds in paper, leather, and glue are known to degrade at predictable rates. As they do, they release a blended scent that carries notes of vanilla (from lignin and vanillin) and almonds (from benzaldehyde). Other implicated compounds include toluene, alcohol, and ethyl hexanol, each of which can produce sweet and floral odors, and which can distinguish older from younger books. Eugene Field, author of *The Love Affairs of a Bibliomaniac*, wrote lyrically on the subject: "Sweeter than thy unguents and cosmetics and Sabean perfumes is the smell of those old books of mine."

Born around 385 A.D. and dying in Bethlehem in 439, Melania the Younger collected an important early Christian library. She was so fond of reading that "she would go through the *Lives* of the Fathers as if she were eating dessert." The attractiveness of books has led other people to go further. Holbrook Jackson devoted two sections of *Anatomy of Bibliomania* to the subject of eating books.

In medieval Jewish society, learning to read was celebrated and ritualized. On the Feast of Shavuot, as Alberto Manguel described in *A History of Reading*, a boy visits his teacher to undertake an initiation rite. The teacher shows the boy a slate containing scriptoral passages written in the Hebrew alphabet, and reads them aloud to him. The slate is then covered in honey, which the child licks. Other modes of bodily assimilation were also used. Teachers would write biblical verses on honey cakes, and on eggs that were hard-boiled and peeled. After proving himself by reading the verses out loud, the child was allowed to eat the cakes and eggs, thereby ingesting the words of God both literally and figuratively in a peculiar echo of the doctrine of transubstantiation.

CHAPTER 7

•

Secret Histories

Tricks and treasures in library design

Acquiring books is a fraught business. In June 1933, the Belfast bookseller James Weatherup wrote to the Rosenbachs, a famous firm of New York booksellers who had helped build America's greatest private and institutional collections.

Dear Sirs,

Bay Psalm Book.

I have a copy of the above book particulars of which I have noted on the enclosed sheet. If you are interested I shall be glad to hear from you. In the meantime I shall hold it for your reply, and if you care to see the book, I shall be glad to forward it—per my daughter, who will be leaving this side for New York about 1st July—for inspection & offer.

The attachment described the book cryptically and matter-of-factly.

> Old Brown morocco.—worn & cracked at hinges. Title-page—missing. Preface a few leaves missing . . . Leaves unpaginated, and number in this copy 135, in addition to an errata leaf entitled "Faults escaped in printing," and the 4 leaves of preface making in all 140 leaves. Four leaves, signature D, are entirely missing and do not seem to ever have been in this copy.

Dr. Abraham Rosenbach replied by cable that Miss Weatherup should indeed bring the book to America. When the volume arrived at 15 East 51st Street, Rosenbach examined it carefully and confirmed what he had only dared to hope. It was a hitherto unknown copy of the first book printed in North America. An extremely exciting and exceptionally valuable book, despite its many faults. (In addition to the missing title leaf, for example, the copy lacked seven other leaves.) As to rarity, no copy had appeared since 1855—and a total of only eleven, from an original print run of about 1,700 copies, were known to exist worldwide. As to value, the even worse Van Sinderen copy, which lacked *nineteen* leaves, would be estimated only a few years later at $50,000.

Rosenbach adopted a shrewd strategy. He sent another cable to Weatherup. "Book received regret condition we do not make offers so kindly cable your price in pounds." Weatherup's reply, "£150," opened the way to a quick sale, one of the greatest bargains ever savored by a book-dealer. The purchase, though, would be bookended by a very different Rosenbach acquisition of a very similar volume.

In March 1879, at the auction of George Brinley's estate, Cornelius Vanderbilt had purchased a complete copy (containing all 148 leaves) of the Bay Psalm Book. At that time, the book cost $1,200. On Cornelius's death the book passed to Alice Gwynne Vanderbilt, then to Gertrude Vanderbilt Whitney, and finally, by bequest, to her Trust. After World War II, the trustees decided to sell the book for the benefit of the North Country Community Hospital in Glen Cove, New York. Gertrude's son Cornelius, known as "Sonny," was determined to keep the book in Vanderbilt ownership.

On January 28, 1947, for the Gertrude Vanderbilt Whitney Trust, the auction house Parke-Bernet held a single-lot sale of the book. Bound by Francis Bedford in dark-brown morocco with elaborate gold decoration, it was in excellent shape, notwithstanding the restoration of the fore-edges of two gatherings (patches of lost text had been inked in). With Henry C. Taylor, chairman of the Yale Library Associates, Rosenbach sought pledges and contributions to buy the book for Yale University. John Fleming, acting for Rosenbach, arrived at Parke-Bernet with pledges—totalling $95,000—plus an understanding, never clearly or formally articulated, that "if more was needed, more would be forthcoming."

Thanks in large part to aggressive bidding by Sonny Vanderbilt Whitney, the price rose quickly from the start. The auction soon settled into a pattern in which Fleming would raise the leading bid by $1,000 and Vanderbilt Whitney would up it by $4,000. This continued until a Fleming bid took the price to $151,000. Sonny was out and the hammer dropped in Fleming and Rosenbach's favor, making the volume at that time the most expensive book ever sold at auction, and taking the price to a level fifty percent higher than the world record amount paid by Henry Folger in

1919 for the Shakespeare "False Folio." The transfer of wealth from Yale's donors to the Vanderbilt Whitney Trust caused jaws to drop. In 1640 the Bay Psalm Book had sold for twenty pence; now, the auction price placed it in the same rank as the world's most sought-after printed books—such as Gutenberg's celebrated forty-two-line Bible and Audubon's sumptuous *Birds of America*.

Fleming's apparent triumph, though, quickly soured. Shocked by the price, several pledgers backed out. An outraged Mrs. Harkness, for example, withdrew her $30,000 contribution. The university, too, refused to condone a bid that was more than $50,000 higher than the total endowment. As a stop-gap measure, a panicked Rosenbach waived his commission and wrote Yale a cheque for $49,500 on the expectation that the university would seek further philanthropic funds and that, as those funds arrived, his own contribution would be repaid. Yale's president and fellows, though, sent him a warm letter of gratitude for the amount they saw as a helpful and timely gift.

Agonized negotiations went nowhere. A full five years after the sale, Rosenbach's brother and partner Philip was still "hectoring" Yale for the money. The university's lawyer Edwin L. Weisel, of Simpson, Thacher & Bartlett, advised him to suck it up. "All of us have many disappointments in life in a business way and there is no sense to tearing one's self up emotionally over such disappointments." The Rosenbachs' own lawyer, Morris Wolf, also recommended dropping the matter. "I feel it would be both useless and undignified to try to pin any legal or moral obligation on Yale." Snookered, Rosenbach thus unwittingly became "the most generous of the friends responsible for donating the volume" that is now a cornerstone of the university's collections.

Rosenbach's unintentional contribution neatly offset the enormous paper profit he'd made at the expense of the Weatherups. In

1954 the Weatherup–Rosenbach copy became part of the founding gift—this time a voluntary one—for the Rosenbach Museum and Library. On November 26, 2013, at Sotheby's New York, another one of the eleven Bay Psalm Books came up for sale. It set a new world auction record for a printed book, realizing $14,165,000. Businessman and philanthropist David Rubenstein, the successful bidder, expressed plans to share the book with the American public "by loaning it to libraries across the country, before putting it on long-term loan at one of them."

Samuel Pepys housed his books in gilded cases so exactingly that his footman, after consulting the catalogue, could locate any book blindfolded. (Pepys's books and cases are now at Magdalene College, Cambridge.) The young Marquis de Sade performed the same trick: he knew so well the aristocratic and hedonistic library of his libertine uncle the Abbé de Sade that, by the age of ten, he could locate almost any volume with his eyes closed. (Years later, while imprisoned in the Bastille, de Sade produced a manuscript, *120 Days of Sodom*, whose format harked back to papyrus scrolls. Jack Kerouac also produced a scroll manuscript for his novel *On the Road*.)

For the young Marquis, this mode of book-finding was the first of many aberrant behaviors. Authors have written about the *sound* of libraries, likening the "whispering of the leaves of books" to "the lisping of lake-waves, or the remonstrance of a shy stream at the overtures of the young wind when the morning or the evening stars sing together." (In pre-alphabet societies, according to Marshall McLuhan, the dominant organ of sensory and social orientation was the ear: "hearing was believing.") In the normal course of events, though, libraries are about *seeing*.

According to an eighteenth-century principle of library design, a viewer anywhere in the library ought to have a direct line of sight to every book. That way, the grandeur of the collection could be displayed at one view. The greatest libraries of that century were designed to delight the senses—especially the visual sense. The Silver Library of Königsberg, the rococo library at Melk, and Austria's Admont library—whose books were rebound in white leather to match the interior color scheme—are spectacular examples; the book world's answers to the Amber Room at St. Petersburg and the Hall of Mirrors at Versailles.

Seeing requires light. That necessity, along with fear of fire, dominated the design and management of early libraries. With candles forbidden and electricity not yet harnessed, the only solution was natural light. Medieval buildings purpose-built to house books can be identified today by their narrow, regularly spaced, south-facing windows, which alternated between lecterns and, later, bookcases.

The windows were narrow for a reason. Light has a disintegrating effect on leather, as can readily be seen when books have stood for any appreciable length of time in direct sunlight. At Oxford and Cambridge and the British Museum, Douglas Cockerell noticed that the leather on the backs of books closest to the light was "absolutely rotten, crumbling to dust at the slightest friction," while the leather on books away from the light was comparatively sound. There are few sorrier sights than a collection of leather bindings whose life has been sucked from them. Surprisingly, Cockerell found that the light affected the vellum bindings worst of all.

After many experiments, the management of light in libraries has been elevated to a sublime science. Armed with hard-won knowledge, library builders have used tinted glass to blunt the sun's impact. Blue and violet glasses are just as bad as untinted glass, it turns out, whereas red, green, and yellow glasses are highly protective of leather bindings. Cockerell recommended pale yellow or olive-green glass in library windows exposed to direct sunlight. He especially favored the "Cathedral" glasses manufactured by Pilkington & Co. Of these, inventory numbers 712 and 812 afforded books almost complete protection during two months' exposure— and they bathed libraries in divine light.

The Sperry & Hutchinson Company of New York City began in 1896 with a simple yet lucrative idea: a type of coupon known as the trading stamp. Merchants bought the postage-sized stamps, then gave them out with customers' purchases. After accumulating enough stamps, the customers exchanged them at redemption centers for fancy products. Sperry & Hutchinson's stamps became one of the most recognizable symbols of postwar consumer culture. The company was widely known for its prominent advertisements in the *Ladies' Home Journal*, the *Saturday Evening Post*, and *Munsey's Magazine.*

The Sperry patriarch, Thomas Sperry, died at the age of forty-nine from accidental ptomaine poisoning while on a European trip. Born in 1886, 1887, and 1888 respectively, three brothers—Edwin, Frederick, and Walter Beinecke—turned the company into a Fortune 500 business. (Two of the brothers married two Sperry daughters.) The brothers earned personal fortunes and put them to good use. Edwin built one of the largest collections of books and manuscripts relating to Robert Louis Stevenson. He also assembled a fine collection of German glass and stoneware. Frederick ("Fritz") was an outstanding collector of original source material relating to the American West. His other interests were broad: model trains, model ships, horology, photography, yachting, fishing. Walter was the sporty brother, a champion gymnast who also played water polo, golf, bridge, and backgammon. Ranked among the best contract bridge players in the world, he helped write the original rules for the game, as well as those for American backgammon.

All three Beinecke brothers were Yale University alumni. The Yale English professor Chauncey Brewster Tinker was a passionate advocate of book-collecting and preservation. He mentored leading collectors such as Paul Mellon, Frank Altschul, Wilmarth Lewis—and the Beinecke brothers. Tinker's mentorees initiated the Yale Library Associates and came to be known as the "sons of Tink." Edwin and Fritz both served turns as chairman of the group, and were among the astute Associates who welcomed Abraham Rosenbach's "donation" towards the purchase of the Bay Psalm Book.

In the middle of the twentieth century, the three brothers funded a major new library for Yale. The Beinecke Rare Book and Manuscript Library, on Hewitt Quadrangle, was designed by Gordon Bunshaft of Skidmore, Owings & Merrill. The most striking feature of the library is its use of light.

Construction was completed in 1963. The library's core is a six story, glass encased tower of book stacks a temple to the book, made from books. The airtight tower is surrounded by a void and a Platonically proportioned, box-shaped outer shell (the width and length are twice and three times the height respectively). The shell was made from Vermont marble panels, three centimeters thick, and Vermont Woodbury granite frames. The alabaster dome of a palace in Istanbul inspired Bunshaft's use of translucent marble. (The box-and-frame design also resembles sheets of Sperry & Hutchinson coupons.) Looked at in daylight from outside, the shell seems opaque, but that is just a trick. On sunny days, honey-colored light warms the interior. At night, the shell glows amber.

The central tower has room for 180,000 volumes. A further 600,000 volumes can be housed in the underground stacks. The storage areas are air-conditioned to maintain constant temperature and humidity. Thanks to the thoughtful and innovative design, sufficient light filters into the interior without damaging the holdings, which now include Fritz's Western Americana collection, Edwin's Robert Louis Stevenson library, and the Vanderbilt–Rosenbach copy of the Bay Psalm Book. Edwin's glass collection went to the Corning Museum in Corning, New York.

St. Gall's rococo library has more than one secret. Extending along either side of the main hall are hinged wooden pillars that, when opened, reveal an ingenious eighteenth-century cataloguing system. The system uses cards and pins to track the movement of books. Also at St. Gall is a hidden staircase that leads to a separate room dedicated to storing the library's rarest manuscripts.

Wiblingen Abbey also has hidden staircases and hidden doorways; in an especially theatrical touch there, niches with statues disguise the doors that lead to the elevated gallery. The baroque library hall of the Biblioteca Angelica was designed by Borromini and remodeled by Luigi Vanvitelli. Each of the hall's four corners features a bust of an eminent personage such as the controversial cardinal and Vatican librarian Henry Noris. The plinths beneath the busts conceal secret doors that open to closets and to spiral staircases leading to the double gallery above.

The Biblioteca Joanina in Coimbra, Portugal, features disappearing ladders. When not in use, they slide into pockets between its bookcases. The great library at Melk Abbey in Austria has little studies hidden behind the shelves. In the main hall, the lower parts of the middle cases in each bay are hinged and set on rollers. When opened, they reveal secret study carrels with private windows. These spaces were probably copied from similar ones at the fortress-like Hofbibliothek in Vienna. Architecture historians James Campbell and Will Pryce remarked of the hidden spaces in the Hofbibliothek: "When the doors of these 'secret rooms' are opened, they provide a glimpse behind the stage set." These secret features are part of an enchanting conceit in library design. In the eighteenth and nineteenth centuries, architects brought to library design the same playful spirit that animates the best fore-edge paintings.

The designers of the Hofbibliothek and the Biblioteca Casanatense in Rome played games with perspective and the perception of height. The library at Melk Abbey is another example. Fixed in position, the shelves there are placed to enhance the sensation of scale. The higher shelves are set closer together, and the very top shelf is so impossibly shallow that real books will not fit. For that shelf, the designers resorted to fake books: little book-shaped blocks made from wood and labeled with playfully literal titles such as *Wood* by Anonymous and *Empty* by Woody.

In interior designer Axel Vervoordt's castle near Antwerp, a secret door lined with sliced-off book-spines leads to a deluxe, marble clad bathroom. Doors inside Austria's Admont Library conceal hidden staircases in the same playful way. The doors are covered with real spines that bear fake titles. Some of the faux volumes are easy to spot: they are impossibly squat, made by a craftsman who thought book spines were like toffee that could be cut to any length. At Chatsworth House in England, the Sixth Duke of Devonshire commissioned a similar door with a similar purpose: to cover the entrance to a secret stairway. Thomas Hood, a humorist and playwright, contributed bogus titles for the fake books, such as *The Scottish Boccaccio* by D. Cameron, *Reflections on Suet* by Lamb, *On Death's Door* by John Knox, and Shelley's *Conchologist*.

In *Crome Yellow*, Aldous Huxley imagined a country house whose library featured a door "ingeniously upholstered" with genuine-looking rows of dummy books that had such Borgesian titles as *Biography of Men who were Born Great*, *Biography of Men who Achieved Greatness*, *Biography of Men who had Greatness thrust upon Them*, *Biography of Men who were Never Great at All*, *Tales of Knockespotch* and *Wild Goose Chase, a Novel*, in six volumes. Beyond the door: a pile of letter-files, old newspapers, and the mummy-case of an Egyptian lady, acquired by "the second Sir Ferdinando" on the Grand Tour.

(Alberto Manguel tells the following story about imaginary titles. The French author Paul Masson noticed that the Bibliothèque Nationale was deficient in Latin and Italian books of the fifteenth century. He decided to remedy this by compiling a list of books that would save the prestige of the catalogue. Masson made up all the titles on the list. His friend Colette asked what was the use of books that did not exist. Masson answered indignantly, "Well, I can't be expected to think of everything!")

The British Museum's domed reading room also has secret doors. To maintain the impression of an unbroken series of books around the walls, the dome's pillars and access doors are painted with false book-backs. In the 2001 Japanese anime film *Read or Die*, the reading room is the secret entrance to the underground headquarters of the British Library's "Special Operations Division"—*daiei-toshokan tokushu-kousakubu*—agents with special powers to fight book-related crime and terrorism, and to acquire rare works for the library. (In Robert Littell's book *The Once and Future Spy*, a villain attempts to assassinate a CIA analyst at the Beinecke Library.)

Secret doors at the Biblioteca Angelica are painted with books, but the secret is an open one: the doors are easy to find because the painted books are more vertical and more uniform in height and width than the neighboring real ones. Schussenried Abbey solves the problem of untidy and uneven volumes (and the problem of damage from light) by storing its books in cabinets whose doors are painted with idealized volumes. At the Central Branch of Kansas City Library, the fake books are on the outside. A signboard facade of twenty-two faux spines, with titles such as *Charlotte's Web*, *The Lord of the Rings*, *To Kill a Mockingbird*, *Catch-22*, and *Fahrenheit 451*, stands more than six meters tall, and has been used to beautify and bookify the exterior of the library's multistory carpark.

Other libraries bulked out their collections with grand-looking volumes that were blank or even empty inside. Maurice Hewlett experienced an intense disappointment when he took from a shelf a volume, "as big and hefty as Liddell and Scott," only to find nothing inside it but air—and a wire clip for holding papers. Book-boxes have also been used as "camouflage" for chessboards. In the nineteenth-century botanical library at Warsenstein, near Kassel in Germany, there were book-boxes made from wood. To make such boxes from *real* books, men scour auction rooms, bookshops, and bookstalls for cheap but early bindings, then turn them into receptacles, for "cigarettes, cigars, liqueurs, jewels, chocolates, *bon-bons*, or note paper." Holbrook Jackson called these men ghouls; and those who encouraged them were no better than body-snatchers.

Another field of fakers make cheap leather bindings look more expensive. Cheap sheepskin, for example, can be treated to add grain and resemble goatskin. And smooth spines can be given a spurious air of quality, seriousness, and antiquity by adding fake raised bands. These ornaments have a long and strange history. On medieval codices, raised bands were a necessity: they revealed the heavier cords that were used to hold gatherings together in a strong text block. In the eighteenth century, though, innovations in binding (such as sewing gatherings on recessed supports) made raised bands unnecessary. And yet, on countless thousands of books, binders in England, France, Italy, and Crete continued to add raised bands, often by inserting unnecessary lengths of cord.

Some of the earliest examples of false raised bands are from Germany. In 1442 they were used on a binding made by the Carthusians of Buxheim. Other examples from the second half of the fifteenth century include a 1457 binding on a manuscript in the Herzog August Bibliothek in Wolfenbüttel; a Strasburg edition, printed not later than 1473, with six false half-bands under alum-tawed pigskin, also in the Herzog August Bibliothek; and a 1497 south German pigskin binding on an Aldus edition in the University of Kentucky.

Some binders added bands to please their clients; others did so to deceive them, supplying a cheaper binding at anything but a cheap price. Esteemed binders felt it necessary to assert that they did not stoop to false bands. The bill for Roger Payne's binding of *The Vale Royall of Chester* states that the binding was "Sew'd in the very best Manner on six bands on the outside (the Bands are not saw'd in and there is not any false bands)." The art of the fake band extended well into the twentieth century. A 1986 advertisement for the ersatz Franklin Library played on the long-standing belief that "real" books should have raised bands. In the advertisement, the senior consulting editor from Doubleday tenderly strokes the spine of a book, ribbed for pleasure, and sighs, "The raised spine is a giveaway. That's quality binding."

In the libraries and scriptoria of Tolkien's Middle-earth, Dwarves write in invisible inks. Their "moon-letters" are runes that can only be seen when the moon shines behind them. For some special moon-letters, the moon has to be of the same shape and season as the one shining on the day they were written. The runes on Thrór's Map, read at Rivendell by the Elf lord Elrond, can only be seen with a midsummer's eve's crescent moon shining through. Made by Thrór—the Dwarf king and grandfather of Thorin Oakenshield—the parchment map is a plan of Lonely Mountain. The ink formulas used to write moon-letters are mysterious, but a hint comes from ancient Byzantium. There, in 250 B.C., Philon brewed an invisible ink using colorless tannic acid. To make his ink visible, a chemical reaction was initiated by over-painting with iron salts.

Books can hide in libraries as effectively as the moon-letters hid on Thrór's Map. Errant volumes fall down behind and between shelves; they hide in archival boxes and distant stacks; and they hide in plain sight. As Lucien Polastron remarked, "the book hides in the library as surely as the tree hides in the heart of the forest." The history of libraries is full of in-house stories of amazing, heartening, and embarrassing discoveries. Found in the Bodleian: a mislaid early pamphlet, rediscovered between shelves. Found in the National Library of Scotland: the lost magnum opus of the poet Hugh MacDiarmid. Found in the Baillieu Library at the University of Melbourne: overlooked mineralogy studies whose rediscovery launched New Guinea's mining industry. At Lismore Castle: the Book of Lismore, an Irish manuscript, found hidden in a wall. At Germany's Württemberg State Library: a seventeenth-century portrait of Vlad Dracul, aka Dracula. And found in the Folger Shakespeare Library in 1984: an exceptionally important early English manuscript that had been used as binder's waste inside the covers of two sixteenth-century volumes on the subject of plague. Libraries, though curated, are quintessentially places of serendipity.

The manuscript discovered in the Folger is a double-page Latin excerpt from a translation of the *Ecclesiastical History* of Bishop Eusebius of Caesarea in Palestine. Up to 200 years older than the Book of Kells (and almost 1,000 years older than most of the other books in the Folger collections), it is the earliest extant manuscript that originated in England. It was probably made by an Irish monk in an English monastery in the first half of the seventh century. Frank Mowery, the Folger's head conservator, noticed it while rebinding the two plague volumes. Professor Bernhard Bischoff later identified it as one of only two known Latin manuscripts in Irish half-uncial. Christopher de Hamel of Sotheby's described the manuscript as "probably the earliest known piece of English writing of any kind." Sotheby's estimated the excerpt at up to $100,000 but the rare-book dealer Hans P. Kraus told the *New York Times* that he found Sotheby's estimate excessive. "It's a little piece of vellum," he said. "A very tiny piece. It is old—very old. It is absolutely not very beautiful." Kraus valued it at about one-fifth of Sotheby's estimate, but he was wrong. When Sotheby's London sold it for the Folger Library in 1985, the tattered, yellowed, crumpled remains brought $105,600.

The Morgan Library holds a similar fragmentary treasure: a single sacramentary leaf, retrieved from inside a binding where it, too, had been used as waste. The original manuscript, featuring a large colored interlace initial and other geometric and inter-lace ornament, was probably written and illuminated at Chur in Switzerland, sometime in the second half of the eighth century. By the ninth century, the manuscript had been moved to St. Gall, whose monks added Latin text on the reverse side.

Books can hide in uncatalogued libraries as easily as binder's waste hides in spines. In his 2007 book, *Books on Fire*, Polastron wrote that 2 million of the works in Argentina's National Library had never even been catalogued, and nor had they been insured. The extent of losses from fires and theft could never be known.

At the Vatican Library, whose catalogue was only recently completed, scholars and librarians are always finding things. In 1926 an important missing letter was rediscovered—under a chair. The letter, to Clement VII, was signed in 1530 by the Archbishop of Canterbury along with five other bishops and twenty-two abbots. The authors complained of the pope's "excessive delay" in annulling Henry VIII's marriage to Catherine of Aragon.

Perhaps the most remarkable discovery in the papal stacks was a smallish Greek manuscript written in or around 550 A.D. by the Byzantine historian Procopius. In the *New Yorker* Daniel Mendelsohn described the discovery in gripping terms. Though the manuscript was largely unknown for 1,000 years, there had been hints about its existence. A tantalizing entry in the Suda, a tenth-century Byzantine encyclopedia, mentioned the manuscript and its incendiary contents, but no one knew for sure where the complete text was, or even if it had survived at all. Then, in 1623, an archivist working in the Vatican Library came upon a fourteenth-century copy of Procopius's text.

The archivist was Nicolò Alamanni and the manuscript he found bore an innocuous sounding Greek title, *Anekdota*. The modern catalogue entry is even more innocuous: "VAT. GR. 1001." "VAT. GR." stands for *Vaticanus Graecus*. The work is more commonly known by its Latin title, *Historia Arcana*, "The Secret History." In two other works, Procopius had chronicled approvingly the achievements of Emperor Justinian, "the last great Roman emperor and a model of European kingship." *The Secret History*, though, told a very different story—the Justinian backstory. With striking freshness and candor, *Anekdota* portrayed Justinian and his circle as "venal, corrupt, immoral and un-Christian." Alamanni prepared a printed edition of the text, though he omitted the shocking tidbits about Justinian's wife, Theodora—the empress who famously complained that "Nature had granted to womankind only three orifices by which to be satisfied." The margins of the Vatican manuscript still feature the inked comments and queries that Nicolò Alamanni himself made while preparing the printed edition. When the edition appeared in 1623, some readers were sure it was a hoax.

In Carlos Ruiz Zafón's novel *The Shadow of the Wind*, Daniel Sempere hides a volume in a great library—the cemetery of lost books, itself hidden in the heart of old Barcelona—by shelving the book between Juan Valera novels and a yearbook of Gerona's judicial minutiae. Gerald Murnane's *The Plains*—a novel as resistant as a *tjurunga* line to simple description—takes the sport of intra-library book-hiding several steps further. *The Plains* is mostly set in the library of a grand frontier home owned by a wealthy plainsman. A young man, about whom very little is known, embarks on several literary projects there, under the patronage of the owner. Perhaps the young man will produce a catalogue of the library, perhaps a history of this district of the plains. The plainsman's wife also visits the library, and the young man engages in a curious, non-verbal, partly imagined conversation with her. Determined to break the silence between them in the ideal way, he makes elaborate plans. He will write a short work, perhaps a collection of essays, to be published privately, under an obscure imprint. Then he will place it in the library where the woman might find it. Or, better still, she ought not to read it, but learn only enough to distinguish him. "In short, she should not read a word of mine, although she should know that I had written something she might have read." The solution is to write the book, have it published, and release only a handful of copies to reviewers, not for circulation, and to place a copy in the library. As soon as the book is catalogued and shelved the young man will remove it. This scheme, though, is also unsatisfactory: in the future, someone might still work out the copy's existence, "and that the woman it was meant for had at least glanced at it." After plotting to include the book in the "list of notable books never acquired by this library but held in other private collections in great houses of the plains," and to add to the list a statement that a copy of the book was housed in an imaginary library in a non-existent district, he finally settles on the perfect strategy, "to write no book" and to broadcast no suggestion that he had done so or ever intended to do so.

Libraries can hide things other than books. Some conceal their true makeup and their true age. The builders of baroque and rococo libraries made plaster and timber look like marble. Nineteenth-century libraries made steel look like stone. Other libraries use deceit and artifice, such as real mirrors and fake windows (an example of these is at the Biblioteca Angelica in Rome), to make the number of books seem larger, or the absence of books less striking.

Looking back on the great medieval tradition of scriptoria and illumination, some modern monks felt pressure to include a library room in their monastic complexes: how else could they prove they were fulfilling their expected duties? The masters of Metten Abbey in Bavaria built a small, single-story library but decorated it "as lavishly as possible," to distract attention from the meager contents. This "incredibly ornate" library features a vaulted roof supported by what James Campbell called, unsympathetically, "contorted allegorical figures."

Rather than resort to a small library room, the abbot and architect at Altenburg built an enormous new wing featuring a triple-domed great hall 9.5 meters wide, 47.5 meters long, and 15 meters high whose sides in large part cannot be seen from the entranceway.

> As there are huge cases in the barrel-vaulted spaces between the domes, the viewer assumes that all the walls are lined with books. In fact, apart from one on the end wall, these are the only cases in the room. The walls of the domed spaces are filled with windows, but once under the domes, visitors are naturally drawn to look upwards to admire Troger's magnificent paintings. The result is a huge library that actually has shelf space for very few books, which is exactly what the monks intended.

The trick is not entirely convincing; the room looks more like a ballroom than a library. The hall's under-story is a vast crypt, for the interment of provosts. "The words of the dead were thus kept above the bodies of the dead."

Found

Apart from flowers, leaves, butterflies, dandruff, dental floss, panty liners, toilet paper, parking tickets, banana skins, lipsticks, stamps, and cash, librarians regularly find bacon, fried eggs, and pancakes inside books—all the ingredients for a flattened and desiccated breakfast. At a major public library in Salt Lake City, Josh Hanagarne recently found a large pair of white underpants wrapped around a copy of *The Dangerous Book for Boys*; and, in a copy of *Guns, Germs, and Steel*, an unused condom. In 1953 a batch of eighteenth-century animal-membrane condoms, each one tied at the open end with silk ribbons, was found inside the British Museum copy of Grose's 1783 *A Guide to Health, Beauty, Riches, and Honour.* The old condoms were transferred to the museum's "Secretum" collection of erotica. No one except Josh Hanagarne knows where the new one went.

Jonathan Swift remarked, "I have sometimes heard of an *Iliad* in a nutshell, but it has been my fortune to have much oftener seen a nutshell in an *Iliad*." A visitor to the Folger Shakespeare Library left behind, on a marble bench, a set of false teeth. He returned the next day to collect them, telling the library staff that he was grinding his teeth and had removed them to rest his gums.

From 1875 to 1884, Richard Garnett was superintendent of the British Museum reading room. He recalled how a lady asked for a particular cookbook, which she was told in a dream she would find in the library. The lady was able to describe the book in some detail. It contained a recipe for curing ham, plus a plate illustrating the carving of various dishes. Happily, Garnett was able to report that a book answering to the description was found.

CHAPTER 8

———— ✦ ————

Keepers of Books

The best and worst librarians in history

The Librarian (c. 1566), by the Italian painter Giuseppe Arcimboldo, is an anthropomorphic portrait of a librarian—a portrait composed of books. A court artist for the Habsburg emperors Ferdinand I, Maximilian II, and Rudolf II, Arcimboldo mastered "composite portraits," the illusionistic art of turning objects into images. This image of a librarian is not just a generic parody; much more is going on. The librarian's "arms" and "fingers" of vellum and silk clutch greedily a stack of books. To the extent that a painted pile of strategically organized books can convey human character, the "librarian" is acquisitive, haughty, careful about his appearance, and somewhat ridiculous. The picture, it seems, is a critique.

Anthony Hobson read the portrait as a satire of the "massive erudition" of the day, while library scholar K. C. Elhard saw in the painting a polemic against "poor bookmanship"—yet another attack on "materialist book collectors" who are more interested in acquiring books than in reading them. But Swedish art critic Sven Alfons was the first to identify the painting's target as an individual: the Austrian polymath Wolfgang Lazius, official historian to Ferdinand I in Vienna's Habsburg court from around 1550 to 1565. Lazius was accused of acquiring records by whatever means possible, including theft. He was also accused of producing self-aggrandizing and inaccurate scholarship. The seemingly innocuous painting is a brutal takedown of Lazius and his methods.

Evolving and solidifying gradually, the practices and conventions of librarianship differed markedly across institutions. The Bodleian Library statutes required the librarian to be a university graduate, "and a Linguist, not encombred with mariage," because "mariage is too full of domestical impeachements." Thomas James, Oxford librarian from 1600 to 1620, threatened to resign unless the celibacy obligation was relaxed; Bodley reluctantly relented. At the Colombina in Seville, the librarian had to be a graduate of Salamanca. His room contained basic necessities—a simple bed, sheets, a blanket, an armchair, a bench, and a book cupboard. Monthly visits, from "a learned person," were instigated to keep him in check, and he would be fined in the case of non-attendance. There was one important perk. Every sixth year, the Colombina librarian was sent all over Italy to hunt for acquisitions.

At the British Museum, James Cates was the first clerk of the reading room. Though Cates was said to resemble a remarkably neat old-style clergyman, in his youth he'd been a champion boxer. Created in 1857, the post of superintendent of the museum's reading room was ideally filled by a man who possessed great stamina, combining the skills of a gentleman, a scholar, and a police officer.

The staff needed to know how to handle themselves, such as when a senior academic invited a deputy superintendent to "step outside" the reading room. When asked why, the academic responded: "In order that I may punch you in the eye, and so relieve my feelings about the inefficiency of this library."

Some library staff have labored in even worse conditions. During the Renaissance, library assistants at the Vatican worked in the cold, half naked. Despite such challenges, librarians have achieved great feats of commitment to the cause of bibliography. In the seventeenth century Adrien Baillet was librarian to François Chrétien de Lamoignon, a magistrate, book collector, and Avocat Général of the Parlement of Paris. According to Holbrook Jackson, Baillet had no life outside of books. He slept no longer than five hours a night, abstained from wine, ate only once a day, and soon became so riddled with ulcers and an "erysipelatous affection," he was hideous to look at. When he died, only fifty-seven years old, he was considered a librarian of "unparalleled diligence and sagacity."

In the fifteenth century Frederick of Montefeltro, Duke of Urbino, laid down principles and guidance for the perfect librarian, who must be "learned, of good appearance, good natured." Not all librarians followed the duke's precepts. Eighteenth-century German librarians were notoriously obnoxious. According to the German traveler and bibliophile Zacharias Conrad von Uffenbach, who wrote at the start of that century, the staff of Germany's public libraries were "ignorant, discourteous, envious and lazy." Nearly a hundred years later, things hadn't improved. The author and historian Friedrich Hirsching contributed to the rich late-eighteenth-century library travel literature. He called the same libraries' directors "arrogant misanthropes who look upon their positions as sinecures." Difficult librarians were an international problem. In a letter to Sir Thomas Phillipps, Sir Frederick Madden of the British

Museum described the Escorial library in 1855: "40 miles from Madrid . . . An ignorant monk is the librarian." Madden himself was known as a famous curmudgeon; Tim Munby called him "probably the ablest, and certainly the most disagreeable, Keeper of the Department of Manuscripts."

Not all librarians were ignorant or misanthropic. When, in July 1575, the Dutch Calvinist Hugo Blotz was put in charge of an illustrious imperial library, the Hofbibliothek in Vienna, he was shocked by what he saw. Everything in the library, which dated from medieval times, looked "neglected and desolate."

> There was mouldiness and rot everywhere, the débris of moths and bookworms, and a thick covering of cobwebs. . . . The windows had not been opened for months and not a ray of sunshine had penetrated through them to brighten the unfortunate books, which were slowly pining away; and when they were opened, what a cloud of noxious air streamed out!

The library was situated on the first floor of the Minorites' monastery, a location that was inherently unsuitable. No air could circulate—because three of the four external walls lacked windows. The building sat directly above the monastery's well; damp seeped implacably into the floors and walls. The internal layout, too, was awful. Visitors had to pass through a corn store and the monks' dormitory to reach the library. When intrepid visitors finally reached their destination, there was no space available for them to consult the books.

Even requesting books to view was well-nigh impossible. The collection "had become so disorganised that the existing index was useless." Blotz had to do something. He press-ganged whomever he could into the task of restoring order. Helped intermittently by his friends Guett, Pudler, and Tanner, and by Pudler's son and Tanner's sons' tutor, he set about arranging the 7,379 volumes and preparing a catalogue. By April 1576, a summary was ready. Blotz kept one copy and sent the other to Emperor Maximilian II in Prague. With the emperor's blessing, Blotz changed the library's policies and configuration. He began lending books, and he increased the collection by negotiating purchases and bequests. "From these uncertain beginnings the library progressed, gathering rarities and reputation." Blotz left behind several invaluable legacies. One of these was his influence on the planning of a new library building to replace the rabbit warren he inherited. Another was his influence on a French librarian.

In the seventeenth century Gabriel Naudé was the beau ideal of library directors. For Cardinal Mazarin, chief minister to the King of France, Naudé assembled a library that he himself called the eighth wonder of the world. Naudé thought the essence of library formation was to collect "all the chief and principal Authors, as well ancient as modern." And then to classify and catalogue them: an unclassified collection deserved the name "library" as little as a crowd of men deserved to be called an army. Thorough in his acquisitions, he once bought for Cardinal Mazarin the entire stock of a bookseller. On another buying trip, he passed through a town and left it "as bare of printed paper as if a tornado had passed, and blown the leaves away." Naudé also recommended sending rich merchants to scour foreign bookshops for treasures and novelties.

As a result of Naudé's work between 1642 and 1651, the Mazarin Library was a wondrous achievement: 40,000 meritorious volumes, beautifully bound in goatskin decorated in gilt with the Mazarin arms. Books old and new, rare and common, orthodox and heretical. In early 1652, however, tragedy struck. During a civil war, thousands of the books were stolen and burned. The librarian cried in anguish, "for he loved his handiwork as a father loves his only child." After recovering many of the lost books, Naudé died in 1653.

Naudé's influence as a bibliographical thinker was enormous. Samuel Pepys's immaculate collection of books included a dedication copy of John Evelyn's 1665 translation of Naudé's 1627 treatise, *Avis pour dresser une bibliothèque*, which "set out a program for a universal library, provided with the most important books in all branches of knowledge in their original languages and in translation."

Blotz and Naudé influenced in their turn another leading figure in the European Enlightenment. In his *Plan for a Public Library that is to be Ordered According to the Classification of the Sciences*, and also his *More Limited Plan for an Ordered Library*, Gottfried Wilhelm Leibniz set down principles for good librarianship. Christian Thomasius called Leibniz a living library. Leibniz sponsored Johann Bernhard Fischer von Erlach, architect of the new Hofbibliothek, the largest rococo library ever built and the most imposing library hall of its time. Becoming librarian to the Duke of Brunswick—whose fabulous Wolfenbüttel library he transferred to a building with a glass roof but no heating—Leibniz was also mooted as a future Vatican librarian. That prestigious post was closed to him when he refused to adopt the tenets of Roman Catholicism.

The legacy of Naudé and Leibniz and their progressive ideas of the scholarly library were taken up by the first curator of the State and University Library in Göttingen. The library was founded as a unit of the Georg-August University in 1734. Its founder and first curator was Gerlach Adolph Freiherr von Münchhausen, the cousin of Hieronymus "Baron" von Münchhausen. Appointed by George II (who was both king of Great Britain and elector of Hanover), Gerlach was an exemplary steward of the library. He appointed outstanding scholars; he sourced books from local and foreign booksellers; he consulted the university's professors on acquisition priorities; he raised funds deftly, including by attracting large bequests; he gave due weight to every major branch of knowledge; he supported scholarly publications and in every respect he put into practice Leibniz and Naudé's principles of librarianship.

Under Münchhausen's leadership, and that of the librarian and neo-humanist philologist Christian Gottlob Heyne, the library grew from 60,000 to more than 200,000 scientifically catalogued volumes. Foundational acquisitions came from Count Joachim Heinrich von Bülow (2,000 maps and 8,952 volumes, forty of which were manuscripts), the Royal Library of Hanover (2,154 volumes) and the Gymnasium Library of Göttingen (708 volumes). Feeding the minds of Goethe, Herder, Heine, Humboldt, and Schopenhauer, the library became one of the most important and influential in Western Europe; "the first realisation of the modern idea of a research library."

Naudé, Leibniz, and Münchhausen were responsible for a key trend in the Enlightenment: the emergence of scientific bibliography and scientific librarians. They were the role models for the greatest librarian of the modern era, "the Napoleon of librarians," the "second founder" of the British Museum: Sir Anthony Panizzi. Panizzi enhanced every major aspect of contemporary library management—access policies, accession policies, cataloguing, funding, and especially architecture. Panizzi broke away from the dominant "hall with gallery" style of library and instead created separate spaces for shelving books and for reading them. He personally planned the British Museum's iconic reading room, which was formally opened, with a champagne breakfast, in 1857. The room's dome fell just short of the Pantheon, and set a new international benchmark for library design and the design of all public spaces.

Vandals

Some people should never be allowed near books. In addition to a neat collection of leather-bound books, Pablo Manguel maintained a secondary collection of paperbacks that yellowed and withered on a wicker patio table, and which his son Alberto would sometimes rescue and take into his room, "as if they were stray cats." The publisher and bookman Nicolas Barker kept a library of paperbacks—mostly Penguins—in the lavatory of his West London home.

Sir Edward Burne-Jones argued books were of no use to a painter, save to prop up models in difficult positions. Théophile Gautier used his folio edition of *Plutarch* as a press for crumpled engravings, and to put under children so they could sit at the table. When Coventry Patmore was a boy, he took from a shelf a thick old Bible so he could sit more conveniently at dinner, earning from his father a memorably stern rebuke.

Tim Munby maintained a private collection of sturdy but imperfect books that he called his "cripples": a Second Folio Shakespeare, first-edition novels lacking leaves or original bindings, and other volumes, equally diminished. Apart from being a great source of pleasure, the impaired books were more practical than pristine copies and sought-after editions: "they can be lent to friends, put in one's pocket and taken up the river; and if they fell into the water it would not be the end of the world."

Passionate about making and sailing paper boats, the poet Shelley could not resist turning fly leaves—along with letters, newspapers, and banknotes—into little ships.

In *Anatomy of Bibliomania*, Holbrook Jackson called out three bibliomaniacs who indulged in a particular species of biblio-abuse: Edward FitzGerald, who regularly cut from his books the sections that gave him no pleasure, retaining only those which were to his taste; Voltaire, who "made such abridgements of celebrated authors, preserving only what he thought good, and frequently reducing several volumes to one"; and the Parisian collector "who tore out so many offending pages that his library contained only one complete volume"; the other volumes "were composed of fragments and remnants magnificently bound."

Dr. Hughlings Jackson, the pioneer neurologist, is a starring figure in Holbrook Jackson's essay "How Not to Care for Books." The doctor owned a unique library of mutilated volumes. Never hesitating to tear a book apart, he frequently sent the torn pages to friends he thought might be interested in the subject matter. Whenever he purchased a novel at a railway bookstall, he would tear off the covers, then rip the book in two, each half going into a pocket. Observing one such sacrilegious performance, the clerk at the stall looked on in shock, causing Jackson to remark: "You think I am mad, my boy, but it's people who don't do this who are really mad."

Charles Darwin adopted the same practical and utterly unsentimental approach to books. When they fell to pieces through rough use, he held them together with metal clips. To make cumbersome books easier to hold, he cut them in half, and was also known to tear out pages of a book, leaving only what interested him, in order to save space. Darwin wrote so many notes in his books that we can now read along with him.

Becky Sharp and Napoleon Bonaparte are two notorious abusers of books, both well known for throwing books from the windows of fast-moving horse-drawn carriages. In the autumn of 1949, one of the rarest and most valuable books in America—the Weatherup–Rosenbach copy of the Bay Psalm Book—was defenestrated from a stationary window. Part of a loan exhibition at the UCLA Library, the 1640 book was snatched from its case by a student, reportedly as part of a fraternity initiation prank. The student then leaped from a second-floor window; the book, but not the student, was recovered unharmed.

In 1962 Sylvia Plath and Ted Hughes shared a thatch-roofed house with their two young children. Unhappy with Hughes's actual or apparent adultery—perhaps with Assia Wevill or, less plausibly, Moira Doolan—Plath made a bonfire in the backyard. She burned more than a thousand pages of Hughes's manuscripts, letters, and other valuable papers—all his correspondence, his work in hand, his drafts, his notebooks. According to Al Alvarez, Plath mixed Hughes's manuscripts with his dandruff flakes and fingernail trimmings, before consigning them to the fire. Plath also "gralloched" Hughes's collected edition of Shakespeare: "Only the hard spine and the end boards had stood up to the onslaught. The text had been more or less reduced to fluff." Hughes managed to salvage a few scraps of his own papers and stuck them back together with Scotch tape.

CHAPTER 9

The Quintessence of Debauchery

Heber, Byron, and Barry

The first English book auction of modern times was held in 1676, for the library of the clergyman Lazarus Seaman. There had been Continental auctions before then, most notably in France and the Netherlands. Librarians and collectors have long prized the records of these and subsequent auctions as public evidence of the contents of private libraries. Auction catalogues help trace the movement of books between collections. In so doing, they capture the pulse of accumulation and dispersal, a pulse ardently measured and lived by bibliophiles.

No man was ever more in tune with that pulse than Isaac Gosset, Bibliographer, Doctor of Divinity, Fellow of the Royal Society. For over thirty years during the reign of George III—a golden era for book-lovers—Gosset was a familiar figure in London's auction rooms, where he often sat to the right of the auctioneer, giving a running commentary on each lot as it was presented. His constant use of the phrase "a pretty copy" caused much amusement. He kept and bound copies of the sale catalogues; eventually his collection of these would number at least three hundred. Reliably he appeared clad in the attire of an earlier generation—exemplified by his three-cornered hat. When a print-seller, aggrieved by some unknown offense, commissioned a satirical print that caricatured Gosset's garb, the bibliophile changed his headgear, but this was met with a second print that showed him in the new outfit.

Reverend Dr. Gosset was unusually short in stature: the editor of the *New Monthly Magazine* called him "squat," and the Earl of Marchmont noticed an uncanny resemblance to Alexander Pope. When he preached, he did so standing on two hassocks. Apart from auction catalogues, his library was rich in Greek and Latin classics. He possessed and expressed opinions on many matters bibliographical, social, and political, and he was well informed about book-world facts and gossip; he allegedly knew, for example, all the secret, ten-letter codes that London's booksellers used to write acquisition prices in their stock—codes like kingalfred (Quaritch), bethankful (Henry George Bohn), and mygodhelps (Francis Edwards).

(In these codes, each non-recurring letter corresponded to a numeral. The word-key was usually told only to the bookseller's staff. The Edinburgh firm R. & J. Balding—so named because the co-owners were losing or had lost their hair—used the code word "motherfuck." One former co-owner, Spike Hughes, wrote of the day when another co-owner, John Price, had to explain the code to the firm's pleasant but proper secretary: "We retreated and left him to it!! She said nothing about it to any of us afterwards and we never asked him how it went.")

At the 1785 Christie's sale of Samuel Johnson's banged, dusted, and buffeted library, Gosset bid alongside Horace Walpole, buying Walpole's 1759 *Catalogue of Royal and Noble Authors*, a French Bible (printed in Amsterdam in 1678), a selection of recent editions of classical works, and William Hutton's *History of Birmingham*—a book rendered unforgettable by Edmond Malone's anecdote of a visit to Johnson's home in March 1783.

> I found him in his arm-chair by the fireside, before which a few apples were laid. He was reading. I asked him what book he had got. He said the *History of Birmingham*. Local histories, I observed, were generally dull. "It is true, sir; but this has a peculiar merit with me; for I passed some of my early years and married my wife there." I supposed the apples were preparing as medicine. "Why no, sir; I believe they are only there because I want something to do. These are some of the solitary expedients to which we are driven by sickness. I have been confined this week past, and here you find me roasting apples, and reading the *History of Birmingham*."

When Gosset was laid up on his own sickbed, the mere sight of the Complutensian Polyglot Bible on vellum was enough to restore him miraculously to health. At least that's what Thomas Frognall Dibdin said in his 1809 book *Bibliomania*, in which he portrayed Gosset in the guise of the book-loving Lepidus. Dibdin's narrator leaps from a chaise and hurries upstairs "into the auction room."

> The clock had struck twelve, and in half an hour the sale was to begin . . . You observe, my friends, said I, softly, yonder active and keen-visaged gentleman? 'Tis LEPIDUS. Like Magliabechi, content with frugal fare and frugal clothing and preferring the riches of a library to those of house-furniture, he is insatiable in his bibliomaniacal appetites.

Gosset, like Dibdin, was a self-appointed arbiter of bibliographical taste. A respected, even loved, figure in the book trade, he would be honored with fond tributes on the occasion of his death in 1812. Stephen Weston composed a poem, "The Tears of the Booksellers," which appeared in the *Gentleman's Magazine*, and a Latin tribute, which appeared in the fourth edition of William Bowyer's *Critical Conjectures on the New Testament*. The auctioneers Leigh and Sotheby sold Gosset's library in 5,740 lots over twenty-three days between June 7 and July 2, 1813, realizing a total of £3,141 7s. 6d.

Though the Bodleian bought well, Richard Heber was the principal purchaser at the Gosset sale. The books were sentimentally important for the man who'd been Gosset's protégé since childhood.

Richard Heber was born in 1774, the son of Reginald Heber, a wealthy rector and landowner. Richard's mother died soon after his birth. During his first years, perhaps as a result of that loss, a virulent strain of bibliomania took hold. According to Holbrook Jackson, the boy was "normal" until he saw a copy of Henry Peacham's 1638 *Valley of Varietie*,

> which he showed to Bindley, who described it as rather a curious book. Why this incident should have set

Heber on his terrible career is not known, but sure it is that, from that hour, the love of books blinded him to everything else.

At the age of eight, Richard prepared a detailed bibliographical catalogue. By the age of ten, he was chasing books with exceptional vigor, making fine distinctions about editions and bindings and formats. By twelve, his father was complaining about young Richard "running up unreasonable bills with Joliffe, the bookseller." Heber's quarry was diverse. Greek and Latin classics. Cook's voyages. The output of the master printers. Multivolume editions of Shakespeare and Johnson.

Heber's associates noticed in the boy an "unnatural gravity." At book auctions he would sit beside Gosset, taking it all in, while the reverend gave his real-time commentary on the proceedings. Under Gosset's mentorship, Heber was a keen bidder at the Pinelli sale of 1789, an event that "caused high excitement among the literati of the Capital."

Richard's father was worried. He wrote a stern letter to his son. "Of multiplying books, my dear Richard, there is neither end nor use. The *Cacoethes* of collecting books draws men into ruinous extravagances. It is an itch which grows by indulgence and should be nipt in the bud." If Richard promised not to bring his father "any more Bookseller's bills of which you know I have too much reason to complain, I will indulge you in laying out five Guineas at the sale you mention, but not a shilling more." The bills, though, continued to arrive. Reginald was forced to forbid booksellers from sending their goods without explicit approval from him or his agents. Why, he asked, could not his son be satisfied with visits to Westminster and other libraries where he could read the classics "and about every other Book you can have any *real* occasion for"? If Richard was to keep buying books, he would have to do so in secret and without his father's blessing.

Richard's secrecy was imperfect. After receiving, indirectly, another bill, Reginald complained in 1791 of Richard's "prohibited Extravagance." By the age of twenty-one, Richard was widely recognized as a formidable bookman. In 1804 he inherited the Yorkshire and Shropshire estates of his long-suffering father. Naturally, he used his new wealth to build a great library—one uniquely strong in Elizabethan and Jacobean poetry and drama—and a reputation as the most ardent, most dogged bibliophile.

Seymour de Ricci, William Roberts, and Thomas Frognall Dibdin all left portraits of Heber the mature collector. He was "a bibliomaniac, if ever there was one"; "a bibliomaniac in the more unpleasant sense of the word; no confirmed drunkard, no incurable opium-eater, had less self-control"; "the great and strong passion of his life was to amass such a library as no individual before him had ever amassed." Holbrook Jackson wrote of how books were Heber's infatuation. To see a book was to desire it, and to desire it was to possess it.

Using his knowledge, learning, accomplishments, and riches, Heber made his life a mortal quest to assemble the perfect library. His definition of perfection had much to do with breadth: his collection was "omnigenous" and he bought books "by all methods, in all places, at all times." The definition was also about repetition. "No gentleman," he remarked, "can be without three copies of a book, one for show, one for use, and one for borrowers." Extending to more than 100,000 books (30,000 of which he acquired in a single purchase), Heber's library filled eight houses. After visiting one of them, Dibdin wrote that he had never seen "rooms, cupboards, passages and corridors, so choked, so suffocated, with books." The piles of volumes extended "up to the very ceiling . . . while the floor was strewn with them." Unusually for a bibliophile, Heber disliked large-paper copies—because they took up too much space, space that other books could occupy.

Heber was a driving force behind the celebrated bibliophile society, the Roxburghe Club, which he co-founded in 1812 during the famous auction of the Duke of Roxburghe's library. Heber came to exemplify the obsessive, psychologically damaged book collector. Yet he endured with grace and wisdom a series of personal scandals, in one of which he was publicly accused of an improper private relationship with a young man, Charles Henry Hartshorne.

In Heber's pleasant dotage there would be much reading and book-talk. With his "cronies" Drury, Haslewood, Wilbraham, and the Boswells, he—much attached to the "lower school of the old Latin Poets" such as Lucan, Claudian, and Silius Italicus—would "moot Greek metres," "fight over derivatives and etymons," "quote long passages" of Johnson's biography, and "ring changes on 'Robin Hood Garlands.'" In October 1833, Heber died among his books, at Pimlico, in the room in which he'd been born. His will, hidden on a bookshelf, was not found for three months. The sale of Bibliotheca Heberiana took even longer, extending over 216 days in London, Paris, and Ghent, and marking the end of the peak period of British bibliomania.

Prior to these dispersals, while still searching for Heber's will, his executors found and destroyed certain volumes with pornographic and homosexual content, among them the Earl of Rochester's scandalous farce, *Sodom, or the Quintessence of Debauchery*. Though it was written in the 1670s (and first circulated in manuscript in

1676 or thereabouts), the book first appeared in a printed version in 1684 (with an Antwerp imprint). On that edition the author of the slim volume was identified as "the E. of R." The book was received with words such as these: "intolerable foulness," "a pariah amongst books," "diabolical humour," "indecent burlesque," "outrageously ribald." Nearly every book in the edition was destroyed, but Robert Harley preserved the text in a manuscript copy, and at least two printed copies survived into the nineteenth century—one of them the copy destroyed by Heber's executors. Though Rochester's contemporaries decried the book (and though there are doubts about the work's attribution to the earl), it did find an audience. The play was supposedly performed, once, before the court of Charles II. At least three French editions were produced in the eighteenth century.

Apart from *Sodom*, Heber's executors also destroyed "one or two other obscene books." The executors' definition of "obscene" was idiosyncratic, and their purge incomplete. A curious book of verse, for example, got through. Dating from 1680, within a few months of Rochester's death, *Poems on several Occasions by the Right Honourable the E. of R.* purported to have been published in "Antwerpen" but was actually issued in London. Also appearing over Rochester's name was a racy adaptation, "in poor taste," of the tragedy *Valentinian*, originally written by the Shakespeare collaborators Beaumont and Fletcher. The full title of the revised work was *Valentinian: a Tragedy. As 'tis Alter'd by the late Earl of Rochester and Acted at the Theatre Royal. Together with a Preface concerning the Author and his Writings. By one of his friends.* The "friend" was Robert Wolseley. *Poems on several Occasions* and the sauced-up *Valentinian* both escaped Heber's executors; they appeared, alongside other Rochester titles, in the 1834 auction sales of Bibliotheca Heberiana.

Posthumous printings of *Sodom* attracted prosecutions for obscenity. (Joseph Streater and Benjamin Crayle were fined for attempting to publish *Sodom* in 1689.) One of the few surviving printed copies—an edition probably dating from early in the eighteenth century and entitled *Sodom, or the Gentleman Instructed, A Comedy*—came to light recently after it was released from "a private European collection." Sotheby's estimated that the octavo volume would achieve between £25,000 and £35,000; in fact it realized £45,600 inclusive of premium. The catalogue described it as the rarest piece of early English pornography on record. John Vincent in the *Independent* called it the last surviving copy of "quintessential" English porn.

Alexander Pushkin's library, too, seems to have been purged of clandestine and pornographic literature after his death. According to Andrew Kahn, the major part of Pushkin's library that now survives contains "virtually no erotic literature of any kind," though the library was rich in meditations on love, including Baculard d'Arnaud's *Épreuves du sentiment*, and "sensational anthologies of anecdotal histories alongside medical works on masturbation." Pushkin is known to have read Diderot, Laclos, the younger Crébillon, and the Marquis de Sade's *Justine*, which Pushkin regarded as one of the best works of depraved French fantasy; the poet admitted he'd become aroused while reading it "and had to put it down."

The executors' destruction of *Sodom* echoed another act that took place less than a decade earlier, and that has been described as the greatest literary crime in history: the burning of the personal memoirs of the poet and libertine Lord Byron. Soon after Byron's death in 1824, three men disposed of the manuscript: the publisher

John Murray; the poet Thomas Moore; and Byron's longtime companion, John Cam Hobhouse. Along with lawyers representing Byron's married half-sister, Augusta Leigh, and his widow, Anne Isabella, these men decided the manuscript would ruin Byron's reputation, it was that scandalous. In Murray's drawing room they tore up the pages and threw them into the fire.

There was much to cover up, including evidence of Byron's relationship with Augusta. (Harriet Beecher Stowe claimed Byron had fathered Augusta's daughter, Medora, a claim backed by Lord and Lady Byron's own letters.) Peter Cochran has recently argued that, apart from "protecting" Byron's reputation, the three men had other, less noble, motivations. Hobhouse was embarking on a political career. Murray was worried that a rival publisher might secure the right to issue the memoirs. And both Murray and Hobhouse grappled with feelings of betrayal and a desire for revenge. Moore, for his part, seems to have been bamboozled into playing along; Corin Throsby pictured him "overwhelmed by what he called the "hoity toity proceeding"—complicated issues of copyright and payment, and Hobhouse's self-righteous bullying."

Another episode of postmortem executorial awkwardness had a happier ending.

Redmond Barry made Melbourne, Australia, his home from 1839. Like most of his fellow settlers, he tried to create in the New World the values and institutions of the Old. His greatest achievements were connected with his prominent roles in the founding of the University of Melbourne and the Melbourne Public Library— two institutions that helped make Melbourne one of the greatest cities of the nineteenth century. The foundation stones for both institutions were laid on July 3, 1854. Barry was chancellor of the university and chairman of the library's trustees until his death.

Strongly influenced by the international public library movement, Barry believed in making knowledge available for the benefit of all. Before the library was built, he threw open his own private library to sundry visitors. When the new library opened, he ensured its management would adhere to liberal principles. Foreign visitors marveled at the conspicuous lack of admission restrictions. Barry's ethos extended to his involvement in the library's operations. Happy to dust shelves and to fill in for the porter, he even stayed late into the night to help staff fill bookshelves after a late delivery.

He helped make the library's regulations, which forbade the mutilation or marking of books. His own library, however, was another matter. Barry marked and annotated his books extensively. Many of those volumes are now held in institutional collections. Forty-four are in the library of St. Mary's College at the University of Melbourne. The books feature vehement underlining and are heavily annotated in Barry's hand with textual comments, cross-references, and quotations from Shakespeare and the Bible. The annotations typically show Barry disagreeing with the author's views. Though Barry made some of the notes in pencil, most are in emphatic ink.

Barry was appointed to the bench of the Supreme Court of Victoria in January 1852. Presiding over the trial of the bushranger Ned Kelly, he sentenced Kelly to death. Barry himself died in 1880, twelve days after the outlaw's execution.

The Melbourne Public Library became one of the world's great civic libraries and is known today as the State Library of Victoria. Early in the twentieth century, John Monash engineered the dome of the library's Domed Reading Room, emulating those of the Pantheon and the British Museum. Monash would soon become a key Allied general in World War I. At the time of its construction, the Melbourne dome was the largest reinforced concrete structure in the world. The Pantheon dome, the greatest concrete structure in antiquity, is still the largest unreinforced one. The British Museum dome is not concrete at all; it consists of cast iron and papier-mâché.

Though the State Library of Victoria is indubitably a solid institution, some of its foundational documents are highly curious. The library has kept Redmond Barry's personal journals—Barry called them his day books—which chronicle with striking candor his "flagrantly nonconforming sexual behaviour." He diligently and matter-of-factly recorded his affairs and trysts and assignations with prostitutes and mistresses and married women.

> September 22. Sunday. church. Mrs S 4 times . . . September 25. Mrs S 3 times . . . October 8 went to Parramatta with Mrs S. Mrs S 10 times.

In her Barry biography, Ann Galbally likened these notes to the scoreboard in a game of cricket. Notwithstanding their surprising content, they are of unarguable value. Had they been burned, their loss would have obscured Barry's character—and falsified his legacy.

Writers' libraries

If libraries have auras, then those of writers' libraries are the most pungent. Oscar Wilde's extensive library housed fishing books, Gothic romances, *éditions de luxe*, periodicals, finely bound Greek and Latin classics, popular literature, more than a hundred French novels, special copies of his own works, and multiple editions of Shakespeare, whom Wilde loved "as we should love all things, not wisely but too well." The chaotic, punitive dispersal of Wilde's library during his obscenity trials was for him the most distressing event in a life marred by tragedies. In prison, books were the first things he asked for. When he passed away in a cheap Parisian hotel, he was surrounded by his latest attempt to re-create his library.

Leo Tolstoy also had strong feelings about Shakespeare, feelings he expressed with words like "repulsion," "tedium," "bewilderment," and "evil." But Dickens was a favorite of Tolstoy's and had pride of place in the Russian's library-workroom. The American diplomat and historian George Kennan visited that room in 1886, describing it as "not much larger than an ordinary bedroom." The walls were lined with bookshelves filled with books, mostly in paper covers.

The floor was bare; the furniture, which was old-fashioned in form, consisted of two or three plain chairs, a deep sofa, or settle, upholstered with worn green morocco, and a small cheap table without a cloth . . . There was a marble bust in a niche behind the settle, but the only pictures which the room contained were a small engraved portrait of Dickens and another of Schopenhauer. It would be impossible to imagine anything plainer or simpler than the room and its contents. More evidences of wealth and luxury might be found in many a peasant's cabin in Eastern Siberia.

Only slightly less austere was Ralph Waldo Emerson's library, "a large, square room, plainly furnished, but made pleasant by pictures and sunshine." The "homely shelves" that lined the walls were well-stocked with books. A visitor noticed the lack of showy covers or rich bindings. Each volume seemed "to have soberly grown old in constant service."

Some writers' books are pressed less gently into service. In 1763 James Boswell visited Samuel Johnson's garret library—up four pairs of stairs in an attic of Johnson's house in Gough Square. The attic window offered a view of St. Paul's Cathedral. Boswell found in the library "a number of good books, but very dusty and in great confusion. The floor was strewed with manuscript leaves, in Johnson's own handwriting, which I beheld with a degree of veneration, supposing they perhaps might contain portions of *The Rambler* or of *Rasselas*." On another visit, in April 1776, Boswell found Johnson putting his books in order, "and as they were generally very old ones, clouds of dust were flying around him." He had on a large pair of gloves, such as hedgers and ditchers used. Clutching his folios and octavos, Johnson "banged and buffeted them together until he was enveloped in a cloud of dust."

This violent exercise over, the good doctor restored the volumes, all battered and bruised, to their places, where, of course, the dust resettled itself as speedily as possible.

R. W. Ketton-Cremer described Johnson's sixteenth-century copy of *The Iliad* as "a great folio as dingy and tattered in outward appearance as most of the books that passed through Johnson's hands and suffered his drastic methods of dusting and buffeting." During dinner, according to Boswell, Johnson kept a book wrapped in the tablecloth in his lap,

> from an avidity to have one entertainment in readiness, when he should have finished another; resembling (if I may use so coarse a simile) a dog who holds a bone in his paws in reserve, while he eats something else which has been thrown to him.

CHAPTER 10

Execration upon Vulcan

Libraries destroyed by fire and war

During the fall of Nineveh around 612 B.C., fire destroyed the library of clay tablets formed by Sargon I, founder of the Semitic Empire in Chaldea. Other ancient book fires include the one that destroyed Rome's Palatine Library in 80 A.D.; fires in Byzantium in 476 A.D. and, possibly, the fires that helped seal the fate of the Great Library of Alexandria. There was no shortage of book fires in the Middle Ages, either. A medieval chronicler penned an account of the burning of a church library: "An inexpressible number of books perished, leaving us deprived of our spiritual weapons."

The English poet and diplomat Matthew Prior fell asleep in the oak-beamed Wimborne Minster Library while reading Walter Raleigh's *History of the World* with a candle. The book was damaged; afterwards a master scribe painstakingly saw to the injuries, reinstating the printed words with his pen. To prevent such incidents, Gabriel Naudé would not permit candles in his library, though he would allow a small stove to keep the air from becoming damp. Ben Jonson wrote the poem *An Execration upon Vulcan* about the books destroyed in his home when, after a night spent drinking, he retired to his paper-filled study and lit candles. John Stuart Mill's maidservant accidentally burned a whole volume of the manuscript of Thomas Carlyle's *French Revolution*. No duplicate of the manuscript existed, so Carlyle had to rewrite it. Tennyson asked him how he felt. "I just felt," Carlyle said, "like a man swimming without water."

Apart from destroying many libraries, the 1666 Great Fire of London also obliterated bulk quantities of unsold books. Shakespeare's 1663 Third Folio, for example, is rarer than his First Folio because many of the Third Folio copies were destroyed in the stock of booksellers. In 1671 at El Escorial in Spain a fire broke out amid the library's 18,000 books and manuscripts while the monks were in church. In a heroic effort, the monks beat the flames back and threw the threatened volumes into the courtyard. Tragedy followed. The dry fabric of a captured Turkish banner caught alight, collapsing and setting it all on fire. About a third of the library's holdings were destroyed, some of them unique. The library was restored but charred panels can still be seen at the *Biblioteca Principal*.

On the night of February 3, 1731, fire broke out in the royal palace in Brussels. The books of the royal library, kept in a tower room, were hastily thrown out of the window; a thick folio reportedly killed an onlooker.

•

In England, between 1536 and 1539, the monastic orders, and all that belonged to them, were annihilated. As John Willis Clark wrote in his 1906 *The Care of Books*,

> Upwards of 800 monasteries were suppressed, and, as a consequence, 800 libraries were done away with, varying in size and importance from Christ Church, Canterbury, with its 2000 volumes, to small houses with little more than the necessary service-books. By the year 1540 the only libraries left in England were those at the two Universities, and in the Cathedrals of the old foundation. Further, the royal commissioners made no attempt to save any of the books with which the monasteries were filled . . . The buildings were pulled down, and the materials sold; the plate was melted; and the books were either burnt, or put to the vilest uses to which waste literature can be subjected.

Those uses included tearing pages from manuscripts to wrap food, scour candlesticks, and polish boots. The protestant John Bale lamented the terrible destruction and the books' careless dispersal to grocers and bookbinders, and by the shipload to foreign nations. To destroy the libraries in such a manner "without consideration" was a national disgrace; a horrible and ineradicable infamy.

Upon the dissolution of German monasteries and religious institutions, the fruits of centuries of zealous collecting were carelessly disposed of or destroyed as "papist literature." Many ecclesiastical libraries, such as the one at Reinhardsbrunn, met total destruction.

The printer, author, philanthropist, landscape architect, and Member of Parliament Thomas Johnes is best known for his development, late in the eighteenth century, of the Hafod Estate in Wales as an exemplary picturesque landscape. Housed in a spacious, octagonal building, the estate's library contained many prizes: Welsh, French, and Latin manuscripts; rare books of natural history; rare editions of the French chronicles of the later Middle Ages; and valuable volumes purchased from the library of the Marquis de Pesaro.

Thomas Johnes married Jane Johnes, his first cousin. From Thomas Banks, Jane commissioned a sculpture for the library: a depiction of Thetis dipping Achilles in the river Styx. The Johneses' baby daughter, Mariamne, provided the model for Achilles. On March 13, 1807, fire broke out in the mansion. Disastrously, the entire contents of the library were destroyed. Mercifully, though, Jane and Mariamne escaped. Thomas was in London attending Parliament when he heard the news.

In 1904 a fire at the Turin University Library destroyed more than 100,000 books and manuscripts—about a third of the total collection—including twenty-one manuscripts from Bobbio, and an important collection of Oriental manuscripts. The fire, which destroyed five entire halls of the library, was blamed on an electrical fault. Fortunately, some of the Turin–Bobbio manuscripts had been photographed. In 1907 Carlo Cipolla published the photographs as *Codici Bobbiesi* in a limited edition of 175 copies.

Another electrical fire was equally devastating. In September 2004, fire gutted Weimar's eighteenth-century rococo library of Duchess Anna Amalia. (Johann Wolfgang von Goethe had once been a director there.) The fire destroyed over 50,000 volumes; the library has since been restored.

In 1731 a fire at Ashburnham House on Little Dean's Yard in Westminster caused mayhem for the old library of Sir Robert Cotton. Thirty years earlier, Cotton's grandson had bequeathed the library to the British people. It was residing temporarily at Ashburnham under the care of the king's librarian, Dr. Bentley. The library of literary, ecclesiastical, legal, and constitutional manuscripts was described by C. J. Wright of the British Library as "arguably the most important collection of manuscripts ever assembled in Britain by a private individual." It contained some of Britain's greatest treasures, including the sublime Lindisfarne Gospels (in which Eadfrith's deliberate errors can be found); the original Magna Carta that Cotton allegedly discovered at his tailor's shop; and "Cotton Vitellius A XV," which contains the only extant manuscript of *Beowulf.*

Many banded together to fight the fire, including Mr. Speaker Onslow. They rescued hundreds of volumes by entering the building and throwing them from the windows. "Cotton Vitellius A XV" was one of the manuscripts thrown onto the lawn.

The fire affected about a quarter of the collection and a tenth of the manuscripts. Almost all the printed books were lost, along with thirteen entire manuscripts and parts of others; some of the "surviving" manuscripts were reduced to fatty lumps or charred fragments, so the true extent of manuscript losses was far worse than these numbers suggest. The manuscript of *Beowulf* was singed around the edges, but fortunately remained intact.

Apart from eliciting a parliamentary committee investigation, the fire was the subject of scuttlebutt in which the Ashburnham librarian Dr. Bentley was himself accused of lighting the fire. Holbrook Jackson thought this unlikely, given Bentley's conduct during the fire-fighting effort.

> The Headmaster of Westminster, speeding to the rescue, saw a figure issue from the burning house "in his dressing-gown, a flowing wig on his head, and a huge

volume under his arm": it was Bentley saving the Alexandrine manuscript of the New Testament.

That manuscript, the fifth-century *Codex Alexandrinus*, was one of three of the earliest manuscripts of the Bible. The accusations seem even less plausible when it is noted that the losses included expensive Greek manuscripts, which Bentley had long been accumulating for his work on the *Greek Testament*.

A massive conservation effort followed, with much hanging, drying, cleaning, flattening and reassembling of leaves—often with highly imperfect results. Some burned, congealed, fatty, lumpy, and brittle fragments of vellum were no longer conservable. (One of the damaged manuscripts, left unconserved, looks like "an irradiated armadillo.") Some volumes were put back together in the wrong order or with pages from elsewhere. Many single leaves and fragments, like scattered puzzle pieces, were put into drawers to await future reunions.

Most of the library was retrieved. The surviving books and manuscripts are now a core part of the British Library. Much has been learned from the fire, about conservation and about fire management. The water used to extinguish the fire caused as much damage as the flames. Modern libraries have gone to great lengths to avoid that predicament. The Oxfordshire library of Paul Getty, for example, was fitted with a "sprinkler" system containing halon gas that would extinguish a fire without recourse to water. The Beinecke Library also avoids the need for water: if the library's smoke detectors are triggered, a fire-suppressing cocktail of halon and inergen gases floods the glass-enclosed stacks.

Eighty years after the Ashburnham blaze, another controversial book fire burned, this time at Clontarf near Dublin. Frederick

Cavendish owned an impressive house that featured an impressive library: a magnificent collection of rare editions in sumptuous bindings. After the death of his wife in 1812, Cavendish moved his family to Dublin and sought a tenant for the house at Clontarf. In advance of a visit by a prospective lessee, Cavendish lit fires in the house to "air" it and to protect the books from damp. In an essay for the *Book Collector*, Tim Munby and Mary Pollard describe how Cavendish spread some of the volumes out on the floor and on a large couch, "so they should get the maximum benefit from the heat of the fire in the grate."

> At about seven-thirty [in the evening] Cavendish, who was pacing the lawn in front of the house, was horrified to see smoke pouring from the library windows. He gave the alarm and the neighbours swiftly came to his help, augmented by a number of casual labourers who were in the area for the harvest.

When finally the fire was extinguished, the library was a scene of devastation. Two hundred of the most valuable volumes had been destroyed. Or had they? Did Cavendish ever actually *own* those books, or did he simply fabricate the catalogue of his library, using other sources such as sale catalogues?

When Cavendish called on his insurers to make good his losses, they refused and the matter went to court. There, Cavendish claimed the fire had consumed utterly the lost books—bindings and all. Yet the court heard evidence that the fire was "relatively small," not intense enough to obliterate large numbers of whole books, and that it caused "comparatively little damage to the fabric of the house." Some burned book fragments were left behind, but those, suspiciously, were only of old magazines and reference works—volumes of little value compared to the Caxtons and Aldines that were purportedly lost.

Equally incriminating was evidence that parts of the listing of Cavendish's holdings seemed to have been lifted from a recent auction catalogue. After a flawed trial in which the jury heard inadmissible evidence and the judge allowed the jury to reach a verdict without hearing his juridical summary or the final remarks of counsel, the insurers won. Cavendish had good reason to think that verdict unfair. The auction catalogue, for example, was not so incriminating after all: several of Cavendish's books had come from that sale, so copying the catalogue would be sensible and innocent. He appealed the judgment, but the new jury again found in the insurers' favor.

As Andrew Madden, Joe Palimi, and Jared Bryson noted in their 2006 paper on the history of literacy, the burning of books has become a symbol of barbarism; people are upset even by routine textual destructions. In 1992 Tim Cullen was appointed librarian at the Natural Resources Institute in Kent.

> Within weeks of his appointment, skips were hired and were soon filled with books and papers. Tim Cullen . . . still recalls with frustration, the outcry that ensued. Those documents, some of his critics argued, went back decades and were part of the Institute's long tradition. Tim Cullen's response was to point out that the documents hadn't been looked at for decades, no one had wanted them when he had offered them around, and he needed to make space for texts that would be looked at.

To the protesters, published texts, no matter how humble or tired or peripheral, still possessed an inviolable potency. They were, as Henry Petroski put it, the basic data of our civilization.

Carrying such enormous cultural and emotional power, the burning of books has become a literary stereotype. Books are burned in *Don Quixote, Titus Groan, Anne of Green Gables, Fahrenheit 451,* Iain Pears's *The Dream of Scipio,* and all the Pepe Carvalho detective novels of Manuel Vázquez Montalbán. In Paul Auster's 1987 apocalyptic novel, *In the Country of Last Things,* the narrator takes refuge in the national library, whose books—mostly sentimental novels, collections of political speeches, and obsolete textbooks—are now worthless. "The world they had belonged to was finished." During a severe winter, the books feed the fire: "everything made its way into the stove, everything went up in smoke."

Winston Smith, the hero of Orwell's *Nineteen Eighty-Four,* lives in a world in which books are routinely hunted down and destroyed; in all of Oceania, books printed before 1960 no longer exist. Smith's task is to update the archives based "on the needs of the moment." Books are continuously rewritten, with no trace or admission that a previous version ever existed. History, in Smith's world, is "a palimpsest," to be scrubbed and rewritten at will.

Carlos Ruiz Zafón's novel *The Shadow of the Wind* explores themes of book destruction and protection. It pivots on the labyrinthine "cemetery of lost books" from which Daniel Sempere must select, then guard with his life, a book. In picturing the book hoard, Zafón took inspiration from real and imaginary precedents: galleries of mirrors; stories within stories; the multi-level bookshop of Francis Edwards; the multi-room bookshop of Wilfrid Voynich, said to have been organized in a deliberate sequence of crammed spaces so as to enhance the sense of drama and discovery; the marvelous abbey library in Umberto Eco's *The*

Name of the Rose; and the epic, tragic *dépôts littéraires* of revolutionary France.

Apart from an intolerable human cost, wars and revolutions have levied a terrible toll on cultural heritage. Along with other cultural artifacts, books are, as William Ewart Gladstone put it, "the bonds and rivets of the race"—and there is no better way to destroy a culture than to destroy its books. Throughout the history of libraries, the wholesale destruction and plunder of books has been an appalling constant.

Consider, for example, the Macedonian royal library, looted by the Roman consul Emilius Paulus in 168 B.C. Or the Roman libraries, sacked by the Goths under their king Alaric. (According to Boethius, Fergus II—the first king of the Scots—served as a Goth commander in the sacking of Rome in 410 A.D. and brought away a plunder of manuscripts, which he presented to the monastery at Iona.) Or the illuminated manuscripts, stolen—probably for the gold in the bindings—by the Danes and Vikings who raided monasteries in Saxon England, including Lindisfarne in the ninth century. Or Korea's Tripitaka library of Buddhist scriptural printing blocks, destroyed by fire in 1232 during a Mongol invasion. (Later, Portuguese Christians also wreaked havoc in the libraries of Buddhist Ceylon.)

In 1298 the English king Edward I defeated the Scottish knight Sir William Wallace, a leader of the rebellion against Edward I during the Wars of Scottish Independence. Edward did all in his power to extirpate the Scots; he burned their registers and the great Restennoth Library that housed the books that Fergus II had brought back as plunder from Rome. In August 1305, Wallace was captured near Glasgow. Handed over to Edward, he was hanged, drawn, and quartered for high treason.

The register of book plunder seems never-ending. An illuminated French Bible was stolen from the tent of the king of France during the Battle of Poitiers on September 19, 1356. In 1424–25 the Duke of Bedford relieved the Louvre library of 843 manuscripts. In 1526 the Turks largely destroyed the fine library of Matthias Corvinus in Buda. And in 1632 Gustavus Adolphus's Swedes looted the picture books in Albrecht's *Kunstkammer*, on the ground floor of the Antiquarium at the Bavarian State Library in Munich.

In pre-Columbian America, the Conquistadors burned Mayan books; as few as three genuine Mayan codices survive today, and as few as fourteen Aztec ones—the other Aztec books were despatched by the Inquisition. Further north, in August 1814, the invading British set fire to the U.S. Capitol and the 3,000 books of its new Library of Congress, which only a short time before had acquired 740 books in London. (That century there would be two more Library of Congress fires, in 1825 and 1851.)

On July 14, 1789, a mob swarmed from the Bastille to the Bibliothèque de l'Arsenal in Paris. The mob's intention was clear: to sack the residence of the Count of Artois, the unpopular younger brother of Louis XVI. The superb library, though, was saved through the quick action of Claude Marin Saugrain. Formerly a bookseller, then keeper of the Arsenal's library—some 100,000 carefully selected works, largely by French writers and especially poets—Saugrain made the porter change into the king's livery, "thus persuading the crowd that it had called at the wrong address."

The story was much worse for the Royal Library. In the first heat of the revolution, Anne-Louis-François de Paule Lefèvre d'Ormesson de Noyseau, the last royal librarian, was arrested, as were his successors Jean-Louis Carra and Sébastien Chamfort. Carra died under the guillotine in 1793, Lefèvre d'Ormesson in

1794. After a stint in a filthy prison, Chamfort attempted suicide, dying months later from improper treatment of his wounds.

The Reign of Terror supplied a horrific new material for book-making. Books covered with the skin of executed prisoners were said to be bound in "aristocratic leather." (A volume at Harvard University's Houghton Library—Arsène Houssaye's *Des destinées de l'ame*—is bound in the skin of an eighteenth-century "mental patient.") Collectors and connoisseurs of such items procured ever more sickening examples, prizing specimens with every kind of human protuberance on the front cover.

The contents of the Royal Library, too, were in mortal danger. In the minds of the revolutionaries, its books had been defiled by the name "Bibliothèque du Roi." There was much enthusiasm for burning the whole collection. A less drastic proposal was drafted as a decree:

> the books of the Public Libraries of Paris, and of the Departments, could no longer be permitted to offend the eyes of the Republicans by shameful marks of servitude, and that all such must be immediately effaced: Fleurs-de-lis, for example, and armorial bearings, whether on the bindings, or in other parts of books, together with all prefaces and dedications addressed to kings and nobles must disappear.

Two booksellers and a printer led a newspaper campaign that ensured the proposal was dropped. Many other books, though, were condemned—along with their owners—on account of their fine bindings.

Author and poet Andrew Lang described the dangers of

broadcasting aristocratic sympathies through a predilection for well-bound books.

> Condorcet might have escaped the scaffold if he had only thrown away the neat little Horace from the royal press, which betrayed him for no true Republican, but an educated man. The great libraries from the chateaux of the nobles were scattered among all the bookstalls. True sons of freedom tore off the bindings, with their gilded crests and scutcheons. One revolutionary writer declared, and perhaps he was not far wrong, that the art of binding was the worst enemy of reading. He always began his studies by breaking the backs of the volumes he was about to attack. The art of bookbinding in these sad years took flight to England, and was kept alive by artists robust rather than refined, like Thompson and Roger Payne. These were evil days, when the binder had to cut the aristocratic coat of arms out of a book cover, and glue in a gilt cap of liberty, as in a volume in an Oxford amateur's collection.

In the two decades after the fall of the Bastille, nearly every book in France changed hands. The law of legal deposit was abolished, then re-established. In Paris, millions of volumes were confiscated from émigrés, churches, prisoners, and other perceived enemies of the state. The confiscated volumes were assembled in eight vast, temporary storehouses—the *dépôts littéraires*. Other French cities such as Dijon and Lyon also set up book depots. In the storehouses, the jewels of France's libraries moldered in verminous dust and humidity.

The authorities arranged book sales to help empty the storages.

At one Paris sale, the bookseller and publisher Jacques-Simon Merlin bought so many books that they filled the two five-story houses he had bought for exactly this purpose. Though many of them were precious and rare, the books were priced by weight— the same as on Corfu. Even at that price, most French bibliophiles couldn't afford to buy. Relatively cashed-up purchasers from England and Germany made a killing. The books that escaped destruction and weren't sold abroad were eventually distributed among France's public libraries, but conditions there were little better. As Alberto Manguel wrote in *A History of Reading*,

> Throughout the first half of the nineteenth century, the hours of access to these *bibliothèques publiques* were restricted, a dress code was enforced, and the precious books once again gathered dust on the shelves, forgotten and unread.

In Madrid, at the outbreak of the Spanish Civil War in 1936, communists and anarchists executed the director of the Escorial library, P. Julián Zarco Cuevas, along with his predecessor, P. Melchor Martínez Antuña, and the monks who'd taken refuge in the library. A precursor to World War II, the Spanish Civil War foreshadowed on a national scale the cultural damage that would be wrought on a global one.

The collage of destruction in World War II included the firebombing of Holland House, London, and its wonderful book collection; damage to Ashburnham Place, Sussex, when a fully loaded Marauder bomber crashed nearby; severe damage to Milan's Ambrosian Library in an Allied air raid (the manuscripts and incunabula had been removed as a precaution and they escaped intact, but 50,000 other volumes, along with Cardinal Federigo's original library room, were destroyed); the bombing, on four occasions, of the Bavarian State Library, which lost a devastating 500,000 volumes, many of them Bibles; the destruction of the buildings and the collection of Leipzig's University in 1943; attacks by German bombers on Slovenian libraries in 1944; a Liberator bomber's total destruction of Verona's Biblioteca Capitolare (when the Capitolare reopened in 1948, the stoic librarian, Turrini, declared the new building to be more spacious and much more beautiful than the old one); and Japanese bombing at Rabaul in New Guinea, followed by a ground invasion that destroyed the town's library. Gordon Thomas, editor of the *Rabaul Times*, "had the sad experience of watching the library's entire bookstock being thrown on a huge bonfire that burnt for days."

The typographer Stanley Morison designed many famous fonts, including Times New Roman. In December 1941, he wrote from the London *Times* offices to the American bookman Daniel Berkeley Updike about the night of May 10, 1941. Morison had lost many valuable books on that night, including Cabrol and Leclercq's *Dictionnaire*. The British Museum was also hit. Liturgical books bore the brunt of the destruction. After inspecting the damage, Morison wrote despairingly that it was nothing short of disastrous. "I simply do not know where to turn for copies of certain books."

After the Anschluss, the monks of the abbey library at Admont were expelled as enemies of the state, their property forfeited to the Reich. Manuscripts and incunabula were sent to Graz. In what Anthony Hobson called one of the most bizarre and sinister whims of Nazi rule, 3,000 medical and botanical works were sent to the concentration camp at Dachau.

In some respects, the ancient Gothic invaders were more civilized than modern combatants. In 267 A.D. the Goths penetrated the

Aegean Sea and sacked Athens. But, as Raymond Irwin noted in the *Encyclopaedia of Librarianship*, the marauders regarded one class of building as off-limits: "they were restrained from setting fire to the libraries by the thought that good scholars made poor soldiers." The Gothic invaders were possibly in awe, and perhaps did not "want to lift a finger at something which seemed utterly mysterious and therefore divine."

Not all Goths showed the same civility. The Catholic church has a long memory when it comes to reinstating books stolen from its libraries. In 1461–63 the papal legate Marino de Fregeno traveled through Scandinavia laying claim to books that had been looted by the Goths during the sack of Rome in 510.

In May 1527, the mutinous imperial army of Lutheran lands-knechts also sacked Rome. Ninety-five years later, a Catholic army marched into the Palatinate "to punish its Calvinist Elector." The nuncio in Cologne made known in Germany the pope's willingness to accept an offer of the famous public library of Heidelberg, which was rich in ancient manuscripts from the abbey of Lorsch. Within five days of the town's capture, Maximilian of Bavaria granted the pope's wish. More than 3,000 manuscripts and 5,000 books were taken to Rome. The Palatina's shelves were cut up into packing cases. Any remaining books were picked through by Bavarian soldiers.

Two centuries later, "consciences were still troubled" by this acquisition. In 1815–16, Pius VII returned to the Duchy of Baden 842 German manuscripts and forty-two Latin ones.

Under Napoleon, books from the greatest libraries of Western Europe started to reach the Bibliothèque Nationale as "cultural trophies" from the conquered territories. Four decades later, most of the flood of accessions remained unarranged, uncatalogued and—in many cases—unreturned. It wasn't until Léopold Delisle's administration, beginning in 1874, that the backlog was finally addressed. Napoleon had ordered that the Vatican's Secret Archive of papal documents be removed to Paris. It was returned, minus some key documents, after Waterloo.

The Bavarian State Library has taken pains to restitute any of its holdings that were improperly acquired or that had problematic provenance. The medieval Plock Pontifical, for example, was returned to Poland in April 2015. The Nazis had stolen that book from the Plock Bishopric in 1940 and placed it in the Königsberg university library. (The Bavarian State Library bought the manuscript in 1973 for 6,200 deutsche marks at an auction in Munich.) The library identified a further five hundred books "whose acquisition is to be regarded as unlawful." Among the restitutions already completed, the library returned to the Thomas Mann Archive in Zurich seventy-eight volumes originating from Mann's research library. The expelled Benedictines went back to Admont at the end of World War II; by 1955 most of the library's books had been restored to their shelves.

During his 1990 pastoral visit to Mexico, Pope John Paul II offered a gift to the Mexican people: the *Libellus de Medicinalibus Indorum Herbis*, an early Latin version of a rare medical manuscript that had been taken from New Spain in the sixteenth century. Martín de la Cruz, an Aztec physician, wrote the original manuscript in Nahuatl, the Aztec language, at the College of Santa Cruz in the new colony. Ultra-protective of the Holy See's collections, the Vatican Librarian Leonard Boyle opposed the pope's offer of the book. Moreover, he made a failed attempt to prevent the offer's fulfillment, remonstrating with John Paul II that the Vatican Library was the pontifical library and did not belong to a single pope. Later, a scandal erupted over Boyle's fund-raising activities;

the gossip at the Vatican, repeated by Daniel Mendelsohn in the *New Yorker*, was that Boyle "found himself without crucial support in the Curia."

The librarians at St. Gall maintain a sorry listing—the *Codices dispersi Sangallenses*—of early manuscripts that were once in the abbey but are now held in other collections. The full list of losses also includes priceless early maps and rare prints. In 1996 lengthy negotiations began, with a view to the return of the manuscripts and other treasures taken from St. Gall during the Toggenburg War of 1712. The negotiations were difficult; many of the international treaties governing the theft of cultural heritage in war (such as the Hague Conventions of 1907, on the Laws and Customs of War on Land, and 1954, for the Protection of Cultural Property in the Event of Armed Conflict) did not apply to the sectarian battle of Vilmegen. The Central Library in Zurich, the Canton and City of Zurich, the Canton of St. Gall, and the state's Catholic administration failed to reach an agreement until the Swiss Federal Council intervened and secured a compromise. (The Swiss Constitution empowered the Confederation to "support cultural activities of national interest.")

The main argument for restitution was that the appropriated items were part of an ensemble. Under the settlement agreement, St. Gall accepted Zurich's ownership of the cultural objects that the National Museum and the Central Library in Zurich had possessed since the end of the war. A total of about a hundred St. Gall codices are now housed in Zurich's Central Library. The quid pro quo was that Zurich would recognize that these objects were integral to St. Gall's cultural identity and, more importantly, would give some of them back. In September 2006, Zurich returned forty precious and exemplary works executed by the monks of St. Gall. Formally, they are "on loan" for an indefinite period, without rent or interest.

Zurich also agreed to lend the original Cosmographical Globe to St. Gall, for a four-month exhibition, and to commission, pay for, and donate to St. Gall an exact and expensive replica. The replica globe arrived at the Abbey Library in August 2009; the original is kept at the Swiss National Museum. The loan agreement can only be amended or terminated after thirty-eight years, "by a joint request from the highest executive of each party." Another requirement of the settlement was that the Canton of St. Gall digitize the loaned manuscripts and make them available on the internet. Holdouts on both sides have criticized the agreement. Some in Zurich deny the Cosmographical Globe was ever taken; some at St. Gall are not satisfied with the facsimile version, arguing that the original belonged to St. Gall all along and that the abbey library was the best place for its permanent exhibition. Which part of "ensemble" did the burghers of Zurich not understand?

Fundamentally, though, the dispute is over. In April 2006, to mark the dispute's end, the Canton of Zurich presented the abbey library with the first biography of St. Gallus, the so-called *Vita vetustissima sancti Galli*, written over the century from 680. The manuscript, kept for many years in the Zurich State Archives, is the oldest originating from St. Gall. It exists only in fragments.

Despite its many past vicissitudes, St. Gall's library remains rich in herbals, breviaries, evangialiaries, antiphonaries, psalters, missals, graduals, hymnals, processionals, pontificals, decrees, edicts, satires, allegories, epics, festschrifts, palimpsests, calendars, and lexicons. Volumes decorated in gold, silver, and ivory. Volumes representing the height of book craft and scholarship in the Middle Ages and the Renaissance. Now a UNESCO world cultural heritage site, the library holds more than four hundred manuscript volumes produced before the year 1000; one of the largest collections of early manuscripts in the world.

The treasures that made it through include the oldest German book; beautiful examples of mediaval manuscript art; botanical books; heraldry; cartography; medicine (one book recommends, as cure for the pain of toothache, pouring chamomile into the patient's ear); important musical manuscripts, including a parchment copy of the "Song of the Nibelungs" and Johannes Heer's "songbook" (dating from his student days late in the fifteenth century, this is a collection of bawdy songs and erotic couplets); and an illustrated *Biblia Pauperum*, which, like a graphic novel, made the stories of the Bible accessible to semiliterate and illiterate audiences.

The library continues to be known for its manuscripts, such as works by Horace, Lucan, Sallust, Ovid, and Cicero, and the surviving eleven pages and eight fragments of the *Vergilius Sangallensis*, a fifth-century volume that was originally written in the first century B.C. by Publius Vergilius Maro and that contained the *Aeneid*, *Georgics*, and *Bucolics*. The library is also famous for the rococo library hall made by Thumb, Loser, and the Giggels—visitors must wear special shoe-covering slippers to protect the beautiful, creaking pinewood floor—and for the mummy Schepenese and her beautiful teeth.

Library fauna

Public libraries are as effective as cheap hotels at spreading bedbugs (*Cimex lectularius*). The U.S. Centers for Disease Control consider these creatures a public health pest; civil authorities have employed bedbug sniffer dogs to inspect infested libraries.

Many species of animal and fungus are inimical to books. The very first libraries had problems with worms: in ancient Mesopotamia, before clay tablets were hardened in the sun or in a kiln, earthworms could bore into them, constructing tunnels in the soft clay. After the tablets hardened, worms could still munch and perturb the surface, confusing the cuneiform markings.

Over millennia, the animal kingdom of book botherers has included termites, mud wasps, snakes, skunks, foxes, cockroaches, and silverfish. Children and house-pets have done unspeakable things to private libraries. Rats and mice are known to gnaw the backs of books to reach the glue inside. Rodents also nibble vellum bindings, and the pages of vellum books that have become greasy with handling. When the Jesuit Order in Belgium was dissolved in 1773, the books from the Jesuit church in Brussels were to be transferred to the city's royal library. The library had no room for the new accessions, so they were left temporarily in the Jesuit church, which was infested with mice. After much debate, the secretary of the Literary

Society adopted a novel solution. Books that were considered useful, principally scientific and historical volumes, were placed on shelves in the middle of the nave, while the remainder were left on the floor. In this way, it was hoped, the outer books would be sacrificed to save the inner ones.

Bookworms have been a scourge in libraries since ancient times. Aristotle wrote of them in his *History of Animals*. The poet and grammarian Evenus of Paros penned an epigram on the "black-fleshed" bookworm, calling the creature, "Pest of the muses, devourer of pages." Evenus lamented, "Wert thou born for the evil thou workest? Wherefore thine own foul form shapest thou, with envious toil?"

In the thirteenth century, the manuscript *Remedium Contra Vermes Librorum* was widely circulated. In the seventeenth century, Christianus Mentzelius was claimed to have heard the bookworm "crow like a cock unto his mate." Robert Hooke provided in *Micrographia* (1665) one of the first scientific descriptions of the creature:

> a small, white, silver shining worm or moth which I found much conversant among books and papers, and is supposed to be that which corrodes and eats holes thro' the leaves and covers. Its head appears big and blunt and its body tapers from it toward the tail smaller and smaller, being shaped almost like a carrot.

Typically, true "bookworms" are insects from the order *Coleoptera*, which are sheath-winged beetles. (The most ravenous of these has a frightening name: *Sitodrepa panicea*.) Precisely identifying book-destroying culprits is difficult. Beetles account for one-fifth of all living species, so the lineup of suspects is wide.

Beetles live through four stages: egg, larva, pupa, and adult. Most damage to books is done at the larval stage, which can extend for years. In one famous infestation, a single insect chomped a straight hole through twenty-seven contiguous volumes. Some species specialize in eating vellum, others paper, hemp, glue, or flax. (Certain types of beetle are capable of eating through plastic and even through lead cable.) In his 1898 *Facts about Bookworms*, John Francis Xavier O'Conor described *Dermestes lardarius*, the larva of the larder beetle, as being "covered with bristles . . . like a tiny hedgehog, curling himself in his spikes to insure protection."

Bookworms flourish in circumstances of quiet neglect; larvae have been known to "rear up" when disturbed. The signs of active infestation are dead beetles and "frass" (larval debris). Though the beetles typically emerge from exit holes to mate, some mating does take place inside books. The prohibition of eating and drinking in libraries is less about protecting books from spillages or sticky fingers than it is about discouraging insects and rodents.

The notorious British Museum flea thrived in the poorly ventilated old reading room. In 1848 a reader remarked that the "flea generated in the room . . . is larger than any to be found elsewhere, except in the receiving rooms of work-houses."

In sixteenth-century China, libraries controlled infestations with herbal treatments. In the Tianyi Chamber, for example, bags of insect-repelling herbs were positioned in the book-cupboards. An early Chinese law required that *huang-neih*, an extract from the seeds of the cork tree, be added as an ingredient in paper as a means to ward off insects. Chinese library-builders also spread gypsum beneath cupboards and shelves, to combat damp.

Termites were a problem in tenth-century Baghdad. There, in 993 A.D., Sabur ibn Ardashir's librarians used chemicals to control the pests. Early insecticides and repellents included alum, cypress wood, clay daubing, clove oil, cedar oil, eucalyptus oil, musk, and red myrrh. A mixture of boracic acid and methylated spirits was said to work well as a protection for books in tropical Australia and New Guinea. According to Jules Cousin, bookworms can be controlled with essence of turpentine, camphor, tobacco, and fine pepper. The patented Keating's Insect Powder is an alternative to pepper, as is snap freezing the infested books. An incursion of Italian bookworms at Yale's Beinecke Library was controlled by freezing the pestilential books at minus thirty-six degrees Celsius for three days.

Portuguese libraries have long relied on biological controls. The eighteenth-century libraries of Coimbra and Mafra host colonies of tiny bats. In summer the bats roost outside; in winter they roost behind the bookcases. Each night they earn their keep by feeding on bookworms and other bibliopests. Each morning the librarians earn their keep by sweeping up droppings. The micro bats might be helpful in Portugal, but larger bats, along with pigeons and damp, did much damage to the manuscripts at Durham Cathedral when it fell into neglect during the sixteenth and seventeenth centuries.

Borroloola is a small settlement on the remote McArthur River in Australia's tropical gulf country. In the 1890s it gained a disreputable status as a frontier town, a center for murderers and alcoholics. By the 1930s it was all but abandoned. And yet it once possessed one of the best libraries in rural Australia.

Late in the nineteenth century, the chief of the Borroloola police—an Irishman with the heroic name Cornelius Power—decided to establish a library for the town. He ordered books from Mudie's Select Library in London, and these formed the nucleus of the collection that was given an equally grand name: the McArthur River Institute. From those origins, the library grew rapidly, though its sources of funding and books after Power's founding purchase are unclear. The Governor of Victoria; the Government of Australia; the National Library of Australia; the Carnegie Foundation; the Carnegie Corporation; the Carnegie Trust—each of these institutions has been put forward as a possible source of the more than 3,000 volumes that the institute had accumulated by 1920.

Rumor and myth surround the library just as Murnane's great plains library was enveloped in mysterious plans and projects. The institute attracted overlanders, stockmen, bandits, and hermits, all of whom used the library for education—and redemption. The drover Charles Joseph Scrutton claimed to have read the whole of the library three times. Roger Jose was said to have walked to Borroloola from Cunnamulla in Queensland. He lived in a shed in the center of town—until the shed was nearly flattened by a cyclone. As the *Sydney Morning Herald* reported:

> He then rolled a damaged 1000-gallon tank from the hotel to the site on top of the hill opposite the present clinic and, with his Aboriginal companion, lived in it until his death in 1963. He was an eccentric who took full

advantage of the Borroloola library and reputedly knew vast sections of Virgil's *Aeneid* in Latin. He also had a good working knowledge of Shakespeare.

Tourists in the area described "stumbling into bush camps at night to find bushmen reciting from the Greek classics, or argumentative swaggies referring to their borrowed copies of Hansard to settle political debates." The Institute library no longer exists. The tropical estuarine environment in which it grew was not unlike Alexandria's river delta, and it had the same destructive impact on the books. The volumes that were not stolen were destroyed by damp and mold, and especially by silverfish, cockroaches, and—just like in ancient Baghdad— termites. In the mythology of northern Australia, though, the library grows larger day by day.

CHAPTER 11

———— ❖ ————

The Count

Book looters and thieves

At Ashburnham Place in Sussex, the Fourth Earl of Ashburnham assembled in the nineteenth century a library that rivaled those of Richard Heber and Lord Spencer. Apart from a superb collection of early printed books—including two Gutenberg Bibles—it contained a fine selection of early manuscripts, of which the earl was a passionate collector. A superbious man—people referred to him as the old Bengal tiger at Ashburnham—he made it very difficult for scholars to access his collection. He was even less cooperative with people who wanted to buy his books. When the earl purchased an important collection of Irish manuscripts, Dr. James Henthorn Todd, librarian at Dublin's Trinity College, wrote asking if he could purchase them. The reply was icy. "If," Ashburnham wrote, "you will send me one of the finest manuscripts now in your possession—for instance the Book of Kells—I will tell you whether I will or will not give my Irish manuscripts for it." Todd replied resolutely that the Book of Kells was not his property—it was part of the Library of Archbishop Ussher, which Charles II presented to the University of Dublin at his Restoration. The heads of the university could not dispose of it without an Act of Parliament, and they would never do so anyhow, but thank you anyway.

According to F. S. Ellis, Ashburnham was "a man rather calculated to inspire fear than love or respect." To the nineteenth-century social trends that were making England's lords more affable and egalitarian, Ashburnham was "wholly impervious." An oft-repeated anecdote from his estate concerned the woodcutter who, after accidentally toppling the wrong tree, fell on his knees to beg the earl's forgiveness. Ashburnham was disliked even by his own son, who would become the fifth earl, and who felt he'd gone without to fuel his father's bibliomania.

Guglielmo Bruto Icilio Timoleone, Conte Libri-Carucci dalla Sommaia, was born in Florence in 1803. A member of a venerable Tuscan family, he studied law and mathematics at the University of Pisa and displayed precocious brilliance in the natural sciences. After obtaining his doctorate, he published a paper on number theory that attracted the attention of the English inventor and computer pioneer Charles Babbage. Upon Guglielmo's graduation, he was offered the chair of mathematical physics at the university—the first of many high offices and honors that would include membership of the Institut de France, a science professorship at the University of Paris, the Legion of Honour, and, in 1841, appointment to the commission overseeing a France-wide audit of every manuscript, in every language, held in every departmental public library.

Guglielmo's passion for books manifested itself early. By 1840 he had amassed a large personal collection—40,000 printed books and over 1,800 manuscripts—that had some spectacular highlights. He also began dealing in manuscripts and rare printed editions. Styling himself as "Count Libri," he cultivated the image, the demeanor and the curriculum vitae of a great bookman.

Late in 1845, Libri decided to sell his manuscripts. The following year, Sir Frederic Madden, keeper of the Department of Manuscripts of the British Museum, arrived in Paris with his assistant John Holmes to appraise them. In Libri's apartment in the Sorbonne the Englishmen found the count a "rather corpulent" fellow who seemed, according to Madden, "as if he had never used soap and water or a brush."

> The room . . . was not more than about 16 feet wide, but filled with manuscripts on shelves up to the ceiling. The windows had double sashes and a fire of coal and coke burnt in the grate, the heat of which, added to the smell of the pile of vellum around, was so unsufferable, that I gasped for breath. M. Libri perceived the inconvenience we suffered and opened one of the windows, but it was easy to see that a breath of air was disagreeable to him, and his ears were stuffed with cotton, as if to prevent his feeling sensible of it!

Though the books were dirty and in a disordered state, Madden concluded the collection was indeed a prize, worth in the range of £8,000 to £9,000. The trustees of the library sought £9,000 from the treasury, but the exchequer refused and Libri had to look elsewhere for a buyer. His first thought was to attempt a sale in Turin. Another English purchaser, though, came forward. Lord Ashburnham sent the bookseller Thomas Rodd to Paris to examine the collection. Rodd returned with a positive report and two samples: a seventh-century Pentateuch, and the *Hours* of Lorenzo the Magnificent. Ashburnham's offer of £8,000 was quickly forthcoming and quickly accepted. In April 1847, sixteen cases of manuscripts arrived at Ashburnham Place.

Apart from the Libri books, Ashburnham made many individual purchases of manuscripts, and two bulk ones: the Stowe manuscripts, bought from the Duke of Buckingham and containing early Irish codices and Anglo-Saxon charters; and the Barrois manuscripts, bought in 1849 from Joseph Barrois of Lille.

Libri's role with the libraries commission had given him special authority to visit and access holdings at all hours, anywhere in France. Armed with his credentials and dressed in a huge cloak— he looked, by all accounts, like a Sicilian bandit—Libri inspected collections across the country. His expertise enabled him to home in on the gems of every library he saw. Indeed, Libri matched his fellow Tuscan Gian Francesco Poggio Bracciolini in book-hunting prowess. But there the similarity ends.

Poggio removed books, but his goal seems always to have been their protection. He treated the books well; he found homes for them in Florentine and other libraries and he worked carefully as a scribe, making copies—several of which still survive—of the rediscovered works. Poggio invented the elegant humanist script (based on the Caroline minuscule) that served, after a generation of polishing, as the prototype for Roman fonts. Libri, in contrast, was a vandal, a butcher of books. Behind his respectable veneer lurked the most ruthless, audacious, and pernicious book thief of all time.

There had of course been thefts ever since the very first books. Property crimes of incredible variety mar the history of libraries. Indeed, the relationship stretches right back to the rationale for books existing at all. The purpose of the first books—those tablets in ancient Mesopotamia and Egypt—was to prevent fraud. They recorded ownership, so property was harder to steal, and they recorded transactions, making it harder for sellers and buyers to renege. The vast majority of surviving tablets are lists of items and payments: who owned what, and who paid whom and how much.

In the millennia since the tablets were made, books have been associated with every conceivable type of racket. A large slice of what we know about books and authorship in the Middle Ages and in early-modern times has reached us because it was documented in legal prosecutions and disputes. As Burnett Streeter noted in his 1931 survey of chained libraries, "in the Middle Ages books were rare, and so too was honesty." Dating from the twelfth century, the earliest definitive reference to a Paris bookseller damns him as a rascal who had double-crossed Peter of Blois. The illustrious bookseller H. P. Kraus remarked (accurately, if somewhat self-servingly), "you expect every great manuscript to have been stolen at least once."

Dr. Francis Wilson, a rector who lived at the deanery with Jonathan Swift, was suspected of filching books and of intimidating "the increasingly defenceless old man." Swift's friends ejected Wilson from the house. Pilfering has been known to reduce libraries to nothing. The collections of Humfrey, Duke of Gloucester, and the Franciscan convent in Oxford both say much about Oxfordshire's thieves, who turned both collections into thin air. At around the same time, thieves in nearby Warwickshire reduced the abbot's library at Stoneleigh Priory to a level that was recorded as *In libraria abbatis, nichil.* "In the library of the abbot, nothing."

Chimney cross-bars, which prevent thieves coming down, are just one of the many devices that custodians have used to prevent theft from libraries. Other libraries have solved the problem of security by locking books behind glass, metal stays, metal screens, and, such as at the Ambrosian Library in Milan, wide-gauge, wirework mesh. At the Bodleian's Arts End, which dates from 1612, the staircases that give access to the upstairs gallery are safely enclosed in timber cages.

When Montaigne visited the Vatican Library in 1581, he saw books chained to desks. The libraries of Peterhouse and St John's College at Cambridge lost their chains late in the sixteenth century or early in the seventeenth. We are accustomed to thinking of chained libraries as medieval, and of chains as a feature that fell out of use long before the modern era. And yet, as Burnett Streeter found from his survey, university libraries were still using chains well into the eighteenth century.

> Fresh chains were being purchased at Chetham College, Manchester, in 1742, and at the Bodleian in 1751. At The Queen's College, Oxford, the chains were not taken from the books till 1780; at Merton not till 1792. Magdalen was the last college in Oxford to retain them; here they lasted till 1799.

These latter chains date from the Enlightenment, not the Dark or Middle Ages or the Renaissance. Another late chained library was installed at Hereford in 1715.

The modern history of library thefts is full of sorry episodes—but also happy reunions. In 1956 the Folger Shakespeare Library returned to the Boston Athenaeum a book reported missing there in 1867. In 1992 the Folger suffered losses of its own. A professor admitted stealing from the library. In the district court, Stuart Adelman, aged fifty-four, pleaded guilty to one count of interstate transportation of stolen property: rare letters signed by Isaac Newton and Voltaire. Adelman was sentenced to a year in prison. He had sold many of the stolen letters and other documents, but all of them were recovered and returned to the library. Another professor, this one from Ohio State University, stole pages from a fourteenth-century manuscript in the Vatican Library. The manuscript had once belonged to Petrarch. From Christ Church College, Oxford, a specialist in baroque music stole a 1552 work by Vesalius, entitled *De Humani Corporis Fabrica*. The thief was a regular on the conference circuit and had appeared as a musical expert on the BBC. After passing through the hands of several owners and dealers, the book resurfaced in Japan, in the library of a dentistry college. Oxford demanded it back. The thief spent two years in prison, where he was able to improve his Latin.

A 1998 audit of the Library of Congress revealed a devastating discovery: at least 300,000 titles were missing. In addition, approximately 27,000 illustrations had disappeared from its nineteenth-century books on travel and botany.

The modernist Beinecke Library at Yale University is all glass and voids and mezzanines and translucence; doing anything surreptitiously there is almost impossible. But Edward Forbes Smiley III did—for a while at least. A well-known dealer in antiques and rare maps, Smiley cut maps from the library's books with an X-ACTO blade. In 2005 his wrongdoing was discovered; the jig was up when he dropped his blade in the reading room and was caught red-handed with recently excised maps. Apart from stealing from the Beinecke, Smiley also confessed to having stolen from Yale's Sterling Memorial Library, Harvard's Houghton Library, Chicago's Newberry Library, the Boston Public Library, the New York Public Library, and the British Library. The extent of his crimes ran to at least ninety-seven rare maps and documents, altogether worth more than $3 million. He was sentenced to three and a half years in prison and ordered to pay $2.3 million in restitution. The Beinecke tightened its security.

According to a 1992 survey of theft and loss, published by London's Home Office Police Research Group, the most stolen subject areas in British public libraries were, in decreasing order: sex, telepathy, foreign languages, occult magic, music, and the arts. The ordering differed by place; sex was more popular among thieves in the big cities, occult magic in the smaller communities.

In the late 1990s John Charles Gilkey stole checks and credit card numbers, then used them to steal books. He was a regular visitor to Heritage Book Shop in Los Angeles. Housed in a converted mausoleum with a vaulted ceiling and stained-glass windows, the shop was stylishly fitted out with cabinets from England and chairs from *Gone With the Wind*. In those surroundings, and already inspired by the old libraries depicted in Sherlock Holmes films, Gilkey dreamed of building his own giant library, in which he would read and write at a desk next to a world globe. Apart from stealing books, Gilkey also collected snuff bottles, musical instruments, baseball cards, crystal, coins, and autographs—he had Stephen King's, Anne Perry's, Princess Diana's, and Ronald Reagan's. Heritage Book Shop closed in 2007, partly due to stock losses.

The author Allison Hoover Bartlett called on Gilkey after he was sent to prison for his crimes. In *The Man Who Loved Books Too Much* she describes a Clarice Starling–esque experience. Arriving at the jail, she has a knot in her stomach. Will Gilkey be hostile? Is it safe to talk to him? Security is tight. Bartlett notices the signs in the waiting area. "No Levi's." "No sleeveless tops." "No sandals." "No underwire bras." Running back across the hot parking lot, she climbs into her car and wrestles off her bra. "I was glad I had not worn a white blouse." She returns to the waiting area. Half an hour later her name is called. She approaches Gilkey through a metal detector and two sets of heavy doors. Dressed in prison orange, Gilkey—age thirty-seven, height 175 centimeters, eyes hazel-brown, hair dark and thinning—sits behind a Plexiglas window. Bartlett tries to look as though this is a routine visit, but she is sweating and nervous. Despite all the precautions, Gilkey comes across as a mild, personable chap, definitely no Hannibal Lecter, clearly enjoying Bartlett's dishabille visit, happy to spill the beans on how he used the Modern Library 100 Best Novels list to know what to steal, and on how stealing books helped him pretend to be Sherlock Holmes.

Over an astounding time span stretching from the 1820s to the 1840s, Count Libri aroused suspicions in Italy and in France. At Florence's Accademia dei Georgofili, for instance, where Libri had resigned after only a year in the position of librarian, his successor "checked the holdings and found that three hundred books were missing." The thefts were an inside job. There and elsewhere, though, official bumbling and cronyism conspired to save Libri's skin. Exiled from Italy after taking part in a botched Florentine conspiracy, he settled in France, obtained French nationality, and was elected to the Académie des Sciences. Keeping up his respectable professorial facade, between 1838 and 1841 he published a four-volume work on the history of mathematics. Meanwhile, the accusations continued. Anonymous denunciations reached the police; damning rumors reached the press—Libri threatened to challenge the editor of *Le National* to a duel. Félix Boucly, the public prosecutor, made inquiries and submitted his findings in an official report. But Libri's friend M. Guizot, president of the Ministerial Council, hushed it up.

All the while, Libri continued to steal books, and to deal in them. Salting down the stolen books with volumes legitimately obtained from fellow dealers, he organized auction sales and composed catalogues rich with misleading information. (At a later Libri sale, notable for its fraudulent Galileo and Kepler manuscripts, the great English collector Sir Thomas Phillipps was a voracious bidder, acquiring nineteen Cicero manuscripts and more than a hundred lots in total. When, in the cold light of day, Phillipps discovered his purchases had been misdescribed, he sought an adjustment to the price. Libri pointed to the conditions of sale. The manuscripts had been sold "with all faults." An adjustment was out of the question.)

Libri stole in a manner that was as ingenious as it was brazen. Impressed by his connections, his appointments, his apparent knowledge, and his title, most librarians were only too willing to oblige him with generous access privileges. (The vigilant librarian at Auxerre in Burgundy was an exception.) He stole entire volumes and—using the stiletto he carried for the dual purposes of self-enrichment and self-defence (the Carbonari, a secret revolutionary group, allegedly had a price on his head)—he cut out valuable gatherings and single leaves.

Libraries at Lyon, Orléans, and Tours suffered his worst depredations. The adaptable Libri matched his method to the circumstances of each library. The Bibliothèque Municipale de Lyon preserved thirteen manuscripts in uncial or half-uncial of the fifth to the eighth century; Anthony Hobson called them "the most important homogenous group in any city except Verona." Most of the bindings were in a terrible state of disintegration. "All that was needed was to slit the sewing thread to remove complete gatherings." In total, Libri stole portions of six early manuscripts from Lyon. From an important seventh-century Pentateuch, he removed the books of Leviticus and Numbers.

The library at Tours was also in disorder, with numerous manuscripts uncatalogued. Libri again exploited the chaos ruthlessly. "Complete manuscripts could be removed and their places on the shelves filled with uncatalogued works of lesser value." From Tours, Libri stole twenty-four manuscripts, including another seventh-century Pentateuch (this volume, featuring nineteen large miniatures, is the one Libri would send as a sample to Ashburnham). At Orléans, Libri pulled off a combination of his Lyon and Tours heists. He cut out gatherings, and he stole whole volumes. In total from Orleans he stole twenty-six complete or partial manuscripts. And this appalling pattern of theft continued elsewhere. At the Mazarin Library—that wonderful collection assembled by Gabriel Naudé—a copy of the *Galeomyomachia*, a Byzantine parody of *The Iliad* printed by Aldus around 1494, had disappeared from a shelf close to where Libri normally sat. A representative of Troyes, a town in the Champagne-Ardenne region, remarked that "after M. Libri's visit, the library of this town offers much less of interest to book lovers."

Once Libri had the stolen books in his possession, he took pains to create false provenances for them. He added call numbers and shelfmarks, he altered identifiers such as colophons and inscriptions, and he replaced bindings. Libri kept a set of Renaissance-style binding tools, which he used to restore and "improve" fine bindings. He also sent some of the French manuscripts to Florence to be rebound in Italianate half-bindings of wooden boards and leather spines. He gave French manuscripts false Italian provenances. With the help of paid forgers, for example, he "relocated" manuscripts from Fleury to Florence by changing "Floriacensis" to "Florentinae." The forgers also erased stamps and seals, washed away incriminating marginalia in volumes that were well known to scholars, and forged ownership inscriptions by copying legitimate ones from other volumes. Libri's enterprise was as thorough as it was despicable.

After the Revolution of 1848, Félix Boucly's report was rediscovered. The new government now knew what Libri had been up to. An official shared the information with Terrien, a reporter at *Le National*, Libri's printed nemesis. The next day, Terrien saw Libri at an Institut lecture. Libri entered, sporting a tricolor cockade, smiling and shaking hands with those he knew. Terrien, convinced of Libri's guilt, penned a bold note that brought the affair to a head.

> Monsieur, you are doubtless ignorant of the discovery in the Ministry of Foreign Affairs of a judicial report regarding your work as inspector of public libraries. Believe me, you must spare the new society reactions they would find repugnant. Come not again to the Institut.

Libri hurried back to his apartment, frantically packed his books, and burned his papers. Using a friend's passport he crossed the Channel with his wife, Guizot's daughters, and eighteen cases of books, valued at 25,000 francs. In England, Libri posed as a political refugee and was welcomed by real exiles such as Panizzi and Guizot.

Back in France, an expert panel published a damning formal indictment. Tried in absentia in June 1850, Libri was sentenced to ten years' imprisonment "and the deprivation of his civil rights."

Despite everything, Libri still had his fans. Prosper Mérimée published "such a loud defence of his friend that the courts ordered him to appear before them, accused of contempt." Though Libri, too, published pamphlets contesting the French verdict, his guilt was increasingly clear to all, including the Earl of Ashburnham, who suspected at an early stage in the affair that "fraudulent attempts" had been made to hide the true provenance of the Libri manuscripts. For three decades the French and Italian governments doggedly pursued the stolen manuscripts. (Tim Munby described the full saga in his 1968 Harvard lecture "The Earl and the Thief" and its 1969 sequel, published in the *Harvard Library Bulletin*, "The Triumph of Delisle.") True to his character, Ashburnham made the recovery of the stolen books as difficult as it could possibly be.

When the French ambassador offered to refund what Ashburnham had paid for the manuscripts, in exchange for their return to France, the earl refused. Unluckily for Ashburnham, the Libri manuscripts were not the only stolen property in his collection. Sixty-four of the Barrois manuscripts had been filched from the Bibliothèque Royale. Léopold Delisle became Keeper of Manuscripts at that library in 1847. He then became Administrateur général of the Bibliothèque Nationale, as it had become, in 1874. After studying catalogues of the Ashburnham holdings, Delisle published an article showing that some of the Barrois manuscripts had certainly been stolen, while those from Libri gave rise to "curious observations." He remarked, generously, that while he lamented France's loss of these treasures, he was comforted to know they were "in the gallery of an illustrious book lover, who appreciates their true value and to whom French erudition already owes so much." Delisle made it his mission to ensure the return of the manuscripts.

Ashburnham's death in 1878 opened the way to more fruitful

negotiations. The new Lord Ashburnham agreed to divide the collection. The British Museum acquired the Stowe manuscripts for £45,000. Italy paid £23,000 for the genuinely Italian Libri manuscripts. And, with help from the bookseller Karl Trübner of Strasbourg, the French government acquired 166 French Libri and Barrois manuscripts.

The manuscripts bought by the Italian government were chained to desks in Michelangelo's Sala until the 1920s. Afterwards, they were kept out of view, their chains still attached, permanently recalling their medieval and Renaissance origins and occasionally haunting the reading room with ghostly rattling. In France, the books of Leviticus and Numbers were restored to the Lyon Pentateuch. The Bibliothèque Nationale retained the other repatriated French manuscripts: Delisle refused to return to provincial libraries the manuscripts that had been lost by the provincial librarians, and for whose recovery the provinces had done nothing. Having never really liked his father's books, the fifth earl spent the sale proceeds on speculative business ideas and, in the words of his nephew, "what may loosely be called fun."

In 1868 an aged and unwell Libri returned to Florence, where he received a warm welcome—and died soon after. Recently, the beautiful sixteenth-century Girolamini Library in Naples, one of the oldest libraries in Italy, endured a sad modern echo of Libri's crimes.

The treasures among the library's 160,000 volumes included Galileo's 1610 *Sidereus Nuncius*, Kepler's *Astronomia Nova* and a 1518 edition of Thomas More's *Utopia*. These were some of the prizes on offer when the library's director, Marino Massimo de Caro, and its curator, Sandro Marsano, began stealing from the library audaciously and on a massive scale.

The two men were aided and abetted by three Argentinians and one Ukrainian. To hide the volumes' provenance, just as Libri had, the conspirators removed seals and shelf-marks, and in some cases whole bindings. The library's incriminating catalogue was also destroyed. A single load of five hundred books earned the gang a €1 million advance from a German auction house. Apart from his involvement in the theft of around 1,500 important books and manuscripts, de Caro also commissioned and disseminated forgeries. In Argentina, for example, he had forgers make copies of *Siderius Nuncius*: de Caro sold one of the copies to the national library in Naples.

A well-known figure in the book trade (he had also worked as an adviser to a Russian energy tycoon), de Caro had political connections in Italy; he used these, again just as Libri had done, to provide cover for his crimes. Those crimes only came to light after a chance encounter. In the spring of 2012, art history professor Tomaso Montanari called on the closed library and was shocked to find inside a busy scene of disarray: piles of books, garbage on the floor, stray dogs, and a stray blonde, reportedly wearing a tracksuit and carrying a beauty-case on her way to the bathroom. Montanari alerted the police, and in March 2013 de Caro was sentenced to seven years in prison. The sentence was commuted to house arrest because he cooperated with the investigators.

With the active support of the International League of Antiquarian Booksellers, the Italian authorities recovered nearly all the stolen books. The library reopened, under tight security, in October 2015 as part of Domenica di Carta (Paper Sunday).

Book wheels and machines

In *Gulliver's Travels*, Lemuel Gulliver describes how, in Brobdingnag, the library of King Glumdalclitch holds around 1,000 volumes in a gallery 1,200 feet long. To enable tiny Gulliver to read the king's books,

> The queen's joyner had contrived [a] wooden machine five and twenty foot high, formed like a standing ladder, the steps were each fifty foot long. It was indeed a moveable pair of stairs, the lowest end placed at ten foot distance from the wall of the chamber. The book I had a mind to read was put up leaning against the wall. I first mounted to the upper step of the ladder, and turning my face towards the book, began at the top of the page, and so walking to the right and left about eight or ten paces according to the length of the lines, till I had gotten a little below the level of mine eyes, and then descending gradually till I came to the bottom.

Other famous library inventions include Father Antonio Piaggio's device for unraveling the carbonized scrolls from Herculaneum; Congreave's book reacher, which had metal jaws and reminded Melvil Dewey of an apple picker; the revolving shelf and revolving bookcase made by Dewey's Library Bureau; St. Jerome's lazy Susan–style rotating book stand; Ramelli's sixteenth-century paddle steamer–style book wheel, which helped gouty old men handle large folios at Wolfenbüttel; Charles Coley's spring-loaded "book ejection apparatus" (U.S. patent no. 4,050,754); Orville Owen's "Wheel of Fortune," an instrument of Shakespearean heresy constructed as a rotating collage of the works of Francis Bacon and his contemporaries; Lord Spencer's wheeled "siege machine," which allowed him to reach high books at Althorp in comfort; Hinman's collator, a device for detecting differences between editions of Shakespeare; the "Penguincubator" vending machine for Penguin paperbacks; and the eighteenth-century "cockfighting" library chair. Dr. Johnson kept in his library an apparatus for undertaking chemical experiments. The most intriguing machine from ancient times, the wheeled "Antikythera Mechanism," seems to have been a mechanical textbook.

CHAPTER 12

———— ◆ ————

"The interior of a library should whisper"

The Pierpont Morgan Library

Fernando Columbus's sixteenth-century library in Seville was the first of many important book collections to be financed with American money. The greatest of these was assembled in New York, late in the nineteenth century and early in the twentieth.

Born in Hartford, Connecticut, on April 17, 1837, John Pierpont Morgan moved to London at the age of seventeen. There, his wealthy and domineering financier father, Junius Spencer Morgan, jointly led the investment house of George Peabody & Co. After a brief stint at a Swiss boarding school, Morgan attended the University of Göttingen, where Gerlach Adolph Freiherr von Münchhausen had been first curator of the University Library, where the brothers Jacob and Wilhelm Grimm had also served as librarians, and where the American author and Hispanist George Ticknor had studied before helping establish the Boston Public Library.

(The first professor of modern languages and literature at Harvard University, Ticknor became president of the Boston Public Library's Board of Trustees. He gave the library money and thousands of books, including, by bequest, his own large collection of Spanish, Portuguese, and Catalan literature, after Harvard pointedly turned it down.)

Returning to New York in 1857, Morgan began his business career under the watchful eye of his father—who thought his son impetuous—and other senior minders such as Charles Dabney and Anthony Drexel. Morgan's professional peers and business associates portrayed him as brusque and abrupt. He did make friends, though, including with Jonathan Sturges and his pianist wife, Mary. Occupying a fashionable town house, the "faintly Bohemian" Sturges household was a gathering place for artists, such as J. F. Kensett, and musicians, such as L. M. Gottschalk. In that environment, Morgan fell in love with the Sturgeses' "high-minded," "refined," "well-educated," "sweet-looking" daughter Amelia, nicknamed Memie. The love affair was doomed from the start.

Amelia's consumptive illness did not show itself at the beginning of the courtship. But, by the spring of 1861, the deadly disease was in full swing. Morgan still told his friends of the couple's engagement, and he expressed a determination to press on with the marriage. Perhaps he had an idea of saving Memie's life by taking her abroad. Whatever his plans, the Sturgeses opposed the match: how could he marry a girl who, in all likelihood, had only a few months to live?

Morgan's own family refused to attend the melancholy wedding that took place at the Sturges home on October 7, 1862. The bridegroom had to carry the bride downstairs to the back parlor, where

Dr. Tyng conducted the brief ceremony. Memie was unable to join the guests for the wedding breakfast. As soon as the formalities were over, the couple left for England, then went on to Algiers and Nice. There, just four months after the wedding, Memie died.

When Morgan returned to New York he attended a Sanitary Commission fair and purchased his first oil painting: a portrait by George F. Baker of a "young and delicate looking woman"—a reminiscence of Memie that would hang for many years over the mantel in Morgan's home. Three years after Memie's death, Morgan married Frances Louisa Tracy, the daughter of a New York lawyer. The marriage produced four children: Louisa, Juliet, Anne, and J. P. Junior, known to everyone as Jack.

In his fifth and sixth decades, Morgan was gradually freed of his minders. Charles Dabney died in 1879. In April 1890, Morgan's father was riding in an open carriage near his Monte Carlo villa while holidaying on the Riviera. A passing train spooked the horses. Junius Spencer Morgan—the man who'd sent Morgan to boarding school and Germany, and who'd boycotted his son's first wedding—was thrown to the stony roadside and died soon after. Hard upon a third departure—Anthony Drexel died in 1893— Morgan changed the name of his New York business from Drexel, Morgan & Co. to J. P. Morgan & Co. His thirty-year probation was over. Morgan was now his own man, and one of the world's most powerful bankers and financiers.

From this point on, his annual visits to London and the Continent ceased to be those of a penitential subordinate and became instead a means to indulge what biographer George Wheeler called Morgan's "growing pleasure in collecting great objects of art." Morgan's business activities attracted scrutiny from investigators and Senate subcommittees. But patrician Morgan had little patience with "the demands of representative government." The banker's priorities were obvious to all. In 1896, in the face of a pending congressional summons, he pursued the magical Gutenberg Bible that was once owned by Cardinal Mazarin and curated by Gabriel Naudé. In a "lordly response" to the subcommittee summons, Morgan made clear his frame of mind:

> "My firm cable me of your notice," he said in a wire to Senator Isham Harris of Tennessee, the subcommittee chairman, sent from London on May 26. "Regret absence from country will delay, but will sail Wednesday next week, *Teutonic*, and hold myself at the call of your committee."

Morgan attempted to create an English or European "gentleman's library" in New York. His buying reflected a Dibdinesque taste: medieval and Renaissance manuscripts, early printed books (preferably on vellum), fine bindings, historical autographs, old master drawings, Shakespeare, and modern literary manuscripts such as Hawthorne's notebooks, Thoreau's journals, and the manuscripts of Keats's *Endymion*, Dickens's *A Christmas Carol*, and Zola's *Nana* (which Madame Zola later tried to buy back). Morgan was so successful that he far surpassed the libraries he sought to emulate.

Apart from becoming America's foremost book-collector, Morgan also acquired art: Egyptian funerary sculpture, Chinese bronzes, and paintings by Raphael, Vermeer, and Fragonard. "No price," he was reported to have said, "is too high for an object of unquestioned beauty and known authenticity." Those words carried an unexpected sting. Sometime in the 1890s he showed five of his Chinese porcelain beakers to art dealer Joseph Joel Duveen.

In a Chatwinesque "it's a fake" frame of mind, the visitor looked at the five, then raised his walking stick and smashed two of them.

To assemble his library, Morgan purchased individual items—like the Mainz Psalter of 1459—as well as entire collections. He bought, for example, the libraries formed by James Toovey, Theodore Irwin, and Richard Bennett (an eccentric Mancunian who, like Heber, preferred smaller books, even going further and refusing to allow large folios in his library). The latter collection included one hundred illuminated manuscripts and thirty-two books printed by Caxton.

Morgan's "inebriate" collecting forays were likened variously to "a sailor on shore leave"; a "tipsy dowager with unlimited credit moving down Fifth Avenue on a riotous shopping trip"; and "a Medici prince or even a pharaoh." Morgan pursued artifacts in the same manner in which he chased books. "He began emptying Egypt of treasure at such a rate that on one of his visits he was scolded by Lord Kitchener."

In 1880 Morgan had moved to a large brownstone at Madison Avenue and 36th Street. To accommodate his growing library and art collection, he began planning a separate structure to the east of his house. He bought every piece of property on the 36th Street block between his home and the Madison Avenue corner. He also bought the home of the architect Cass Canfield, on the Park Avenue corner. He then had the buildings demolished, and engaged Charles F. McKim, of McKim, Mead & White, as principal architect for the library project.

The resulting structure is a beautiful, if architecturally confused, mansion. Completed in 1906 and executed in pinkish white Tennessee marble, the building blended Peloponnesian, Italianate, Elizabethan, and Edwardian elements. The facade features Doric pilasters, Ionic columns, and an arched portico based on Bartolomeo Ammannati's garden loggia of the Villa Giulia, and Annibale Lippi's Villa Medici.

Though McKim expressed the view that the interior of a library should "whisper and not shout," the opulently colored and ornamented interior makes a certain amount of noise. Three rooms embrace a monumental vaulted foyer known as the Rotunda. McKim conceived the largest room, the East Room, as a space for book storage and display. The West Room was Morgan's private study, the North Room the librarian's office. In the Rotunda, Skíros marble pilasters adorn the walls, and columns of cipollino marble flank the doorways. The marble floor was modeled on the Villa Pia in the Vatican gardens. Inspired by Pinturicchio and Raphael, the artist H. Siddons Mowbray decorated the Rotunda and the East Room with Renaissance-style paint and stucco.

The East Room's walls soar ten meters high and are lined floor to ceiling with triple tiers of bookcases of inlaid Circassian walnut. Hidden spiral staircases give access to the galleries. An enormous sixteenth-century Pieter Coecke van Aelst tapestry—purchased by Morgan in 1906 and depicting, truthfully, the triumph of Avarice—hangs over the fireplace. The elaborate ceiling paintings feature classical imagery and references to Europe's great artists and thinkers, such as Dante, Botticelli, Michelangelo, Socrates, Herodotus, Galileo, Columbus, and Caxton. Zodiac signs on the ceiling correspond to Morgan's date of birth, the date of his second marriage, the sign Morgan assumed as a member of the New York Zodiac Club, and the sign under which Memie died.

In the West Room, whose ceiling Morgan purchased in Florence, he displayed his collection of porcelain, sculpture, paintings, and other *objets d'art*. Channeling Gabriel Naudé, Francis Henry

Taylor called the Morgan library one of the Seven Wonders of the Edwardian World. It was finished just in time to provide Morgan "with a setting of truly anachronistic magnificence" during the stock market panic of 1907. Hosting a series of all-night meetings, the library served as Morgan's nocturnal command post during the weeks of panic.

In 1905 Morgan appointed Belle da Costa Greene as his librarian and "general aide-de-camp." The surname "da Costa" was a pseudo-Portuguese fiction. "Greene," too, was a falsity; Belle's name at birth was Belle Marian Greener. She'd gone straight from public school to a job at the Princeton University library. Morgan's scholarly nephew Junius may have met her there; it was he who introduced her to Morgan. Exotic Greene was even more bohemian than the Sturgeses. She was also promiscuous; the Renaissance expert Bernard Berenson headed the long list of her lovers. (When later asked if she was Morgan's mistress, she answered candidly, "We tried!") Designer clothes were another well-known taste. "Just because I am a librarian," she declared, "doesn't mean I have to dress like one."

Greene's goal was to make Morgan's library one that was renowned for classics, as well as for bindings and manuscripts. From 1908 she traveled regularly to Europe, staying at the Ritz and other deluxe hotels and befriending the leading bookmen of the era. As an acquirer of books, she was startlingly effective. On one successful buying trip to London, she snaffled up Lord Amherst's seventeen Caxtons in "private negotiations" the night before they were to be sold at auction.

Morgan died in Rome on the doubly unlucky date of March 13, 1913. His legacy, though, was in good shape. His collection of books and art accounted for half the estate's $128 million value. The great bulk of that estate passed to Morgan's only son. (Among other specific bequests, Morgan left Belle Greene $50,000.) Jack Morgan sold some of the art to pay taxes and improve cash flow. But he enhanced rather than eroded the book collections. In 1915 Greene wrote to the London bookseller Quaritch. "I am glad to tell you that [Jack has] a strong interest in the library and promised that I may go on collecting books and manuscripts when the war is over." Jack added 206 illuminated manuscripts as well as important incunabula, one of them an indulgence printed by Gutenberg. Jack's acquisitions brought the total number of Morgan incunabula to about 2,000.

In 1924 Jack turned the book collection into a public reference library, the Pierpont Morgan Library, which he vested in trustees, and gave $1.5 million. His goal was to render the collections permanently available to the American public, so that people could enjoy and learn from them. Belle Greene stayed on as the library's first director.

One of the Morgan Library's most intriguing books played a central part in a medieval scandal. Jacquemart de Hesdin worked as an illuminator for the Duc de Berry. In 1398 Hesdin accused a rival illuminator of stealing his colors and his pattern sheets. Aided by his brother-in-law Jean Petit, Hesdin murdered the rival. The killers were tried—and pardoned. The pattern-book is now in the Morgan.

Another highlight of the library is an evocative group of manuscripts that came from an unlikely place. In the spring of 1910, villagers were digging for fertilizer at the site of the destroyed Monastery of the Archangel Michael, in Egypt's Fayyum oasis, near present-day Hamuli. In an old stone cistern the villagers found sixty Coptic manuscripts. The following year, J. P. Morgan acquired fifty-four of them. Written in Sahidic (a Coptic dialect) and ranging in date from 823 to 914 A.D., they formed the oldest, largest, and most important group of early Coptic manuscripts with a single provenance. Evidently, early in the tenth century, the monks had buried the monastery's entire library in the cistern for safekeeping, shortly before the monastery closed for good.

The manuscripts feature simple, even crude depictions of the Holy Family; the thought might have crossed Morgan's mind that they were forgeries. (Chatwin and Duveen would no doubt have denounced them as such.) But the find was well documented and authenticated. The manuscripts passed through the hands of J. Kalebdian and Arthur Sambon, a French numismatist and dealer. Henri Eugene Xavier Louis Hyvernat, a Franco-American Coptologist, Semitist, and orientalist, studied and photographed them. Further supporting their authenticity, nearly all the manuscripts were found in their original bindings. About twenty have decorative or pictorial frontispieces, typically a large ornamented cross with interlace patterns. One of the manuscripts—John Chrysostom's *Encomium on the Four Bodiless Beasts*, illuminated by Papa Isak and dated 892–93 A.D.—contains one of the earliest extant images of the Virgin nursing Christ.

Morgan also gathered a treasure of manuscripts from Europe, including examples from St. Gall and nearby Lindau. His first major medieval acquisition was the ninth-century Lindau Gospels, which rank as one of the great masterpieces of his collection. He acquired the volume in 1901. Its richly jeweled gilt, silver, and enamel cover is one of the best surviving examples of a medieval treasure binding, and one of several examples of that art form in the library. The inside covers are lined with precious patterned silks from Byzantium and the Middle East. The book itself was made at St. Gall. It features twelve richly illuminated canon tables. Each of the four gospels begins with a marvelous double-page spread featuring the opening words of the gospel text. The copying of the texts involved the work of as many as seven different scribes. A monk named Folchart, one of St. Gall's preeminent artists, seems to have been responsible for some of the richer illuminated pages.

Another Morgan prize with a St. Gall connection is an illuminated epistle lectionary and missal for Holy Saturday. Purchased by Morgan in 1905, it features ninety-two vellum leaves decorated with three large illuminated interlace-pattern initials and 144 smaller initials. The manuscript was made at St. Gall in about 880 A.D. Morgan also acquired important printed books, including the Gutenberg Bible printed on vellum, the first English prayer book (which was also the first English book printed on vellum), the earliest surviving book that was printed in Italy, and all four Shakespeare folios.

Helene Hanff, visiting in 1976, was unimpressed with the Pierpont Morgan Library. "You enter a dark, airless hall with heavy mahogany doors." The red plush and mahogany made the West Room "suffocating," an "oppressive mausoleum" that gave Hanff the cold horrors. The nearby mansion that housed the Frick Collection— assembled by Henry Clay Frick, the Pittsburgh coke and steel industrialist—was a contrast and a relief: "white stone outside, white stone and marble inside . . . almost a shock, coming to it as we did from the sombre darkness of the Morgan. The Frick is all light and air."

When disaster strikes

A scene from the 1999 film *The Mummy* is set in a Cairo library in which the hapless librarian causes a shelf to topple over. The falling bookcase causes a chain reaction. In its turn, every bookshelf in the library falls over and loses its books.

Something similar happened in 1968 at Northwestern University. A heavy, freestanding section of empty shelving fell against shelves that were full of books. John Camp and Carl Eckelman reported on the incident in their technical paper on library book stacks: "a domino effect toppled twenty-seven ranges, spilling 264,000 volumes, splintering solid oak chairs, flattening steel footstools, shearing books in half, destroying or damaging more than 8,000 volumes."

No one was injured, but an employee was killed in 1983 by the collapse of similar shelving at the Records Storage Center of Ewing Township, New Jersey.

In the same year, at the Coalinga District Library in California, an earthquake scattered the collections. According to Camp and Eckelman's paper, "The card catalogue toppled over, wall shelves collapsed, some stacks twisted, and two-thirds of the library's 60,000 books spilled to the floor." The same tectonic risks led the Huntington Library in San Marino to use bungee cords to restrain the contents of its shelves.

In 1726, King John V of Portugal purchased the manuscript collection of Charles Spencer, Third Earl of Sunderland. The

Lisbon earthquake of 1755 destroyed many of the valuable manuscripts—including treasures that Sunderland had purchased in Venice in 1720 and, most tragically of all, Gian Francesco Poggio Bracciolini's handwritten copy of the St. Gall Quintilian, which Sunderland had acquired in 1712 from the library of Nicolaas Thomas van der Marck at The Hague.

Ladders were a late arrival in the history of libraries: the number of books had to reach a critical level before high shelves were warranted. (Before resorting to a ladder, Christopher Wren used a stool with safely splayed legs.) The hooked ladder was a nineteenth-century innovation. Melvil Dewey described an example that he first saw in Birmingham and later in the Locust Street branch of the Philadelphia Library, where it was installed in 1880. The ladder was suspended from bronze hooks running along a pipe, which made "an annoying metal-on-metal sound whenever the ladder was used."

As soon as librarians climbed ladders they fell from them. At the Tripitaka Koreana, ladders lead to a perilously narrow suspended plank which gives access to higher shelves. At one eighteenth-century German library, the books were so shelved that, to reach them, librarians needed "the agility of a tight-rope walker or a roofer." Tim Munby wrote of a Cambridge library in which a volume of Hansard was shelved high above an entrance door that managed to move the ladder away every time it was opened: "It is not for nothing that mountaineering has a major part in the pursuits of the Fellows of the College."

In 1834 Friedrich Adolph Ebert, formerly head librarian at Wolfenbüttel, returned to his old town of Dresden, where he fell to his death from a library ladder.

CHAPTER 13

———— ❧ ————

For the Glory

The Folger Shakespeare Library

Eugene Scheifflin, one of the first Americans to collect Shakespeare, loved birds as much as he loved the bard. Scheifflin introduced European starlings to New York as one stage in his epic plan, to naturalize in the United States every bird mentioned in Shakespeare. He imported the starlings from England and released sixty of them in Central Park in 1890. A further forty took flight in 1891. Scheifflin hoped the birds would thrive and breed. They did. Today, there are almost as many European starlings in North America as there are people.

J. P. Morgan collected Shakespearean highlights in the face of strong competition from other bibliophiles and bardologists. Harry Elkins Widener was one of those competitors. In 1907 Widener bought, from a New York stockbroker via Abraham Rosenbach, a well-preserved copy of the First Folio. Five years later, Widener attended the Sotheby's London auction of the library of Henry Huth, co-founder of the Bibliographical Society. There, Widener bought the second edition of Francis Bacon's *Essays*. "I think I'll take that little Bacon with me in my pocket," he said, "and if I am shipwrecked it will go down with me." A few days later, he and the book sank with the *Titanic*. Widener's mother donated his First Folio to the Harvard Library.

During J. P. Morgan's life, his fellow New Yorker Henry Clay Folger had been another competitor for bookish treasure. Folger possessed less money but more focus, especially in the market for First Folios. In fact, Folger was gripped by Foliomania of the most acute kind. Not that Folger lacked money: as an executive at Standard Oil, a firm that enjoyed a near monopoly on domestic fuels, he rubbed shoulders and played golf with the Rockefellers. (Folger invented a new type of golf putter, which he used like a croquet mallet.) Paradoxically, Folger benefited when the antitrust authorities split Standard Oil into multiple businesses; at that moment, his annual income rose from about $50,000 to around $650,000. A large part of this income went towards Shakespeareana, and especially towards the acquisition of First Folios.

Though some prizes did get away, Henry Folger became the world's greatest collector of Shakespeare. (One copy that escaped him was the famed "Bodleian Folio." The Bodleian Library had sold that copy of the First Folio in the 1660s when the "better" Third Folio came available—just as the unsentimental monks of St. Gall had replaced their *Vetus Latina* with a "better" Bible. In hindsight, the sale caused grave embarrassment. When the Bodleian Folio resurfaced, in poor condition and having fallen into the ownership of the Turbutt family of Derbyshire, the new masters of Oxford's library were determined to get it back. A public appeal was launched. More than eighty subscribers pledged money and a total of £3,000 was paid to return the book to its rightful place.) Apart from Shakespearean books, Folger also bought musical instruments and other artifacts of Elizabethan and Jacobean interest.

In August 1915, German submarine U-24 torpedoed the White Star Line's RMS *Arabic*. In just nine minutes the ship sank, taking with it forty-four lives (390 were saved) and a cargo, en route to Folger, of twenty-five letters written by David Garrick. The following year, Standard Oil launched a tanker to transport fuel to Europe. The company called the ship SS *H. C. Folger*. Protected by naval escorts, it survived dozens of wartime voyages, mainly to British and French ports; in the ship's worst brush with danger, a torpedo passed within fifty meters of the hull. Folger did not attend the ceremony to launch his namesake: he was "busy at his desk at 26 Broadway, filling out a loan application to borrow $20,000 . . . to buy more Shakespeare."

Henry Folger would eventually assemble a collection that was more than twice the size of Lord Spencer's at Althorp. He bought so many books and paintings and artifacts that he forgot what he owned. When finally the collection was decanted and tallied up, the numbers involved were large: in excess of a million items of Shakespearean interest; more than 250,000 books; 60,000 manuscripts; 200 oil paintings; 50,000 other images; and a vast collection of theater ephemera, sculptures, instruments, and costumes.

Phobic, even paranoid, about publicity, Henry Clay Folger stored his books in bank vaults and lockups, and strove to keep his purchasing and his collection secret. This was, of course, impossible. Sidney Lee, president of the Shakespeare Society in England, was attempting an up-to-date census of the surviving copies of Shakespeare First Folios. Lee knew of many of Folger's purchases, but the American's voracity and secrecy drove Lee to distraction. For Lee, Folger's conduct was almost as vexing as that of the Irish "Dragon" who deliberately bought the books everyone else wanted, then hid them away. Inquiries about Folger's holdings were continually rebuffed. A young Rhodes Scholar grumbled that, when researchers wrote to Mr. Folger asking to see rare manuscripts, Folger would reply:

> I am sorry that I cannot let you see the manuscript you refer to, for I bought it some time ago and with my other first editions and manuscripts I have wrapped it in brown paper and put it away in a vault. As I keep my brown paper parcels in twenty different banks and I do not remember which is in which, I cannot comply with your request.

Lee complained that Folger "seems to think First Folios ought to be put in a bin in cellars like fine vintages." He bemoaned the Americans like Folger who were "stripping this country of rare early editions of Shakespeare's plays and poems—editions which had long been regarded as among its national heirlooms."

Folger for his part was frustrated by Lee's census busywork, which tended to drive up values as owners learned what they possessed, and what their possessions might be worth. Late in life, Folger and his wife, Emily, made plans for a suitably grand building that would house their collection. They would fund the library with the fortune they held in Standard Oil shares. For the jobbing artist who painted likenesses of George V and Mussolini, Henry sat—holding a book—for a portrait that he would hang in the library. He had taken the subway to the artist's studio, carrying the chosen volume wrapped not in brown paper but in newspaper. The volume was the so-called "False Folio," the first collected edition of Shakespeare's plays, a hundred times rarer than the First Folio. Henry had paid $100,000 for it, making it the most expensive book in the world. This is what Folger wrapped in newspaper and carried on the subway.

In Washington, D.C., Folger bought and demolished a row of brownstones on East Capitol Street, a block away from the Library of Congress. Throughout the planning of the new library, Folger consulted his more established neighbor. Americana and other English-language works were an obvious focus, but the Library of Congress also built early strengths in Slavic, Hispanic, and Asian languages. George Herbert Putnam was an "epoch-making" director at the library. His approach and methods influenced the management and operation of libraries in Scandinavia, the Holy See, and elsewhere in Europe and North America. He and Henry Folger struck up a cordial relationship and agreed to maintain complementary footprints and collection scopes. Folger commissioned a building that, outwardly at least, harmonized with the other institution's architectural style.

Just as Michelangelo had done at the Laurentian Library, Henry attended to every detail of his new building: the systems for heating, cooling, and fire prevention; the uses of each room; the style of the furnishings; the placement of artworks; the height of the ceilings; the timber used for paneling; the musculature of the sculptures; the sumptuousness of the toilets; the recycling of bricks from the demolished brownstones. He specified that the sculpture in the

"Elizabethan garden" would feature Puck, "embowered in shrubbery." He also placed great emphasis on fire prevention. Though ultimately he opted for real timber, he found and considered asbestos panels that had been used in home libraries "to simulate ancient oak."

Most planning for the library was completed before the 1929 Wall Street Crash. With books stored at dozens of locations across the city, tracking them down and moving them into the library took six months and required a massive logistical effort. All this work had a splendid goal, but Henry never experienced the delight of unpacking his books and seeing them all together. Less than a year after the crash, the library not yet built, Henry died during what was supposed to be routine surgery. In the shadow of the stockmarket collapse, the value of his shares halved and the cost of the library doubled. Henry's Shakespeare project was at risk of its own collapse.

Emily, though, vowed to continue the project as she and her husband had envisioned it. Construction was overseen by the man who supervised erection of the Flatiron skyscraper in New York and the Tomb of the Unknown Soldier in Washington. The building was completed in 1932, just two years after the cornerstone had been laid. With an Art Deco exterior in white marble, the two-story library looked as modern and streamlined as a Bakelite radio. And the contrast between the exterior and interior was even greater than that between the Morgan and the Frick. The interior was all dark wood and faux Elizabetheana. People entering the Folger Library were struck by the jarring, instantaneous transition from a high-modern aesthetic to an early-modern one. Henry and Emily had conceived of the interior as "the First Folio, illustrated."

A deeply evocative place—ranking alongside the Winterthur Library as one of the world's best examples of a specialist center for historical and documentary research—the finished library is a remarkable monument to the Folgers, and especially to Henry's Shakespeare mania. Washingtonians, and indeed all Americans, embraced the library as a premium stake in the Shakespeare story, and an emphatic representation—physical, political, teleological— of America's claims over Shakespeare and his world. America was, after all, a Jacobean project—just like the First Folio.

Ceremonies to dedicate the Folger Library were held on April 23, 1932, the anniversary of Shakespeare's death and, according to tradition but not documentation, his birth. Present were Emily Folger, some of America's most noted scholars and educators, President and Mrs. Herbert Hoover, and a gathering of other distinguished statesmen, officials, and ambassadors. According to press reports, the opening was the largest cultural gathering ever to be held in Washington. The event was broadcast nationally on radio. The main speaker, descended from Presidents John Adams and John Quincy Adams, taught English literature at Cornell University. One of the most ardent Shakespeareans in the Americas, Professor Joseph Quincy Adams Junior announced that, with the new library, America's capital now had three great memorials that stood out, "in size, dignity and beauty, conspicuous above the rest": the memorials to Washington, Lincoln, and Shakespeare.

Musicians from the American Society of Ancient Instruments played at the opening ceremony. The playlist included Thomas Morley's "It was a Lover and his Lass," transcribed from the Folger Library copy of Morley's *First Book of Ayres*. The society performed on the library's own treble viol, viola da gamba, virginal, and clavichord. The "handsome new Folger Shakespeare Library" was celebrated in the press as a noble shelter for "Shakespeare Treasures." The *Washington Post* published a Folger Shakespeare

Memorial Library Supplement. "The Folger Shakespeare Library," the supplement cooed, "is conceded by critics of architecture to be one of the noblest small buildings in the world. Of delicate and harmonious lines and of graceful proportions, the structure may be likened to a fine gem, skilfully cut and polished by a lapidary genius."

Art critics declared the library "a true work of art"; a "temple to Shakespeare appropriate in all ways"; the newest and fairest diamond in the crown of beauty around Capitol Hill: "glistening white marble fashioned into a form of the utmost simplicity, set in a square of foliage and flowers, makes an appeal to the mind and heart." Thomas M. Cahill wrote appreciatively in the *Post*:

> Word jewels of a master poet now repose in a casket, the excellence of which he may have dreamed but his day never saw. These gems, whose facets often were brightened in a rush-strewn tavern, now are guarded in a house finer than that of good Queen Bess, their fashioner's most exalted patroness.

The builders and tradesmen on the project gloried in having reared the library. "They were like the old craftsmen of the Middle Ages. They loved their work, they were proud to do their best and they are proud of the result." (A construction worker who helped build Yale's Beinecke Library expressed a different sentiment about that building, telling a reporter in 1963, "The whole thing's built crooked.")

Six years after Henry's death, Emily passed away. She bequeathed what remained of her fortune to the library's ongoing management. She also left behind instructions for the making of a special passageway in the library. It would have secret staircases and a cavity wherein would repose her and Henry's ashes. The cavity would be covered by a brass plaque bearing the somewhat impious words, "FOR THE GLORY OF SHAKESPEARE AND THE GREATER GLORY OF GOD." (Due to an unfortunate typographical error, almost as bad as the Wicked Bible, the inscription is rendered very impiously indeed in Henry Folger's 2015 biography as, "FOR THE GLORY OF GOD AND THE GREATER GLORY OF SHAKESPEARE.")

Henry had bought scores of First Folios. Today, the Folger Library stores them in the same way that the first codices were stored: lying down. On its face, this obsessive acquiring of multiple copies seems a decadent, even vulgar pursuit. But scholars comparing the folios have made striking discoveries. Textual changes occurred during the printing process. Differences between copies reveal much about the birth of the canonical texts, and about the editors and compositors who were the midwives to that birth.

Five distinct compositors emerge, each with his own style and character. The five are now identified by the letters A to E. Compositor A was a master of practical presswork, B was sloppy, E an accident-prone apprentice. Scholars have subjected the compositors to a plethora of typographical, grammato-logical, and psychomechanical tests. There are many mysteries in Shakespearean bibliography, but what we know about his compositors provides a priceless patch of certainty. The Folger Folios demonstrate beautifully the fractal nature of bibliography. Every detail matters; every entry point is valid and rewarding.

On the subject of duplicates, the experiences of a Manchester library are salutary. Havana-born Enriqueta Augustina Rylands was the second wife of John Rylands, a prosperous Manchester cotton merchant. When her husband died in 1888 she inherited an estate of more than £2 million. This she spent on philanthropic and cultural causes, among them the John Rylands Library in Manchester.

The core of the Rylands collection was formed through the purchase of one of the finest private libraries ever assembled: Bibliotheca Spenceriana, Lord Spencer's splendid library at Althorp. As First Lord of the Admiralty from 1794 to 1801, Spencer had largely been responsible for giving Nelson the independent command in the Mediterranean that led to the victory of the Nile. Among his many book-world achievements, Spencer was founding president of the Roxburghe Club and a celebrated bidder at the Roxburghe sale. The library at Althorp filled five adjoining rooms: the Long Room, the Raphael Room, the Billiard Room, the Marlborough Room, and the Poet Library. "A Shetland pony might be conveniently kept," Dibdin suggested, "to carry the more delicate visitor from one extremity to the other." Richer than many princes, Spencer collected tens of thousands of fine books and manuscripts dating from the sixteenth to the eighteenth centuries. His library also contained 3,000 incunabula, among them Caxtons, de Wordes, Gutenbergs, and Schoeffers. Spencer had an eye for type.

Enriqueta negotiated the purchase in secret, ultimately paying £210,000 in 1892. Before then, no one had ever paid that much for a collection of books. The acquisition saved the Althorp Library from dispersal and brought a treasure to Manchester—a superb example from the golden era of English private libraries. The Rylands purchase included the Roxburghe *Decameron*, the most expensive book in the nineteenth century.

Apart from buying Spencer's collection, Enriqueta paid for a suitable place to put it: a purpose-built, Gothic pile that became the elegant home of the John Rylands Library. She also acquired other major collections of printed and manuscript material, and gifted those, too, to the library. Upon her death in 1908 she bequeathed a further £200,000, as well as further private collections of books. The library spent the cash rapidly on acquisitions, rather than slowly on operations.

In 1972 the Rylands Library merged with the library of the University of Manchester. The following decade was a time of tight funding and government austerity. The managers of the merged libraries decided to sell ninety-eight "duplicates" that were among the best books from the combined collection. Two-thirds of the books slated for sale had come from Spencer's library.

The sale took place a century after John Rylands's death. Some books were damaged by rough handling in transit and at the pre-auction viewing. Despite spirited bidding by an Italian bookseller under the *nom de vente* "E. P. Benson," the sale was a lackluster affair. The books realized low prices.

Worse still, the library trustees realized too late that the books were not duplicates at all. The copies in the ninety-eight pairs differed meaningfully in illustration, annotation, composition, binding, and provenance. One Spencer incunabulum in the sale featured unique author corrections; one had a unique leaf inserted; several had unique and important fifteenth-century provenance. After the disposal, visitors to Manchester could no longer make textual and typographical discoveries by reading differences between stellar copies of ninety-eight of the first printed books.

The sale caused an outcry. Though measured in different units, the cost to the library's reputation was higher than the revenue raised. Manchester became a less significant place for the study of early typography such as fifteenth-century printing of Ancient

Greek. As a book refuge, it had broken faith with the past. In the aftermath of the uproar, donors elected to send their money and their books elsewhere. The Earl of Crawford withdrew thousands of volumes that he and previous earls had deposited at Manchester. The books went instead to the National Library of Scotland.

Writing in the *Independent*, Nicolas Barker called the sale of the ninety-eight books an unparalleled "rape of the country's literary heritage." Writing further in *The Book Collector*, he said the sale had "destroyed the integrity of a great part of the bibliothecal wealth of this country." The sale, he said, was like pillaging a trilith from Stonehenge.

When Emily Folger passed away, she left behind at the Folger Library a devoted staff that included a dirt-hating, workaholic maid, and Charles Rogers, the nightwatch engineer who had helped dig the Panama Canal. Rogers arrived at the library each day at four in the afternoon, resembling a dapper U.S. Senator who would not be seen without a scarf and gloves.

The collections were notionally open and accessible, but in many respects the library was not very welcoming. Guards stood at the front door. The catalogue was incomplete. The lights in the reading room were not conducive to reading. One observer described the overall atmosphere as "funereal." By changing policies, staff, and operations, and by acquiring gap fillers, complementary books, and better lights, successive librarians unlocked the Folger and made it work more fully as a research library.

The Folger's postwar director Louis Wright broadened the acquisition strategy, particularly in books from the second half of the seventeenth century, such as Jacques Boileau's 1678 work, *A Just and Seasonable Reprehension of Naked Breasts and Shoulders, Written by a Grave and Learned Papist* and *The Compleat English and French Cook* (1690), which contains recipes for many remarkable dishes such as "Eels Boiled" and "Pig-pye after the newest fashion."

Wright was anxious that the Folger be seen as a friendly place. He transformed the front-door sentries into cleaners. In decisions about staffing, he steered clear of a certain type of woman librarian, which he described as "owl-eyed and awkward, wearing spectacles and an air of gloom." Wright searched the northern hemisphere for "bright young women" genuinely interested in books and the operations of a research library. "We are not impressed," he wrote, "when some young thing gushes that she 'just loves Shakespeare.' A love of Shakespeare is less important than common sense and an ability to type." In England, Hungary, Greece, and California he found what he was looking for. One of his prize recruits, a "cheerful young lady" named Janice Jacques, brought a welcoming, Franco-Californian atmosphere to the front office.

Wright painted a picture of staff conditions—and the newly installed roof garden where "girls sunned themselves"—as idyllic as Poggio's water nymphs of Baden. This picture stands in stark contrast to the Vatican Library's cold and "half naked" assistants. Though crows rather than starlings cawed in the magnolias, the Folger's beautiful gardens became an intrinsic part of how the library was experienced.

(Crows infiltrated the Folger in more ways than one. A note in a Folger volume, a 1574 history of the doges of Venice, warns, "Whoever snatches this book, let ravens snatch his guts.")

A network of tunnels, crypts, pseudo-dungeons, and oubliettes lurks beneath the Folger. At the height of the Cold War, some Washingtonians believed atomic destruction was imminent, civilization "hardly worth saving, much less studying." But the Folger's staff, refusing to flee to some "God-forsaken Patagonian refuge," continued to curate and study. Wright knew where he wanted to be when the bombs fell. "The really safe spots are going to be crowded with people we won't like. We'll just stay here and keep our air conditioning going as long as it will run, and read solid Renaissance sermons on innate depravity—a theme which somehow cheers us." Just in case, Wright's team made plans to use the Folger's catacombs as a bomb shelter, where the staff could "sweat it out in highbrow comfort."

(At Yale University, rumors circulated that, in the event of a nuclear attack, the Beinecke Library could descend and become an ultra-modern, über-bookish shelter. The stream that runs beneath the library is just one of several damning problems with that rumor.)

The formal launch of the Folger had coincided with the opening, in Stratford-upon-Avon, of the new Shakespeare Memorial Theatre (now the Royal Shakespeare Theatre). The Folger, too, had a replica playhouse, intended to host academic lectures while evoking Elizabethan England. The theater was not intended for performances; it had no dressing rooms, for example, and did not comply with the fire code. But the Folger did eventually hold plays there. After Wright persuaded the municipal authorities to make an allowance, the theater hosted its first play in 1949: a production of *Julius Caesar* by the Amherst Masquers. Many performances followed, including of some of the more obscure plays from the First Folio.

Like the librarians of Alexandria, and like Herr Doktor Peter Kien of Vienna, Henry Folger was gulled by unscrupulous dealers and artifact pedlars. Many of the First Folios he bought were in poor shape. ("A good copy," "well read," "not in collectible condition," "a reading copy"—these are all book-trade euphemisms for clunkers.) Some Folger First Folios had been scrawled in by children, or were made up with pages from Second Folios and facsimile leaves. Some lacked title pages or other prelims; some lacked whole plays. One copy that Folger purchased in 1907 lacked more than half its leaves—not really a First Folio at all. Cropped, bumped, canted, wormed, worn, food-stained, oil-stained—Folger's folios were a catalogue of woes. In addition to copies that were "too dirty," some were "too clean"—ruined by overzealous washing, a common practice in the nineteenth century. Booksellers smiled when they saw Folger coming.

Apart from being duped into paying over the odds for genuine items, he was also sold forgeries and worthless trifles. For an exorbitant price, a dealer sold him a small picture of David Garrick. The dealer called it an original sketch by Sir Joshua Reynolds. In fact it was a cheap photographic print that a backstreet bookman had dipped in watercolor to add the appearance of age. The value? Maybe twenty cents on a good day. Folger vacuumed up Shakespeare busts whenever they came on the market. One such purchase was an oversized replica, rendered in modern concrete, of Shakespeare's death mask. Long after Folger's own death, Wright offered to trade the mask for something more useful: perhaps "a few loads of good topsoil" for the Folger gardens. Wright offloaded other items of similarly dubious value. The Folger Library's attic bulged with poster-portraits of actors and actresses, "which formerly hung in theatre lobbies and are too big to hang anywhere on our premises. They are just about right for a Texas oil millionaire's mansion, and we shall be receptive to a good offer."

Many visitors to the Folger asked Wright and his staff about an enchanting object in the collection: the corset, which Henry

Folger purchased and which was supposed to have belonged to Queen Elizabeth I. To sate the public's curiosity, Wright had it put on display along with an acknowledgment that the staff could not verify its authenticity.

> It was acquired years ago from a dealer anxious to sell Mr Folger anything of human interest dating from the period. The only provenance the dealer could supply was the statement from an old lady who brought it to his shop that "a tradition in the family said it once belonged to Queen Elizabeth."

Wright sent images of the corset to the Victoria and Albert Museum. Donald King, assistant keeper in the Museum's Department of Textiles, looked closely at the underwear and concluded that it dated from the first half of the eighteenth century, and that "no such corsets are known from the Elizabethan period." Wright reported with regret,

> We cannot even attribute it to Queen Anne or to one of the mistresses of George I, for their known girths were too great for our corset to encompass. We shall have to change our exhibition label to read "One old corset, late Queen Anne or early Georgian."

Other dubious Folger relics include a collection of objects supposedly made from a mulberry tree that Shakespeare planted in Stratford-upon-Avon. A chair, a thimble, a ring, a rolling pin, a tobacco box, a pipe tamper, an inkstand, a goblet, a caddy, and a cassolette. If all the mulberry objects were piled up, they would account for more timber than all the fragments of the True Cross.

The list of forgeries foisted on the Folger also includes fake bindings, several of which pretend to be from the sixteenth century—and are attached to genuine sixteenth-century texts—but were in fact made in the nineteenth century. The library holds, for example, a fake "Apollo and Pegasus" binding (on a 1515 volume of Cicero) that was expertly executed in goatskin. The binding was thought to be authentic, until Anthony Hobson, the world's greatest expert on Renaissance bindings, noticed minute details that gave the game away. In the gilt block on the upper cover, the wheel of Apollo's chariot has four spokes—instead of the requisite six—and the inscription around the central medallion was applied as an integrated part of the block, rather than being tooled separately. The binding, it turns out, was as fake as J. P. Morgan's smashed pots. Vittorio Villa made it (possibly for Demetrio Canevari, a Genoese doctor) by taking a simply decorated sixteenth-century cover and adding gilt decoration to mimic the grand bindings made in Rome in 1545–47 for Giovanni Battista Grimaldi.

Notwithstanding these impostors, the Folger collections are rich with bookish gold. Important manuscripts, fine early editions, sumptuous bindings, extensive ephemera, striking realia. Items of great beauty and incalculable scholarly value. In spectacular fulfillment of its founders' goal, the library is a marvelous memorial to Shakespeare. It is also a first-class research institution. The Folger attracts scholars from around the world and runs a rich program of events. It is no exaggeration to say that the library has become the global head office of Shakespeare studies.

The riven nature of Shakespeare scholarship, though, makes that honor a dubious one. The field has been likened to a shark tank and a snake pit. A thousand controversies persist, and the hottest of these is the so-called Authorship Question—the question of whether Shakespeare wrote Shakespeare. The authorship controversy presents a conundrum for the Folger. What if the unthinkable happens and the question is resolved in favor of one of the many claimants—perhaps Francis Bacon, Christopher Marlowe, Edward de Vere, or Henry Neville? If the heretics are right, then the Folger is a ridiculous institution, dedicated to a lie. This possibility has certainly occurred to the Folger's directors, who have adopted a variety of "risk mitigation strategies" over the years. Broadening the acquisition of early texts is one. Acquiring both orthodox and unorthodox Shakespearean works is another. Several key figures of heretical Shakespeare scholarship are American. Delia Bacon was from Ohio, Orville Owen hailed from Michigan, and Diana Price from Connecticut—and their books are in the Folger.

Though far from being a Shakespeare skeptic, Louis Wright was a key hedger at the Folger. He consistently de-emphasized Shakespeare as the library's focus and rationale. Instead, he augmented the collection to such an extent that it became important worldwide as a sixteenth and seventeenth-century English collection per se, with multiple author and subject strengths. Vocally, Wright opposed Stratford-upon-Avon's "Barnum and Bailey" version of bardology—and this stance won him friends on the side of unorthodoxy. In 1956 a "well-meaning and worried friend of the Folger" asked whether Wright was concerned about the devaluation of the library's assets, "in case the promoters of Christopher Marlowe proved that he wrote Shakespeare's plays." Wright assured the friend cheerfully that the Folger "had hedged years ago by acquiring one of the finest Marlowe collections in the world." As a consequence, the Folger was "sitting pretty"; the friend appeared relieved.

Another Folger Library strategy is to strive to be the go-to place for debating and deliberating on Shakespearean controversies and discoveries. An example is the recent "discovery" by two booksellers of "Shakespeare's Dictionary." The thought processes of the Folger's leaders are easy to picture. How should the library react to what is surely a double try-on by the booksellers—to pump the value of the book, and to secure a publishing deal for the story of their research? The Folger worries about validating bad paleography and bad bibliography, and wants to avoid damage by association. But it also likes to create a buzz around Shakespeare, and to spur and capture the enthusiasm that such finds can generate. Most important of all, the Folger wants to be the destination for people with questions and material like this. By arbitrating and adjudicating the validity of contested Shakespeareana, the Folger can solidify its position as the global Shakespeare authority.

And the final mitigation strategy for the library is a simple one. Be ready, just in case, to change the business cards, the letterhead, the marble frieze, and that unfortunate brass plaque.

Birth

About 85 million years ago—in the time of the dinosaurs—primates diverged from tree shrews and other mammals. About 20 million years ago, the apes diverged from the gibbons. About 8 million years ago, our human and chimpanzee ancestors diverged from gorillas. Between 6 and 4 million years ago, those ancestors diverged from each other—but only after a slow breakup featuring more than a million awkward years of recidivist interbreeding and hybridization. Between 250,000 and 100,000 years ago, humans began to speak. About 5,000 years ago—after the domestication of horses, the cultivation of chili, the brewing of beer, the hoisting of sails, and the spinning of clay—humans began to write. Four years ago, paramedics and librarians helped deliver a baby girl in the children's section of Edmonton Green Library in Lancashire.

———— ❦ ————

CHAPTER 14

Killing a Monk

Fantasy libraries

Marvelous libraries are a staple of fantasy and science fiction. Iain Banks, Philip K. Dick, Terry Pratchett, Douglas Adams, Jack Vance, Jon Sladek, and J.R.R. Tolkien all created striking visions of fantastical libraries. In *Tik-Tok*, Sladek imagined a vast, interplanetary, mobile library. "Tik-Tok," Sladek's humanoid robot antihero, finds himself aboard the Liberian-registered *Doodlebug*, a gargantuan spaceship that was designed to enable the super-wealthy to tour the solar system. But, after an economic slump, the ship was repurposed to transport livestock. Union rules prohibited robots from working on the ship, so Tik-Tok had time on his hands. He frequented the silent ballroom, the deluxe bathrooms, the first-class coffee room, and the first-class library.

To properly explore the library's "incomparable" book collection, Tik-Tok established rules. This day, he could only consult volumes that featured a robot character named Robbie. On another day, books about Mars, or autobiographies of former nuns, or titles beginning with U—titles "often seeming to conceal profane meanings," like *Unspeakable Practices, Unnatural Acts*; *The Urinal of Physick*; *Up the Junction*; *The Unpleasantness at the Bellona Club*; and *Uncle Tom's Cabin*.

In the *Doctor Who* episode "Silence in the Library," the Doctor is trapped on a planet-sized library infested with "tiny piranhas that live in the shadows." At Unseen University on Terry Pratchett's Discworld, magical codices struggle against their chains, and the orangutan librarian is a formidable protector of three things: silence, the library's lending policies, and the physical laws of the universe.

In *Night Lamp* by Jack Vance, the characters Jaro and Skirl find, in the abandoned palace of Somar, a great library crowded with books more than 1,000 years old; "ponderous and thick, with covers of carved board and pages alternating text and hand-wrought illumination." Some of the volumes exhale pleasant fragrances of wax and preservative. A local cavalier explains how each book is a personal record that tells the story of a life. Part diary, part revelation, part poetry, each book is a statement, a repository of secrets and private theories. And each book is richly illustrated by its creator in a revealing personal style. In this way, the books both express and achieve their authors' wishes to live forever. By capturing the creative essence, each book can "clasp time and make it a static thing, so that the person who created the book would forever be alive, half dreaming his way back and forth through the pages he had created so lovingly." Behind the library walls are secret passages, some of which lead to safe-houses, others to the homes of ghouls.

Like *Night Lamp*, Audrey Niffenegger's *The Night Bookmobile* is a fantastical treatment of the themes of books and death. In Niffenegger's book, a young woman has a mysterious nighttime encounter—with a mobile library. The library is a Winnebago–Tardis that contains every book she has ever read, or grazed, or dipped into. The librarian, Mr. Openshaw, carefully curates the collection. After this first encounter, the woman searches for the Night Bookmobile but does not see it for another nine years. When she again meets Openshaw she begs him to employ her as his assistant. He refuses but she enrolls in librarianship studies and goes to work at the Sulzer branch of the Chicago Public Library. Twelve years later she sees Openshaw and the Bookmobile again, but he repeats his refusal to hire her. Only after her death does the answer change. Taking her own life, she finds herself with Openshaw in the "Central Reading Room of The Library." Thereafter, she becomes a Bookmobile librarian and curates the collection that her own designated reader is forming.

The 2014 film *Interstellar* explores the same themes as *Night Lamp* and *The Night Bookmobile*. The film's climax takes place inside a library, which in turn is inside a black hole. The library is a hyper-real version of the brown-toned, ultra-modern, perfectly geometrical Beinecke Library. (From the perspective of the film's astro-pioneer Joseph Cooper, the books are shelved spine-inward, like Odorico Pillone's.) The film has been criticized as overlong, overblown, and, worst of all, implausible. Cooper's entry into the black hole stretches believability but not the spaceman himself; he avoids being splattered in three dimensions or smeared across four. But the climax works exceptionally well. Through the Borgesian metaphor of an infinite library of stacked bookshelves, the film's director solves the problem of depicting unlimited space-time on a limited cinema screen.

Shelves of books are an apt metaphor for communication across time, linking past and future, and an apt signifier of infinity and immortality. The black-hole library is narratively powerful but it also contains physical truth. Curiously, multidimensionality and information both have central places in black-hole physics. A recent theory, for example, proposes that the observable universe is a three-dimensional projection on the event horizon of a four-dimensional black hole. Theories such as this disrupt the frontiers between digital and analogue, and virtual and reality. And they animate a sixth-century Cabbalistic vision, in the *Sefer Yezirah*, of the universe as one created from letters and numbers.

The Smithsonian—"America's attic" or *Kunstkabinett* or mathom house—contains an excellent collection of rocket science books, including rocket pop-ups and sci-fi pulps. The Folger Shakespeare Library, though, is the place to go to see the first book in English to suggest gunpowder as a rocket propellant. "Murtagh McDermot" (a pseudonym) dedicated his 1728 novel *A Trip to the Moon* to Lemuel Gulliver. The book tells a remarkable tale. While climbing the peak of Teneriffe, the narrator is caught in a whirlwind—Dorothy-leaving-Kansas style—and elevated beyond the earth's gravitational pull. Suspended between earth and moon, he fears starvation, but weather again comes into play when he is rescued by a hailstorm. The spaceman has the good fortune to fall into a lunar fishpond, in which the moon king's fisherman hooks the traveler's buttonhole.

The narrator solves the problem of terrestrial reentry by using a crude form of rocketry. He places himself inside ten concentric wooden tubs, the outermost strongly hooped with iron, and blows himself off the moon with the 7,000 barrels of gunpowder he'd buried under his tubs. Again reaching the midpoint between the moon's and the earth's attraction, he crawls from his cockpit, puts on his wings, and follows a flock of migrating birds to Africa. In Guinea he boards a ship bound for Europe, and ultimately returns to Ireland. "Even for a daring Irishman, the trip was difficult." A whirlwind, the narrator remarks, "is not the easiest Vehicle; and being blow'd up is but little better."

For more than a century, science fiction has supplied marvelous visions of future libraries. But the two most marvelous fantasy libraries are pictures of the past.

Author, scholar, and bibliophile Umberto Eco assembled a private library of more than 40,000 volumes, which he stored, Heber-style, in multiple homes in Milan and elsewhere. His academic career centered on the study of words, books, and libraries. At the age of sixteen he explored the Gothic and Romanesque cloisters of a Benedictine monastery. In the monks' library he found, open on a lectern, the *Acta Sanctorum*. Therein he read of his namesake, St. Umberto, the bishop who converted a lion in a forest. Leafing through the folio "in supreme silence, amid shafts of light entering through opaque windows that were almost grooved into the walls and ended in pointed arches," Eco had an epiphany that ultimately led him to create the most captivating library in fiction: the abbey library of the Benedictine monastery in his debut novel, *The Name of the Rose*.

The library is the heart of the book and the fulcrum for its plot. To picture the library, Eco studied and drew hundreds of library plans, abbey plans, mirror galleries, and mazes—Greek, rhizome,

Mannerist, imaginary. The floor labyrinth of Rheims cathedral was one of several especially helpful benchmarks. Known today only from drawings and paintings, that labyrinth was in the shape of an octagon, and had a smaller octagon in each corner, similar in shape to a corner tower. (Canon Jacquemart destroyed the maze in the eighteenth century, allegedly because he was annoyed by children playing there, seeking out the pathways during services.) Particular inspiration also came from Durham Cathedral, Yale's Sterling Library, the monastery of Bobbio, the monolithic St. Michael's Abbey in the mountainous Susa Valley, Piedmont, and St. Gall's ninth-century plan of the ideal monastery and library.

When constructing the abbey library, Eco also had in mind Borges's infinite library. Two years before *The Name of the Rose*, Eco wrote the entry for "Codice" (Codex) in the *Einaudi Encyclopaedia*; the entry includes what Eco called "an experiment on the Library of Babel." His interest in Borges became a benign obsession. As finally conceived, the abbey library in *The Name of the Rose* resembles in many respects Borges's infinite library of interconnected hexagonal rooms. Eco would give his medieval library a blind librarian, and name him "Jorge da Burgos."

When Eco finally began writing the novel in March 1978, a seminal, homicidal idea was in his mind: "I felt like poisoning a monk." Influenced by Conan Doyle and the English detective novel tradition, Eco was fascinated by the idea of a monk absorbing a fatal toxin while reading a book in the library. He asked a biologist friend to suggest a compound that could be absorbed by the skin when handled. The biologist knew of no such poison, and Eco promptly tore up his friend's letter of reply: "it was a document that, read in another context, could lead to the gallows."

Some of the book's first readers were confounded by the

untranslated strings of Latin text. Others were confused by the book's apparent seriousness and genre transcendence. The great majority of readers, though, saw the book for what it was: an intelligent re-take on the mystery genre, set in a medieval world of striking verisimilitude, and containing the most enchanting library ever captured in words,

> the place of a long, centuries-old murmuring, an imper-
> ceptible dialogue between one parchment and another,
> a living thing, a receptacle of powers not to be ruled by
> a human mind, a treasure of secrets emanated by many
> minds, surviving the death of those who had produced
> them or had been their conveyors.

Situating the story and the large library in the late Middle Ages made sense; collections were larger at that time than they had been for most of the medieval period. But the library still attracted charges of anachronism. The "larger" late medieval libraries were not very large: the Sorbonne's collection, for example, one of the world's largest in the late Middle Ages, numbered only 1,720 volumes in 1332. The number of volumes in Eco's abbey library was an order of magnitude larger: 87,000 volumes, a figure that drew criticism from medievalists who, as Polastron noted, "could not help but denounce the heresies of Eco's novel." The number of manuscripts would have required at least 8 million calves and all the world's copyists working for two generations. "Nevertheless, dream and fantasy laugh at accountants."

Tolkien, like Eco, was a medieval scholar. He built much of his academic reputation by editing, translating, and reinterpreting early texts such as *Beowulf* and *Sir Gawain and the Green Knight*. Both Tolkien and Eco were enthralled by early libraries, and by mazes. Both were influenced by Borges. Both, like Borges, wove rich fantasies and were meticulous "world builders." They shared a love of philology; they wrote in multiple languages, they played with the texture of words, and, when their novels appeared, each took pains to help translators render their texts into other tongues. When it came to ornamenting their fictional worlds, both Tolkien and Eco created awe-inspiring libraries.

Tolkien's works are set in the most exquisitely realized and enduringly appealing fantasy world. Middle-earth is a land of Hobbits, dragons, and goblins. It is also a land of libraries. Tolkien invented languages, and he invented books and libraries in which to house them. Intricately wrought by their creator, Middle-earth's libraries come in many different forms. Collections of books are housed in towers, citadels, studies, treasuries, strongrooms, and bedrooms. Tolkien's fiction is a sustained hymn to bibliophilia.

Occupying a pleasant region called the Shire, Hobbits are one of the most bookish races in Middle-earth. Smaller even than most Dwarves, they are genetically human and culturally have much in common with the normal-sized inhabitants of human communities far to the east and southeast. A key difference, though, apart from their height, is that most Hobbits live underground, in neatly excavated and fitted out hillside homes called "smials."

A clever and nimble-fingered people, Hobbits are naturally capable scribes, zealous conservators, and talented craftsmen. In Middle-earth's tumultuous Third Age it is Shire Hobbits who shelter and nurture the noble arts of making and preserving books—just as Irish and Scottish monks did in our Dark Ages. Hobbit book craft peaks early in the Fourth Age, partly as a result of the involvement of Shire folk in the War of the Ring, and partly as a result of the long peace brought about by the war. *The Red Book of Westmarch*, *Herblore of the Shire*, and *The Tale of Years* all date from that period.

The famous Hobbit Bilbo Baggins keeps his book collection in his study. His home, Bag End, is one of the finest smials ever to be dug, and the study is the best room at Bag End. It has everything a civilized Hobbit could ever need: paneled walls, a tiled floor, carpet, fireplace, polished table and chairs, bookshelves, a wooden strongbox, and a single, deep-set, round window that overlooks the garden, the meadows, and the river beyond. The study window is curtained and shuttered to control the light. Bilbo stores in the strongbox his most valuable books and his own works-in-progress. The rest of his books are kept in the shelves. These are built low, because Hobbits are afraid of heights and will never climb a ladder to reach a book.

Hobbit books have leather covers, most of which are brightly colored. An example is *The Red Book of Westmarch*. Unlike Mao's book, the hobbitish *Red Book* is large—and enormous in Shire terms. Like the *Codice Atlantico*, it consists of multiple folio volumes. It is an account of the end of the Third Age and a record of Bilbo and Frodo Baggins's adventures with the One Ring. The book's title is suitably long. Bilbo called the first part of *The Red Book* "My Diary. My Unexpected Journey. There and Back Again. And What Happened After. Adventures of Five Hobbits. The Tale of the Great Ring, compiled by Bilbo Baggins from his own observations and the accounts of his friends. What we did in the War of the Ring." Bilbo's nephew Frodo Baggins then crossed out the old title and added "THE DOWNFALL OF THE LORD OF THE RINGS AND THE RETURN OF THE KING (as seen by the Little People; being the memoirs of Bilbo and Frodo of the Shire, supplemented by the accounts of their friends and the learning of the Wise.) Together with extracts from Books of Lore translated by Bilbo in Rivendell."

Bilbo's own books are all uniformly bound. The four he authored are precisely the same height, and bound in the same style, in the same color leather. Bilbo's book collection is a scaled down model of an English gentleman's library—as befits the status of Bag End: an English country house in miniature, and underground.

The largest Shire libraries are at Undertowers, Great Smials, and Brandy Hall. Undertowers is the home of the Wardens of Westmarch. Great Smials, in Tuckborough, is the mansion of the extended Took family. Brandy Hall, near Bucklebury, is the residence of the Brandybucks. Peregrin Took founded the Great Smials library. Many of the books there were written by scribes from the distant kingdom of Gondor, the most famous being Findegil's copy of *The Thain's Book*, the best facsimile of *The Red Book*. It lacks the original volume's section of genealogies—these were not reproduced in *The Thain's Book*—but it includes all the improvements and additions to *The Thain's Book*, as well as a copy of the whole of Bilbo Baggins's *Translations from the Elvish*. Most of the other books at Great Smials are facsimiles and synopses of histories and legends relating to the ancient island of Númenor, the godlike warrior Elendil and his heirs, and the rise of Satan-like Sauron.

Fondly known to Hobbits as "Yellowskin," *The Yearbook of Tuckborough* is bound in blazing yellow leather. One of the few ancient documents preserved in the Shire, "Yellowskin" pre-dates *The Red Book* by 900 years. It records the births, marriages, and deaths of the Took families, along with various other notable Shire events, and details of land sales in and around Tookland.

The library at Brandy Hall specializes in books concerned

with the history of Eriador (a region that includes the Shire) and Rohan (a region far to the southeast). Many of the books were written or at least begun by Meriadoc Brandybuck, a member of the Fellowship of the Ring. *Herblore of the Shire*, for example, is Merry's history of pipeweed and treatise on smoking methods and connoisseurship. He also wrote a *Reckoning of Years*, which relates the calendars of the Shire and Bree to those of Gondor, Rohan, and the Elvish city of Rivendell; and *Old Words and Names in the Shire*, a volume whose title is self-explanatory. All these books are kept in Brandy Hall's library.

Apart from preserving key books like Yellowskin and *The Thain's Book*, the family seats of all the major Hobbit clans collect the types of shelf-filling volumes that can be found in every second-hand bookshop in Britain: genealogy, local history, poetry, cooking, gardening, sport, and true crime. Shire readers especially delight in tales of burglars, heroes, and "things never seen or done." More popular still are books filled with things that Hobbits already know, "set out fair and square with no contradictions."

The writing of Umberto Eco's first novel took the better part of a decade. In preparing the book, Eco spent whole years writing nothing at all, while he painstakingly scouted imaginary locations. Compared to *The Lord of the Rings*, though, *The Name of the Rose* enjoyed a smooth and speedy pathway into print. Professor Tolkien's epic, eschatological masterwork took so long and went through such trials that it very nearly was not published at all.

The tale of the book began in 1937, when Tolkien's children's story *The Hobbit* was published. He wrote *The Hobbit* as a diversion from his academic work, and from his passion project, a new "mythology for England." He worked on the mythology all his life; eventually it would develop into *The Silmarillion*.

The Hobbit was an instant bestseller, and hard on its release the book's publisher, Stanley Unwin, pressed Tolkien for a follow-up. Tolkien answered that he had "squandered" so much material on *The Hobbit*, which he had not meant to have a sequel, "that it is difficult to find anything new in that world." Nevertheless, he began *The Lord of the Rings* late in 1937. Unwin looked forward to publishing the "*Hobbit* sequel" within three years. He would have to wait somewhat longer.

Tolkien delivered nothing until 1947, a full ten years later, when he showed a typescript to Unwin's son, Rayner. By this time, Tolkien was Merton Professor of English Language and Literature at Oxford. (Bag End's cozy, bookish spaces recall Tolkien's favorite Oxford haunts, such as Arts End at the Bodleian and the rabbit room at the Eagle & Child pub.) The manuscript he submitted was a peculiar work, much longer than the Unwins had anticipated, and aimed at adults rather than children. The first people to read the manuscript were unsure what to make of it. But Rayner urged his father to publish, calling the book brilliant and gripping. In the meantime, Tolkien continued to redraft and redraft, arriving in late 1949 at a version with which he was satisfied.

Around this time, Tolkien flirted with Collins publishers in the belief they would publish both *The Lord of the Rings* and an early version of *The Silmarillion*. In 1937 Unwin had rejected *The Silmarillion* as a sequel to *The Hobbit*, but Tolkien was determined to bundle his mythology with his newest work. He was also dissatisfied with Unwin's efforts to sell his medieval fable *Farmer Giles of Ham*. Hence his dalliance with Collins, who had eyes for *The Hobbit* as well as its siblings.

In April 1950, Tolkien gave Unwin an ultimatum: publish *The Silmarillion* and *The Lord of the Rings* together or he would take both works elsewhere. Unwin refused, and Tolkien cooled his heels for two years while Collins equivocated. Then, in June 1952, the professor wrote to tell Rayner that he had changed his views. "Better something than nothing!" he concluded. Could anything be done to unlock the gates that he had slammed?

Fearing a loss of as much as £1,000 on *The Lord of the Rings*, Stanley Unwin offered Tolkien a contract under which the author would receive no advance and no royalties until the publisher covered his costs. Tolkien had divided the book into six titled parts, but had always intended it to be issued as a single volume. To reduce Unwin's financial exposure, the book was instead split into three volumes. This kept the retail price low, and allowed the water to be tested by volume one, entitled *The Fellowship of the Ring*. From his firm's printers, Unwin ordered 3,500 copies of *Fellowship*, and it was published in July 1954. Tolkien's painstaking color illustrations were omitted, much to his lingering annoyance. Naomi Mitchison, Richard Hughes, and C. S. Lewis all provided quotes for the dust jacket.

Before publication, proofs were sent to English booksellers. Unwin, looking back in 1960, remembered how J. G. Wilson of Bumpus recognized the book immediately as a great work. Some booksellers were almost wildly enthusiastic while others were left completely cold. The critical reaction was similarly mixed. In the more negative reviews, Tolkien's imagination was labeled simplistic and shallow. The *New Yorker* reviewer found Tolkien blind to the danger of becoming tedious, "and so he is tedious a good deal of the time." From the beginning, though, ordinary readers' reactions were much more uniform.

The inclusion of supplementary antiquarian material—Elvish and Dwarvish grammars and Hobbit family trees—delayed publication of *The Return of the King* until October 1955. Unwin was inundated with begging letters from readers trapped in agonizing suspense. The appendices may not have been the sole cause of the delay. Unwin was not above showmanship, nor was he blind to the benefits of fermenting a little longer the appetite of readers. He moaned about the burden on his staff of answering all the letters, but he was crying crocodile tears; when finally the book was released, it broke all records. Sales of *The Lord of the Rings* would soon vastly exceed the total number of books written in the Middle Ages plus the number produced in the first decades of printing.

From 1954 to 1956, Dan Wickenden heaped praise on *The Lord of the Rings* in the *New York Herald Tribune*, but it would be a decade before the book really took off in North America. In 1965, the year of an American Tolkienian explosion, Ace Books published a pirated edition as a single volume which sold for seventy-five cents. This was made possible by Houghton Mifflin's failure to secure U.S. copyright. The Ace version spurred Tolkien's publishers to produce their own paperback, in collaboration with Ballantine. These two cheap editions fed a Tolkien craze in America. Every college student had a copy of the paperback on his or her bookshelf, and dreamed of being or bedding Arwen Evenstar or Aragorn son of Arathorn. (In the same year, Ballantine also released a softback edition of *The Hobbit*. It was received with bemusement. The cover featured two emus, a lion, and an unidentifiable tree with bulbous fruit. The tree, according to Ballantine, was "meant to suggest a Christmas tree." The designer, it seems, had not read the book.)

A Dutch edition of *The Lord of the Rings* appeared in 1956, a Swedish version soon after, and the book is now in print in most living languages. On its own, the book has underwritten more than one publishing firm and many other titles. All Tolkien's minor works have been published and republished. There are whole franchises of Middle-earth games, comics, songs, films, cookbooks, diaries, lexicons, atlases, pop-ups, calendars, bestiaries, and parodies. Every skerrick of draft manuscript has been published in the series *The Making of Middle-earth*, edited by Tolkien's son Christopher. And scholars and fans have painstakingly reconstructed Tolkien's own library, much of which was dispersed, and all of which was rich in literature, philology, and mythology.

When they come on the market, volumes from Tolkien's reference library attract much interest and high prices. The highest Tolkienian prices, though, are achieved by pristine, first edition copies of *The Hobbit* and *The Lord of the Rings*. In 2015, for example, a copy of *The Hobbit* sold at Sotheby's in London for £137,000 against an estimate of £50,000 to £70,000. Two factors helped drive the exceptional price: an inscription written by Tolkien in Elvish; and the presence of the original dust jacket in excellent condition. The singular value of Tolkien's first edition dust jackets has led to them being protected in archival plastic and in bank vaults. It has also led to them being stolen and faked.

Tolkien died in 1973, aged eighty-one. He did not live to see *The Silmarillion* in print. Published in 1977, more than fifty years after Tolkien first put pen to paper, it is a turgid work and bears only a slight family resemblance to *The Lord of the Rings*. A 2004 parody by Adam Roberts (writing as "A. R. R. Roberts") was titled *Sellamillion*, but in truth Tolkien's attempt to write a "mythology for England" failed. Readers did not take *The Silmarillion* to their hearts. Tolkien's real success lies elsewhere, in his linking generations of disparate readers through shared experiences in an unforgettable secondary world.

The history of Middle-earth contains an alternative but recognizable history of libraries—libraries large and small, classical and medieval, public and private. Three types of book are found there: tablets, scrolls, and codices. In the great human kingdoms of Númenor and Gondor, the most valuable tablets are made from silver and gold. The earliest documented scroll from Middle-earth was *The Scroll of Kings*. It named all the kings and queens of Númenor, and was destroyed when that island sank. After that disaster, the survivors settled in Middle-earth.

In Tolkien's world, Elvish culture serves as an idealized version of ancient Greece and Rome. Books are central to that cultural ideal. The second letter of the Elvish alphabet is *parma*, "book." (The first letter is *tinco*, "metal.") Elves received the art of book-making as a gift from a god—the divine master craftsman, Aulë.

At Ost-in-Edhil in Eregion, Nargothrond in West Beleriand, Gondolin in Tumladen, and Menegroth in Doriath, Tolkien depicts Elvish scribes making books. Situated in the Misty Mountains, the Elf city of Rivendell is, like St. Gall, a place of books. The city houses a central library, with places for scribework, study, and contemplation. The library contains some of the oldest written material extant in Middle-earth. Most adult Elves at Rivendell also maintain private libraries in their homes.

At the start of the First Age, the Dwarf king Durin I established a library at Moria (also known as the Dwarrow Delf and Khazad-dûm), a Dwarvish city excavated in stone far beneath the Misty Mountains. Dwarvish books are straightforward chronicles and records of royal administration, expeditions, trade, and calamities. Moria's records are stored in the Chamber of Mazarbul—one of the oldest libraries in Middle-earth. The chamber is a large, square room secured by stone doors and lit by a single wide shaft cut high in its eastern wall. The tight security that surrounds the storage of Dwarvish records reflects their rarity and value. Other

Dwarvish cities have similar rooms, where communal books and documents are secured in iron-buttressed chests inside subterranean niches.

In the Chamber of Mazarbul, alongside the tomb of Balin, the Ring Party finds the remains of a Dwarvish codex, *The Book of Mazarbul*. Begun in Third Age 2989 and written by several Dwarves over a five-year period, the book records the fortunes of the city. The last lines, written just as Moria fell to invading orcs and trolls, are hastily scrawled. Badly damaged during the invasion, the book reveals the skillful use by Dwarves of foreign scripts. Numerous sections of the book are written in Elvish characters, for example. Other parts are written in Khuzdul, the secret language of the Dwarves.

Several early manuscripts seem to have influenced Tolkien's description of *The Book of Mazarbul*, among them the scorched Cottonian *Beowulf* manuscript; the Codex Argenteus or Silver Bible, held in the Uppsala university library; and now at Fulda, Germany, the Ragyndrudis Codex, which St. Boniface is said to have taken up as a shield, and which bears incisions that might have been made by a sword or an ax.

There are no public lending libraries in the Shire, or elsewhere in Middle-earth. Lending does take place, however. Hobbits routinely lend their own volumes to friends and relatives. Bilbo was generous with his books, often to a fault. Many of them were never returned. Hugo Bracegirdle borrowed and kept such a quantity of Bilbo's books that, when Bilbo left the Shire in Third Age 3001, he pointedly gave Hugo one of his bookcases in which to store them.

Apart from the sharing of books, there is much sharing of book-making techniques. The noblest human communities seek to emulate Elvish culture. At Minas Tirith, the capital of Gondor, there is a "writing house" that resembles a medieval scriptorium. Gondor's professional scribes are attached to the royal household and work under a chief scribe, called the king's writer. The scribes are employed primarily as copyists, producing faithful facsimiles for the king and his family.

This and other Middle-earth libraries are part of an international tradition of scholarship and research. Examples of that tradition include the wizard Gandalf consulting *The Scroll of Isildur* in preparation for the last battle with Sauron; Bilbo Baggins preparing at Rivendell his *Translations from the Elvish* and Meriadoc Brandybuck collating information for *The Tale of Years*. Elrond was happy to allow foreign Elves and Elf-friends to peruse his many books and documents. He welcomed Aragorn's and Gandalf's interest in his maps, and he assisted Bilbo's and Merry's researches.

Like the Chamber of Mazarbul, Minas Tirith's library is well secured: it resides in the treasury, which in turn is inside a guarded citadel. Númenórean émigrés established the library in the Second Age. At the end of the Third Age, it contained a wealth of codices, scrolls, and tablets, many of them ancient. A few had been made in Númenor. Others had been rescued from Minas Ithil and Osgiliath before those cities were sacked by Mordor's armies.

Minas Tirith's books are locked in cabinets and chests, again like those of the Chamber of Mazarbul. Some of the tablets and scrolls are kept in cloth and leather pouches to further protect them. No one knows exactly what the collection contains. There are uncatalogued books in many different scripts and languages. It takes the wizard Saruman years to comb through the holdings in search of information about the One Ring. When Gondor has no king, the steward Denethor II begrudges Gandalf's petition to use Minas Tirith's library. Under the restored king and his heirs, access becomes easier, and the library is greatly expanded, with the city's own scribes contributing many volumes. There is an international book trade in Middle-earth—books are imported into Gondor from distant regions like the Shire, for example—but there are no printers, and commerce doesn't dominate the production and distribution of books.

For Tolkien, libraries signified civilization. All the civilized peoples of Middle-earth regard their books as precious. The demonic goblins he called "orcs" represent a dangerous, mindless, industrial future. They and all the other evil races are destroyers of books, and never make them. (Dragons such as Glaurung and Smaug the Magnificent are exceptional among evil creatures in so far as their treasure hoards probably include libraries of a sort: plunders of Dwarf-made treasure bindings.)

This, then, is Tolkien's fantastical vision of Middle-earth's book world. His writings are full of fantasy, as well as the occasional anachronism, like the odd references in *The Hobbit* to pop guns and in *The Lord of the Rings* to express trains. Paradoxically, however, Middle-earth's libraries, with their scant holdings of tablets, codices, and scrolls, are more medievally correct than the abbey library of *The Name of the Rose*.

Death

Andreas Wilhelm Cramer was chief librarian at Kiel in Germany. In the early 1820s he visited the precious collection of books at the marvelous rococo library of St. Gall. Afterwards he noted in his family chronicle: "One would not mind being buried in such a library." Tim Munby called at a home in Blackheath after the bibliophile owner had died. Many years before, the owner had lost control of his book purchasing. Now, in every room, "narrow lanes ran between books stacked from floor to ceiling." Almost all the books were inaccessible. In one room there was a small clearing just wide enough to accommodate a bed, "and there the owner had died, almost entombed in print."

In 1374, at the age of sixty-nine, Petrarch died in his own library at Arquà near Padua. His body was discovered the following morning, his head resting on an open codex—the manuscript of his *Life of Caesar*. (Plato is said to have died similarly, "with his head on Sophron's *Jests*.")

Charles Van Hulthem perished much as he had lived. "Carried away by a sudden apoplectic fit, he died on a pile of books like a warrior on the battlefield." Thomas Rawlinson likewise departed, "among his bundles, piles, and bulwarks of paper." Tennyson was buried with the volume of *Cymbeline* that he had held during his last moments. The editor and bibliophile Gustave Mouravit related a story about pompous Monsieur

Servien, who on his deathbed realized he was bookless. So disturbed was he by the thought of what people would say of him when they found no books among his effects, he gave orders that a library be purchased at once.

When Aldus Manutius, "the prince of Renaissance printers," died in 1515, the humanists at his funeral at the church of San Patrinian surrounded his coffin with soldier-like towers of the books he had printed in his lifetime.

CHAPTER 15

———— ✦ ————

A Love Letter

Libraries for the future

In ancient Rome, public libraries were plentiful. Trajan founded several of them, including the large Ulpian Library, which endured until the fifth century A.D. Augustus also instituted significant public libraries. The irony of Rome's first public libraries was that they closely followed Greek models and were largely built from the spoils of war, including plundered Greek manuscripts.

The tradition of public libraries was revived in the European renaissance. In the sixteenth century, Nuremberg's civic authorities established a municipal library; by the 1550s it contained some 4,000 volumes, manuscript and printed. In the centuries that followed, most European nations would have national and municipal libraries, built to varying degrees around an ethos of accessibility.

Anthony Panizzi believed it was the state's responsibility to fund a national library for the benefit of everyone.

> I want a poor student to have the same means of indulging his learned curiosity, of following his rational pursuits, of consulting the same authorities, of fathoming the most intricate inquiry, as the richest man in the Kingdom, as far as books go, and I contend that Government is bound to give him the most liberal and unlimited assistance in this respect.

In twentieth-century America, free public libraries opened up a lifetime of reading, and made possible—for authors such as Eudora Welty and John Updike—a literary existence. Also in that century, Britain's municipal libraries were a prominent feature of postwar reconstruction and social reforms.

In the late 1950s some of those libraries were the stage for a grandiose, surrealist prank. Joe Orton and his partner, Kenneth Halliwell, surreptitiously removed books from several Islington libraries. Adding spurious blurbs and modifying the dust jackets with perplexing and shocking artwork, the pair then smuggled the books back inside and returned them to the shelves. The blurb on Dorothy L. Sayers's *Gaudy Night* had the writer "at her most awe inspiring. At her most queer, and needless to say, at her most crude!" According to the cover of her *Clouds of Witness*, borrowers should read the book behind closed doors, "and have a good shit while you are reading!" Monkey and baboon pictures were added to the *Collins Guide to Roses* and other volumes. The biography of John Betjeman was illustrated with an elderly tattooed man in swimming trunks. The cover of *Queen's Favourite* by Phyllis Hambledon featured two men wrestling. The jacket of *The Collected Plays of Emlyn Williams* informed readers of Poggio-ish titles such as "Up the Front," "Up the Back," and "Knickers Must Fall." One of the *Three Faces of Eve* was a kitten.

Orton and Halliwell decorated the walls of their flat with pages and plates cut from art books; the pair called it "library wallpaper." The pair also tormented local libraries and other institutions via the geriatric letter-writing alter ego Edna Welthorpe. The pranks had a political edge, an acid reaction to the priorities of modern libraries. "Libraries might as well not exist," Orton wrote in 1967. "They've got endless shelves for rubbish and hardly any space for good books."

Municipal officials soon came to suspect Orton and Halliwell. The council's law clerk, Sidney Porrett, was an English version of Jerry Seinfeld's diligent Mr. Bookman. Porrett devised an elegant sting to "catch these two monkeys." He wrote to Halliwell asking him to remove an illegally parked car. The typed letter of reply, an intemperate sermon on municipal small-mindedness, matched the irregular typeface that the perpetrators had used in their creations.

In April 1962, Orton and Halliwell were arrested and charged with the theft of seventy-two books and 1,653 plates. Pleading guilty to five counts of malicious damage, the pair were fined and sentenced to six months in separate prisons. In Orton's view, the sentences were more severe because of his and Halliwell's homosexuality.

During his imprisonment, Halliwell attempted suicide. In the five years after the pair were released, Orton built a reputation as an author and playwright. Tragically, in August 1967, Halliwell attacked and killed Orton with a hammer, taking his own life, too, with an overdose of pills.

One of the remarkable aspects of this ultimately terrible episode is that the Islington librarians kept a substantial number of the book covers that Orton and Halliwell had vandalized. The covers, and other artifacts made by the pair, have since become valued parts of the collections of the Islington Local History Centre and other nearby institutions. In 1995 the creations were put on display in the same libraries the pair had raided. A local librarian explained how "over the years, we have become proud of Joe Orton as a leading literary figure with local associations."

Born between the world wars, the poet-librarian Philip Larkin lived the social changes that made modern Britain. As a boy, he was implicated in the destruction of a friend's collection of cigarette cards. Glyn Lloyd was Larkin's fellow pupil at a Coventry preparatory school. Lloyd was an avid collector; when his cigarette cards went missing, he called at the Larkin house and accused Philip of taking them. Larkin did have them, and he did return them. Lloyd later wrote of the incident, and how the cards had been defaced: "all the beautiful red, white, blue and green shirts . . . obliterated beneath a pattern of fine cross-hatching in blue-black ink!" Decades later, Larkin placed much of the blame on his parents. "I wouldn't know about that," Lloyd wrote, "but certainly in terms of fucking things up, he did a Grade A job on my cigarette cards."

As an adult, and as a poet of deprivation and "being on the edge of things," Larkin championed public and university libraries. Though sympathetic to Toryism, he came to oppose the 1980s trends—new public management and neoclassical economics—that were antithetical to libraries. For many years, Larkin was university librarian at Hull University's Brynmor Jones Library. When Larkin first met a new vice chancellor there, the VC asked for the library's payroll/non-payroll breakdown. "Mind your own fucking business" was the poet's muffled reply. Larkin served on the board of the British Library, but resigned because of the early starts, and because the "fire-trap" meeting room gave him claustrophobia.

•

Today, Britain's public libraries are caught in a downward spiral of reduced funding and the de-professionalization of library services. In *The Strange Rise of Semi-literate England*, Bill West decried the dispersal of public collections, the neglect of the literary classics, and libraries' disproportionate emphasis on matters other than the acquisition of good books. That emphasis has led to a series of unexpected calamities.

Suppose a library decides to dispose of much of its paper texts, relying instead on microfilm and digital copies, on the grounds that the originals are held elsewhere. And suppose, too, that other libraries make the same judgment. Nicholson Baker made a terrifying discovery: in the drive for efficiency, whole categories of physical texts had been destroyed. Many newspapers, for example, were "simply no longer available within the library system other than as surrogates"—a situation he blamed on "cost-sphinctering coneheads."

Over the past decade, Britain's municipal authorities have closed hundreds of branch libraries. In response to plans to shut ten of Newcastle's eighteen libraries, the playwright Lee Hall recalled the efforts of workingmen and -women to fight for those same libraries, and "for the right to read and grow intellectually, culturally and socially."

> It is a heritage that took decades and decades to come to fruition but will be wiped out in a moment. You are not only about to make philistines of yourselves, but philistines of us all.

Authors Malorie Blackman, Julia Donaldson, Anne Fine, and Philip Pullman penned an open letter in which they called the plans to close the libraries wrong and immoral. Focusing government austerity cuts on libraries was misguided, the authors said.

"The cost in educational underachievement would far outweigh any savings made by cuts."

Campaigning in 2015 to save sixteen libraries in Fife, Ian Rankin related how the Bowhill Library had been his "refuge and a place of constant wonder" during his childhood, where he'd borrow as many books at a time as possible. He remembered "the thrill of being told I'd reached the age where I could have an adult ticket and take books from the adult fiction section." Paul Mason spoke for a whole slice of Britain's working-class children when he wrote in 2016, "We had been headed for university since we picked up Ladybird books." The history of libraries is rich with stories of how ready access to books meant access to work and social mobility, and the awakening of intellectual lives. Shutting down libraries, people feared, would prevent the chairs from jumping on the tables.

In 2014 a group of poets and authors put their names to a "love letter" to Liverpool's libraries, the loss of which would devastate the city: "it's a massacre, and at the expense of the children of Liverpool most of all." On a national day of protest, Mary Warnock fought the closure of her local library. "In times of economic misery and unemployment," she said, "we need more not less consolation from libraries."

Warnock's battle cry raises an important question: what exactly are libraries *for*? Scores of rationales have been put forward; scores of stories have been told. Libraries are an attempt to impose order in a world of chaos. They are signifiers of power (consider the libraries of Mesopotamian kings and American presidents) and prestige (remember the libraries of America's robber barons). They are an aide-mémoire of the species, a network of sanctuaries, a civilizing influence in the New World, places of solace and education, sources of nourishment for the human spirit, cultural staging posts in which new arrivals can be inducted into their adopted countries. They are places for social connection and the creation of "social capital." They are places in which to give birth. They are places of redemption.

For Umberto Eco, the ideal library was humane and light-hearted, a place where two students could sit on a couch in the afternoon and, without doing anything too indecent, "enjoy the continuation of their flirtation in the library as they take down or replace some books of scientific interest from their shelves." For Panizzi, the British Museum Library was a portrait of Britain's soul. "What mattered to Panizzi was that every aspect of British life and thought be represented, so that the library could become a showcase of the nation itself."

Much more than accumulations of books, the best libraries are hotspots and organs of civilization; magical places in which students, scholars, curators, philanthropists, artists, pranksters, and flirts come together and make something marvelous.

Yet none of these descriptions fits comfortably in the arid, clinical, neoliberal, managerial paradigm of inputs and outputs and outcomes. And therein lies a problem. Throughout most of the modern world, that very paradigm guides how public funds are spent. The inputs for libraries (books, librarians, capital) are easy enough to identify, and to count. But what are the "outputs" of a library, and how might the "outcomes" be measured? The "performance" of libraries resists evaluation as much as the "customers" of libraries resist classification.

Those customers—some of them certainly classifiable as "casual strollers"—are typically and uncooperatively diverse. In *The Library at Night*, Alberto Manguel recorded this remark from an observer at the British Library:

Every day the library is filled with, among others, people sleeping, students doing their homework, bright young things writing film scripts—in fact, doing almost anything except consulting the library's books.

"Investing in a library," another observer said, "requires an act of faith." But leaps of faith are precisely what the cost-sphinctering managerialist paradigm is meant to prevent. The people of Alexandria and Athens knew the value of books for scholarship and culture and civil society. In large part, the history of libraries is the history of how that value was forgotten, then rediscovered, then forgotten again.

The *Star Wars* prequels introduced the Jedi temple and, at its heart, the Jedi library—a digital collection of books and star maps and other inter-galactic media. As author and book historian David Pearson noticed, the design of the Jedi library is strikingly reminiscent of the Long Room at Trinity College, Dublin. So reminiscent, in fact, that the library issued a "please explain" to Lucasfilm. The resulting legal skirmish provided a curious metaphor for how traditional libraries are grappling with digitization and the internet. In 2018 libraries are at a digital crossroads. Most of the printed books in the Vatican are now electronically tagged, and many of them have been digitally scanned. Around the world, such technologies are transforming how books and archives are held, and how they are shared and accessed.

The digitization of bibliographical treasure is a valuable means through which rare books and manuscripts can be discovered, studied, appreciated, and enjoyed. Digitization, combined with online publication, gives easy access to texts from anywhere in the world. Ease of access to rare materials is a boon, as is ease of discoverability. Digitization is also a technique of conservation. The case for digitizing early and precious materials is obvious, particularly for especially delicate books that cannot be handled without endangering them.

The seeming permanence of digital data, though, is not entirely reliable. Some digital storages are even more ephemeral than paper ones. David C. Pearson and Alberto Manguel have recounted the story from the 1980s of the electronic Domesday Book, a venture funded by the BBC to record digitally 250,000 place names, 25,000 maps, 50,000 pictures, 3,000 data sets, and 60 minutes of moving pictures, plus scores of accounts of daily life. The project, to which over a million people contributed, serves as a salutary lesson about the limitations of digital preservation. The resulting "book" was stored on laser disks that could only be read by a special BBC computer. Sixteen years later, these computers had all but disappeared, superseded by other technologies. When readers attempted to recover the digital data, the attempt failed. Only after a massive recovery effort—that involved painstaking unpicking of hexadecimal data, and resorting to the original analogue master tapes—could the "book" be read. All the while, the original, thousand-year-old Domesday Book housed at the National Archives in Kew remained entirely readable.

There are other reasons, too, why digital conservation can be unsatisfactory. Many aspects of books are alien to digitization: indicators of provenance, marginalia, bindings, paper, watermarks, edition variants, the feel of impressed type, and the physical experience— including the smell—of handling a book; each of these is an intrinsic part of every story of every book. An encounter with an old book is miserably dimmed-down if the reader cannot savor the tactile experience of rotating a delicate volvelle, or folding out a map, or seeing a color plate in context. Not surprisingly, the rise of digitization has coincided with a rise in physical bibliography and other book-history disciplines that are founded on real, non-digital book-objects.

Something else is lost, too, in the experience of digital browsing. Browsing books on a screen is utterly alien to the delight of browsing and getting lost in a physical, fractal, serendipitous library of real books. This book has walked through many different species of the wonder of libraries: secret, hidden spaces; marvelous chance discoveries; high art in paint, stucco, timber, and stone; and every aspect of the human drama, from triumph to despair. The physicality of books in libraries—spines, fore-edges, verticality, shelf-marks, bookcases, stacks, stalls, halls, domes—all these may be read so that we may know the histories of the books and the libraries: when and how they were made, how they were used and appreciated. In the case of digital texts and digital libraries, such a mode of reading is impossible or irrelevant.

Before Google Books there was Project Gutenberg, which placed tens of thousands of texts on the internet. Alberto Manguel lamented that many of the texts were duplicates, and many more were unreliable, "having been hastily scanned and badly checked for typographical errors." Paul Duguid noticed another problem of curation. While in many ways Project Gutenberg resembled—and even improved upon—a traditional, analogue library, it also resembled "a church jumble-sale bookstall, where gems and duds are blessed alike by the vicar because all have been donated."

In an unpublished survey conducted in March 2003 (and cited by Andrew Madden, Joe Palimi, and Jared Bryson in 2005), Andrew Madden asked 176 students at a Sheffield school to indicate, on a five-point scale, the extent to which they agreed or disagreed with a series of statements about the internet. Eighty-six percent of the students (aged eleven to sixteen) agreed that "The internet is like a library." The same questionnaire was circulated among delegates of the "Internet Librarian" International Conference in 2003. There, only a third of the respondents disagreed with the statement.

Madden and Palimi and Bryson, though, contested the analogy, arguing that the internet was better understood as a collection of monologues, or even as a bar room, "because most of its users are men, and most of the talk is of sex and sport." These unbounded monologues are inherently uncuratable, which brings us back to the central message of Borges's infinite library. Without boundaries and selection and navigation, libraries are useless. Whether bar room or jumble sale, the internet is both a curse and a blessing for libraries. The world wide web is traditional libraries' principal competitor, but it is also their savior because, in the internet era, there is an urgent need for selection and curation.

Behind digitization, there has always been anxiety about a bleak future, in which libraries would become "content management centers," books would be replaced by screens, and a rump of codices would be consigned to ancillary museums as book-artifact curios. In 1966 a delegation of librarians and scholars from Oxford and Cambridge visited Louis Wright at the Folger Shakespeare Library. On their trip the visitors had seen example after example of how new technologies were transforming libraries. "For two weeks," one delegate said, "we have heard nothing but computers, computers, computers. A book would comfort me." In moments of gloom, Wright foresaw dreary hordes of students punching away at computers and reading machines, unaware of the pleasures of handling a book. Machinery, he feared, would ultimately estrange people from life's humanistic interests. Reading a book on-screen or in microfilm was an unsatisfactory experience, like kissing a girl through a windowpane.

Afterlife

Two blocks from Nevsky Prospekt, in an apartment on the southeast bank of St. Petersburg's Moika River, Alexander Sergeyevich Pushkin—Russia's most celebrated poet—assembled a private library of some 4,000 books. B. L. Modzalevsky later catalogued 1,505 of them: more than 400 were Russian, and the remaining "foreign" books were mostly in French. The library was rich in the classics. Shakespeare, Machiavelli, Leibniz, Dante, Byron, Bunyan, the Bible, De Quincey's *Confessions of an English Opium Eater*, Tocqueville's *On Democracy in America*. There were also plentiful books on horses, philosophy, art, medicine, cooking, the civil war in England, and the revolution in France. There were books published in Paris, Perpignan, Brussels, London, Rome, Venice, Dijon, Lyon, Naples, Dublin, New York, Philadelphia, Constantinople—and a book from a Tunbridge circulating library. Many volumes in the library featured Pushkin's marginalia, penciling, underlining, inscriptions, laconic observations, question marks, and sharp nail marks.

Pushkin married Natalya Goncharova in 1831. Six years later, Baron Georges H. D'Anthès—the husband of Natalya's sister Ekaterina—attempted to seduce Natalya. The adopted son of the Dutch ambassador, D'Anthès was a French officer serving with the Chevalier Guard Regiment. Despite the likely differences in marksmanship, the poet challenged the warrior to a duel. In the days leading up to the contest, Pushkin visited the Hermitage gallery, where, according to George Steiner, he sang nursery rhymes to the granddaughter of the poet Krylov, saw D'Anthès and his own sister-in-law across the room at a soirée, struck friends as "merry and full of life" and went to Countess Razumovskaya's glittering ball.

On January 27, 1837, the combatants and their "seconds" met on a field of snow outside St. Petersburg. D'Anthès shot Pushkin in the lower abdomen and was himself also wounded. Pushkin's friends loaded him on a sleigh, took him to his apartment at 12 Moika, and summoned the lexicographer and naval doctor Vladimir Dahl.

Pushkin died slowly and in agony over the next forty-eight hours, attended by Dahl and surrounded by books. At 2:45 p.m. on January 29, 1837, the poet's heart stopped. He was only thirty-seven. His apartment, carefully restored, is now the Pushkin Apartment Museum. More than a century after the poet's death, forensic scientists studied his leather sofa and confirmed—after exhaustive testing that included making and dressing a paper model of his corpse—that the bloodstains were his.

Multiple versions of Pushkin's last words have reached us. One version has him pressing Dahl's hand and begging, "Lift me up, let us go higher, still higher." Another has him saying, "It is finished. I am going, I am going," then, falling back on his pillow, "I can hardly breathe, I am suffocating." The most fitting and arresting version, though, has him pointing to his bookcases and saying to Dahl, "It seemed to me that you and I were climbing up those shelves." Pushkin then addresses his final utterance to his books: "Farewell, friends."

Acknowledgments

This book owes its existence in large part to the generous support of the State Library of New South Wales (SLNSW), Ashurst Australia, the Monash University Centre for the Book and the Monash School of Languages, Literatures, Cultures and Linguistics. Professor Wallace Kirsop and Joan Kirsop have long been leading figures in the Centre, the School, and the wider book world. Wallace and Joan introduced me to leading librarians around the world, and provided unstinting support in countless other ways. They and others read the manuscript and gave valuable comments; all the remaining errors are of course my own. The award of the Ashurst prize, administered by the SLNSW, allowed me to visit libraries in Zurich, Sankt Gallen, London, Oxford, Boston, Cambridge Massachusetts, New York, Washington, D.C., and Sydney. My hometown of Melbourne, too, is well endowed with libraries—including the State Library of Victoria (SLV), the Matheson Library, and the Baillieu Library—and I made full use of them as well.

I am grateful to the current and former custodians of all these libraries, and specifically to Des Cowley, Sue Hamilton, and Kate Molloy of the SLV; the State Library User Organisations' Council;

the Friends of the SLV; Richard Overell and Stephen Herrin of the Monash Rare Books Library; Philip Kent and Shane Carmody of the University of Melbourne libraries; Dr. Francesca Galligan and Richard Ovenden of the Bodleian and Weston Libraries; Giles Mandelbrote of the Lambeth Palace Library; Peter Accardo of the Houghton Library; Susanne Woodhouse of the British Museum; and the librarians and staff of the British Library, the Wellcome Library, University College London, the National Library of Australia, the Swiss National Museum, Zentralbibliothek Zürich, the Pierpont Morgan Library, the New York Public Library, the Boston Athenaeum, the Boston Public Library, the Widener Library, the Folger Shakespeare Library, the Library of Congress, the Smithsonian libraries, and the abbey library at St. Gall, where reverently I donned the special slippers that everyone must wear to protect the marvelous floor. I also gratefully acknowledge the National Library of China, the National Library of Indonesia, the National Library of Mexico, the Bibliotheca Alexandrina, Tsinghua University Library, Nanjing University Library, Friends of the Williamstown and Newport Libraries, the Goldfields Libraries, Yarra Plenty Regional Library, the Abbotsford Convent Foundation, Humanities 21, and the UNESCO City of Literature.

I further acknowledge the work of prior authors on the libraries explored in this book, including Maria Siponta de Salvia, Daniel Mendelsohn, and John Preston on the Vatican Library and Secret Archive; P. R. Harris on the history of the British Museum reading room; Al Alvarez and Dido Merwin on the destruction of Ted Hughes's personal papers; Nicolas Barker on the sale of books from the John Rylands Library; Ann Galbally, Fiona Salisbury, and the SLV librarians on Redmond Barry's personal library and day books; Eileen Chanin and Charles Stitz on David Scott Mitchell and the Mitchell Library; Jonathan J. G. Alexander on medieval manuscript illumination and scriptoria; Alberto Manguel on the *dépôts littéraires* and *bibliothèques publiques*; George Steiner, B. L. Modzalev-sky, and Andrew Kahn on Alexander Pushkin's library; Carl J. Weber on the art of fore-edge decoration; James Campbell regarding Metten Abbey in Bavaria and the Altenburg library in Lower Austria; J. M. Clark, Anthony Hobson, Johannes Huber, Karl Schmuki, Ernst Tremp, and the staff of the abbey library of St. Gall and the Swiss National Museum on the abbey library's history; Anthony Hobson and Lucien X. Polastron on the biblio-crimes perpetrated at Christ Church College, the Ambrosian Library, the Colombina Library, Dublin's Trinity College, the Jesuit church in Brussels, the public libraries of Heidelberg and Paris, the abbey library at Admont, and the Monastery of Saint John the Theologian; Alan Johnston and the International League of Antiquarian Booksellers regarding thefts from the Girolamini Library in Naples; Allison Hoover Bartlett on the subject of John Charles Gilkey; Umberto Eco for his reflections on *The Name of the Rose*; George Wheeler, Ron Chernow, and the Morgan librarians (including the curators of the *Master's Hand* exhibition) regarding the Pierpont Morgan Library; Peter Gilliver, Jeremy Marshall, and Edmund Weiner regarding Tolkien's "mathom houses"; Nicholas Pickwood on the history of false raised bands; Christine Fernon and the *Sydney Morning Herald* on the McArthur River Institute; the Islington librarians and Joe Orton's diaries for details of his library "creations"; Arnold Hunt, A. N. L. Munby, Alberto Manguel, and Anthony Hobson on the Earl of Ashburnham, Count Libri, and Bibliotheca Heberiana; Holbrook Jackson on the Irish "Dragon" and, along with Andrew Prescott, Sir Robert Cotton's library and the fire at Ashburnham House; A. N. L. Munby and Mary Pollard on the Cavendish fire at Clontarf; the Beinecke Library, Yale, and the Rosenbach Museum and Library, Philadelphia, for details of the Vanderbilt–Rosenbach and Weatherup–Rosenbach copies of the Bay Psalm Book; Leigh Hunt, Peter Cochran, and Corin Throsby on Lord Byron and the burning of his papers; Nadia Khomani, Lee Hall, Mary Warnock, and Bill West on local library closures in Britain; Louis Wright, Andrea Mays, Stephen H. Grant, and the Folger librarians and newsletters regarding the Folger Shakespeare Library; and Nicholas Shakespeare and the *Australian Dictionary of Biography* on Bruce Chatwin, Theodore Strehlow, and the oral libraries of ancient Australia.

The following general works were helpful compasses: Nicolas Barker (ed.), *The Pleasures of Bibliophily*, 2002; James Campbell, *The Library: A World History*, 2013; Thomas Frognall Dibdin, *Bibliomania; or Book Madness*, 1809; Helene Hanff, *Apple of My Eye*, 1977; Anthony Hobson, *Great Libraries*, 1970; Raymond Irwin, *The Heritage of the English Library*, 1964; Holbrook Jackson, *The Anatomy of Bibliomania*, 1930; Andrew Lang, *Books and Bookmen*, 1886; Michael Leapman, *The Book of the British Library*, 2012; Alberto Manguel, *A History of Reading*, 1996, and *The Library at Night*, 2005; Robin Myers, Michael Harris, and Giles Mandelbrote (eds.), *Against the Law*, 2004; David Pearson, *Books as History*, 2012; Henry Petroski, *The Book on the Bookshelf*, 1999; Lucien X. Polastron, *Books on Fire*, 2007; Harold Rabinowitz and Rob Kaplan (eds), *A Passion for Books*, 1999; and Don Heinrich Tolzmann, *The Memory of Mankind*, 2001.

My agent, Sheila Drummond, and the teams at Text Publishing and Counterpoint—particularly Michael Heyward, Elena Gomez, W. H. Chong, Jack Shoemaker, Wah-Ming Chang, Jennifer Alton, and Donna Cheng—did a marvelous job of turning the manuscript into a book. My wife, Fiona, and my daughters, Thea and Charlotte, visited many libraries with me and provided a thousand kindnesses and accommodations. My friends Elizabeth Lane, Louise Lane, Dr. Anna Blainey, Dr. Lisa Ehrenfried, Dr. Ed Schofield, Andrew Schofield, Amanda Wendt, Greg Harbour, Tony Pitman, Charles Stitz, and Professor Ian Gow conducted additional fieldwork in France, Germany, Switzerland, England, Russia, the United States, Mexico, and Australia—and indulged my unrelenting enthusiasm for libraries; many thanks all.

ABOUT THE AUTHOR

STUART KELLS is an author and book-trade historian. His 2015 history of Penguin Books, *Penguin and the Lane Brothers*, won the prestigious Ashurst Business Literature Prize. *Rare*, his critically acclaimed biography of Kay Craddock—the first female president of the International League of Antiquarian Booksellers—was published in 2011. An authority on rare books, Kells has written and published on many aspects of print culture and the book world. You can find him at www.stuartkells.com.